Why America Needs a Left

In memory of Allen Zaretsky
A sweet giving nature, easy laughter and emotional depth

Why America Needs a Left

A Historical Argument

———————

Eli Zaretsky

polity

Reprinted in 2012 (twice)

Polity Press
65 Bridge Street
Cambridge CB2 1UR, UK

Polity Press
350 Main Street
Malden, MA 02148, USA

ISBN-13: 978-0-7456-4484-4

A catalogue record for this book is available from the British Library.

Typeset in 11 on 13 pt Sabon
by Servis Filmsetting Ltd, Stockport, Cheshire
Printed and bound in the USA by Edwards Brothers, Inc.

For further information on Polity, visit our website: www.politybooks.com

Contents

Acknowledgments

This project began with me puzzling over the problem of the left in general. I benefited from invitations from Hendrik Geyer of the Stellenbosch Institute of Advanced Study in South Africa, Christian Ingrao of L'Institut d'Histoire du Temps Présent in Paris, and Ross Harrison, Provost at King's College, Cambridge, which allowed me to present preliminary ideas, and supplied me with research facilities. I also gratefully acknowledge The New School for Social Research and Lang College, which provided me with a sabbatical and other research support. After a while I realized that I needed to separate off the problem of the American left from the more general problem with which I began. Alice Kessler-Harris invited me to prepare a version of my ideas for the Organization of American Historians, which allowed me to do just that. John Thompson was convinced that I could make his book deadline for that version, and he helped me to do that. Two other friends, Leonard Helfgott and Jeremy Varon, gave me superb, last-minute readings. Michael Kazin sent me the proofs of his *American Dreamers: How the Left Changed a Nation* long before I completed my book. Nancy Fraser, as always, was luminous and inspiring; whatever lucidity the book possesses comes from her. My obligations to so many great historians can be traced in my notes. Finally, I want to acknowledge an older debt to James Weinstein, who first introduced me to the problem of the left.

Men fight and lose the battle, and the thing that they fought for comes about in spite of their defeat, and when it comes, turns out not to be what they meant, and other men have to fight for what they meant under another name.

William Morris, "A Dream of John Ball," 1886

Introduction

America's Three Great Crises and Three Lefts

From the beginning of the republic, most of America's thinkers and political leaders have argued that the country neither had nor needs a significant left. The so-called liberal consensus school, including Louis Hartz and Richard Hofstadter, has argued that the country has always enjoyed agreement on such matters as private property, individualism, popular sovereignty, and natural rights. Others claimed that it did not have the leftist working class or peasantry other nations had, a claim often termed American exceptionalism. Still others claimed that the country didn't need a left because it already believed in, or had even achieved, such goals as democracy and equality, goals that other nations were still striving toward. This view has been associated with Cold War liberalism, and with neoconservatism.

This book argues that these are all false and misleading ways to understand America. The country has not only always needed, but has typically had, a powerful, independent radical left. While this left has been marginalized (as it is today) and scapegoated (especially during periods of emergency or "states of exception"), the country's history cannot be understood without assigning a central place to the left. The indispensable role of the left has come during periods of long-term crisis, when the country's identity is in question. In what follows I will argue that the country has gone through three such crises: the slavery crisis culminating in the Civil War; the crisis precipitated by the rise of large-scale corporate capitalism, culminating in the New Deal; and the present crisis, the crisis of "affluence" and global power, which began in the 1960s. Each crisis generated a left – first the abolitionists, then the socialists, and finally the New Left – and together, these lefts constitute a tradition.

At the core of each left stood a challenge to the liberal understanding of equality – the formal equality of all citizens before the law. In place of that understanding, each left sought to install a deeper, more substantive idea of equality as a continuing project. In the first case, the abolitionists, the issue was political equality, specifically the abolitionist belief that a republic had to be founded on racial equality. In the second case, the socialists and communists, the issue was social equality, specifically the insistence that democracy required a minimum level of security in regard to basic necessities. In the third case, the New Left, the issue was equal participation in civil society, the public sphere, the family and personal life. Central to our history, then, is a struggle between liberalism and the left over the meaning of equality. More even than the struggle between left and right, the struggle between liberalism and the left is at the core of US history. Without a left, liberalism becomes spineless and vapid; without liberalism, the left becomes sectarian, authoritarian, and marginal. In great eras of reform, the struggle between them strengthens both. Only when the liberal/left dynamic is weak does a strong right emerge.

To make this argument I first need to clarify two concepts: the left, and crisis. What is the left? Derived from the spatial situation of the body in nature, the distinction between left and right was originally used to ground social power in nature. In every society, the right symbolizes dominance, authority, and God; the left symbolizes rebellion, danger, discontent, and the plebeian status.[1] The words themselves often suggest this: *recht* and *droit* versus maladroit, *gauche* and *sinistra*. In this sense, the existence of a left is a universal characteristic of all societies. Nonetheless, there is a difference between earlier forms of rebellion, based on cyclical time, and the modern left, based on the idea of progress. In earlier societies rebellion took the form of "anger at the failure of authority to live up to its obligations, to keep its word and faith with the subjects." Essentially, writes Barrington Moore, this type of protest "accepts the existence of hierarchy and authority while attempting to make it conform to an idealized pattern." The modern left, by contrast, has questioned whether we need particular forms of hierarchy or authority, such as kings, capitalists, or "experts," at all. It doesn't seek to return to an idealized past, but rather to move toward a utopian but nonetheless ultimately realizable future.

The existence of a left of the modern sort has been inseparable from the project of self-government from the first. According to Christopher Hill, there were *two* revolutions during the English Civil War, out of whose refugees the original New England colonies were populated:

> The one which succeeded established the sacred Rights of property (abolition of feudal tenures, no arbitrary taxation) . . . gave political power to the propertied (sovereignty of Parliament and common law, abolition of prerogative courts) . . . and removed all impediments to the triumph of the ideology of the men of property – the protestant ethic. There was, however, another revolution which never happened, though from time to time it threatened. This might have established communal property, a far wider democracy in political and legal institutions, might have disestablished the state church and rejected the protestant ethic.[2]

Hill's remarks suggest the interdependence of liberalism and the left, as well as the tense but productive relation between them. While liberals like John Locke were attacking extremist, utopian sects, a nagging radical tradition was born, concerned with enclosures (land privatizations) political democracy (voting and the army), women's subordination (reform of the family and of sexuality) and the demand for "true and pure undefiled religion," (the sanctity of the individual conscience), all aspects of a deepened ideal of equality.

Although we can trace many "leftist" ideas back to the Reformation, the *term* left (*gauche*) is indelibly associated with the creation of the National Assembly in France during the 1789 revolution. Over time, those who sat on the left (the Jacobins, the Montagnard) came to represent the egalitarian social revolution, while those who sat on the right (the Gironde) stood for the liberal political revolution. As Napoleon's conquests spread revolutionary ideals throughout Europe, the left/right distinction began to order seating arrangements within all parliamentary democracies.[3] As Jean Laponce has noted, being "visual and spatial . . . [the left/right dichotomy was] immediately understandable and easily translatable across cultures."[4]

What was the idea of a left that descended from the age of the democratic revolution? The two major theorists who have addressed this question, Norberto Bobbio and Steven Lukes, both gave the same answer: equality. In Steven Lukes's summary,

> What unifies the left as a tradition across time and space is its very rejection of the symbolic hierarchy [i.e. the universal subordination of the left] and the inevitability of the inequalities it sanctifies. What this suggests is that the left denotes a tradition and a project, which found its first clear expression in the Enlightenment [and] which puts in question sacred principles of social order, contests unjustifiable but remediable inequalities of status, rights, powers and condition and seeks to eliminate them through political action. Its distinctive core commitment is to a demanding answer to the question of what equality means and implies. It envisions a society of equals and takes this vision to require a searching diagnosis, on the widest scale, of sources of unjustifiable discrimination and dependency and a practical program to abolish or diminish them.[5]

As this quotation suggests, the liberal tradition stands for formal equality, the equality of all citizens before the law, whereas the left probes the social and cultural conditions that lie behind formal equality, and may serve either to eviscerate it or to realize it. But the difference runs deeper than that. Behind the left's commitment to equality is a passion for emancipation from entrenched forms of domination. Criticizing forms of domination that liberals tolerate or ignore, the left stands not only for equality, but also for an enhanced conception of freedom.

Unlike France, America does not have a parliamentary system with left, right and center parties. In its place America developed an originally nonideological two-party system. As a result, the term "left" was not widely used in a political sense in the United States until after the Bolshevik Revolution (1917). In fact, the first American book that I have been able to locate that uses the term in its title in the political sense, David Saposs's *Left-Wing Unionism*, only appeared in 1926. This did not mean, however, that America lacked a left before the Bolshevik Revolution. On the contrary, there existed powerful US counterparts to the radical democrats, utopian socialists and communist revolutionaries of the nineteenth-century European left. These included the radical wing of the abolitionists, as well as many other nineteenth-century reformers, labor organizers, communalists, and the so-called "lyrical left" of John Reed and Randolph Bourne.

In both Europe and America, the place of communism within the history of the left was deeply ambiguous. The reason was the communist break with liberalism. Marx argued that the democratic revolutions were bourgeois revolutions and thus should be followed by socialist revolutions. Whereas the idea of the left before Marx presupposed the existence of a center and a right, Marxism (and especially Leninism) wanted the left to occupy the total political space. After Marxism developed, Marx's followers tended to use the terms left, right and center to describe intrasocialist differences, as in Lenin's 1918 polemic "'Left-Wing' Communism: An Infantile Disorder," or in descriptions of the conflicts between Trotsky (left), Stalin (center) and Bukharin (right).[6] Thus, Marxism conflated the left with socialist revolutions, whereas in many societies, such as our own, the left presupposes liberal and democratic institutions and is committed to preserving, albeit deepening them.

Nonetheless, Marx's contribution to the history of the left is indispensable. When Marx described all of history as the history of class struggle, he gave us a conception of emancipation as a continuous struggle, a project with a deep past, and an extended future. In this way, he countered the notion, central to the liberal tradition, that we are already free, or that we live in "free societies." Equally central, Marx is the only thinker who has provided a clear and lucid theory of capitalism, a social system organized through the division between capital and labor, and utterly distinct from a market or exchange society, as described, for example, in Adam Smith's *Wealth of Nations*, or in the works of contemporary economists such as Joseph Stiglitz or Paul Krugman. Such a theory of capitalism lies behind the second term I promised to clarify, crisis.

Marx's theory of capitalism, like his refusal to accept capitalism as a historical end point was inseparable from his insistence on seeing it as intrinsically crisis-prone. The American left inherited the idea of a crisis from Marx, not just the kind of "economic crisis" that characterized the Great Depression and that afflicts the country today, but also broader, long-term crises reflecting Marx's influence on modern historiography, such as "the crisis of the Middle Ages," "the general crisis of the seventeenth century," or "the crisis of the modern state."

We can learn much about the character of crises by considering the Greek word *krino*, from which the word *krisis* derives. *Krino* means to pick out, to choose, to decide, to judge. A crisis is not simply an economic breakdown or a war, from which one needs to recover. More deeply, it is a turning point during which fundamental decisions are made as to the society's future direction. Crises have narrative structures, as in the Greek tragedies, where the subject arrives at a decisive moment and must directly confront his or her fate. The heart of a crisis lies not in its objective character but rather in the subjective self-awareness of the one who is undergoing it, in our case the American people. It is during periods of crisis that the left becomes indispensable to the nation, so indispensable that the crisis cannot ever be truly resolved without the left's active involvement.

To understand why, we must distinguish "normal" periods, emergencies, and crises in American history. During normal or everyday periods the country does tend to get along with such ideas as individualism, pluralism and private property, and with calls for "pragmatism," "bipartisanship," and passing beyond "obsolete" left/right conflicts. During short-term emergencies, like the Alien and Sedition Acts of the 1790s, the Red Scare of 1919, or the McCarthy period in the 1940s and 1950s, the country reveals a surprisingly strong communal, religious and ethnonational core; it comes together as a whole people, but in a panicky way, joining to expel the "alien element." In crises, by contrast, Americans strive to form a new or revised agreement, an agreement on values, not a mere deal, compromise, or horse-swap. While the left is present during normal periods, and can be very important in resisting group pressures during states of exception, its special value lies in periods of crisis. The reason is that during these periods the nation has to look inward and summon up its unconscious and inherited powers, not just rely on its everyday, commonsensical fund of assumptions. When it does look inward, it needs the deep conception of equality – equality as the nation's telos, as its very raison d'être – to which the left adheres.

Crises invariably have a structural dimension. They occur because of epochal transformations in the deep structure of American capitalism. Still, such crises are not merely "economic" crises, resolvable by allowing the value of goods and services to decline sufficiently, in other words by inflicting sufficient pain.

Rather, they are tectonic shifts in which the nation's assumptions, values and direction are rethought. Thus, they have an identity dimension as well.

The United States has undergone three crises of this sort. Importantly, the American Revolution, which established independence, was not one of them. As figures like Thomas Paine suggest, the Revolution is important to the American left, which has as part of its birthright abiding concerns for national independence and individual liberty. Nonetheless, the American Revolution was not concerned to establish equality; on the contrary, most of the "founding fathers" envisioned a relatively hierarchical society, and not simply because of slavery.

The three crises I have in mind constitute a kind of counternarrative to the one that begins with Independence. They were, first, the slavery crisis, which came to a head in the struggle to abolish slavery and the Civil War; second, the crisis surrounding the rise of large-scale corporate capitalism, which came to a head in the struggles of the 1930s and the creation of a modern administrative state that could regulate business and ensure the general welfare; and third, the crisis opened up by the neoliberal revolution in the 1970s, but with roots in the preceding decade. Each crisis was associated with a particular stage in the history of capitalism: primitive accumulation in the form of slavery and Indian Removal; large-scale corporate accumulation in the case of the New Deal; and finance-led globalization in the case of the New Left. The shift from each stage to the next was not socioeconomic alone. Each shift, rather, brought a crisis of authority, identity, and governing purpose that could not be resolved by reference to the political thought of the Revolution, or to the American Constitution (with which in fact progressive forces were frequently at odds).

Understanding American history as a series of three successive crises and not in terms of a unilinear unfolding gives us a different conception of the nation. The actual founding of the United States, I will argue, should be seen to lie in its commitment to equality and justice, not simply to independence. Thus, each crisis involved a *refounding* of the country, a transformation of its identity and of its conception of legitimate order, one that placed equality at its center. In each case the left supplied an indispensable idea, namely a conception of equality that spoke to the country's identity. In each refounding, moreover, the left's role was quite specific.

Slavery would have been abolished without the abolitionists. A modern state bringing some degree of rational administrative steering to the otherwise dysfunctional irrationality of corporate capitalism would have been created without the socialists. A postindustrial, consumerist America, and the end of Jim Crow and the family wage, would have emerged without the New Left. What the left did was to give an egalitarian meaning to each of these transformations – to articulate racial equality as the meaning of the Civil War, social equality as the meaning of the New Deal, and a wider participatory democracy as the meaning of the 1960s.

The left was indispensable because without it the meaning of each reform was ambiguous. Consider the abolition of slavery. As David Brion Davis has written, the "sense of self-worth created by dutiful work" that replaced slavery could have become either "a way of disguising exploitation" or a spur to redeeming the "equality [of] people of subordinate status."[7] The abolitionists, the first American left, forced the latter meaning, to the extent that it has been forced. Similarly, the powerful mechanisms of the New Deal state could have been used either to help rescue Wall Street from its continuing disastrous errors, or to advance the condition of industrial workers, immigrants and Southern blacks. To the extent that the New Deal did the latter, it was due to the efforts of the socialists, understood broadly to include a great range of American reform, including the communists. Finally, the sixties could have produced a meritocratic, sexually liberated, consumption-oriented world of gated communities, mercenary armies and exquisite cafés, or a worldwide democratic transformation centered on an expanded ideal of equality. The New Left sought to establish the second outcome; if it failed, the long-term meaning of the episode remains to be seen.

In each case, the left did not create the call for equality. That call arose, rather, from social movements, such as the labor movement, the various African-American freedom movements, and the women's movement, movements sparked by the large-scale shifts I have termed crises. The history of these movements reveals that the call for equality changes historically, often in quite unpredictable ways. The abolition of slavery, a form of labor that was essentially unquestioned for thousands of years, is one example of the unpredictable course that the demand for equality follows; the New Deal's overthrow of "the Protestant Republic" (i.e.,

WASP domination) was another; Gay Liberation is still another. Although the social movements that demand equality create new values, often surprising ones, they are not themselves on the left. The left's job is not to create these movements but to be responsive to them, to relate them to an overall telos of equality, to participate in them as a left, and to critique them when necessary from that point of view. In Karl Marx's youthful formulation, the left aims at "the self-clarification of the struggles and wishes of the age."

In each of the three crises, too, the left contributed its part by placing the ideal of equality at the center of the country's collective memory. We have been reminded in recent years of how important collective memory is to politics. The Tea Party movement, for example, argues that activist governments contradict the founding fathers' sacred writ. Originalists insist that the Constitution has an eternal status. The left by contrast argues that the nation's identity is an ongoing project, constantly being redefined, but in the direction of greater equality. Thus a crucial moment for the first American left occurred when Lincoln insisted that the Declaration of Independence's assertion that "all men are created equal" "was of no practical use in effecting our separation from Great Britain ... it was placed in the Declaration not for that, but for future use," by which Lincoln meant the emancipation of the slaves. Likewise, Eleanor Roosevelt understood the nation's identity as an ongoing project when she arranged for the black soprano Marian Anderson, denied access to the Daughters of the American Revolution Constitution Hall, to sing on the steps of the Lincoln Memorial. The Lincoln Memorial, she grasped, had been put there for "future use." In his speech to the 1963 March for Jobs and Freedom, Martin Luther King observed that the Negro after emancipation had been given a "promissory note," and that the note had come due. Barack Obama ran for President in 2008 as a "community organizer," implicitly drawing on subterranean recollections of the civil rights struggle, even if his Presidency failed to act on this association. In each case, the left connected the present to a telos of equality, seeking to refound the country on an egalitarian basis. Far from being irrelevant, then, the left has been central to the country's effort to establish a coherent history based on its deepest resources.

The left's commitment to a searching ideal of equality explains the basic asymmetry in the relation of left and right. The really vital relationship in twentieth-century history – the one that drives its political dynamic – is not the relationship between left and right, but rather between the left and the classical liberal doctrines that emerged during the seedbed of modern, democratic politics. The right, by contrast, is a reaction to the left. When we get a right that has genuine intellectual force and charisma, as we got in the US after the quasi-defeat of the New Left in the early 1970s, it necessarily dressed itself up in the leftist vernacular of protest, discontent, minority voice, and exclusion. Any attempt to exclude the left, and to form "bipartisan deals" coalition between liberals and the right, cannot resolve the country's crisis, as we shall see. Only a revitalized left, which further deepens America's egalitarian commitments, can move in that direction.

Why America Needs a Left makes this argument in three chapters. The first centers on the crisis provoked in the early republic by the existence of slavery. The ownership of one person by another not only outraged the conscience, it also gave rise to the first American left, a left that included abolitionism, pioneering feminist breakthroughs, evangelical reformers of the "burnt-over" districts, and the densest proliferation of utopian and communist communities in the world. Because of its stress on participation, I call the first American left "republican," but the left cannot be reduced to classical republicanism, which was associated with masculine "virtue" and character rather than rights, as well as with landholding and aristocracy.

The original impetus for the modern left, I will show, was the problem of slavery, hence the problem of races and peoples, and not as Marx later argued, the problem of industry and the working class. This was the case everywhere in the world, not just in the United States. Chattel slavery placed issues of violence and social reproduction as well as labor on the agenda of the left. While many Americans became opposed to slavery in the years during and after the Revolution, the abolitionists were unique in their concern with racial equality. In pursuit of that goal, they introduced into American democracy, or at least revitalized, almost all the political tactics that later lefts have used, including leafleting, public demonstrations and agitation. In their relations with Lincoln and the Republican Party, especially, they taught future lefts how a minority could strengthen the moral spine of a country seeking baseless compromise.

As the leader of the Republican Party, at a time when the US was becoming an engine of commercial and industrial capitalism, Lincoln had to weld together many diverse interests – Southern Whigs, newly emancipated freedmen, Northern industrialists, land-grabbing Westerners, and the like. Thus, he felt a need to compromise with antiwar elements in his own party, in other words to keep moral issues out of politics. It was his tense and conflicted relationship to the abolitionists that changed the character of his Presidency. In 1776, when Jefferson wrote "all men are created equal," he had no intention of challenging the institution of slavery; rather he had the condition of men in the state of nature in mind. In his 1863 Gettysburg address, however, Lincoln turned Jefferson's abstract proclamation into a national project: not that all men were equal, but that they would be made equal. Without the abolitionists, slavery would have been abolished, but then we wouldn't have the attempt – however flawed – to refound the country on the basis of racial equality.

The second American crisis was provoked by the rise of large-scale corporate capitalism, which destroyed the sense of liberty and independence on which the earlier, family and small property centered market republic had relied. Not merely economic, the second crisis arose from the perception that the rise of the large corporations or "trusts" had created a new system of quasi-feudal estates. While a small, mostly white, mostly Protestant middle class was able to provide for the contingencies of life, the vast majority of Americans, above all the immigrants, the African-Americans, and large numbers of white Southerners, lived under conditions of profound material insecurity. The crisis of the 1930s required, as Franklin Roosevelt put it, "a reappraisal of values," in other words, a new direction for the society. The goal was not "recovery" but rather a refounding in the same sense that the Gettysburg address had been a refounding.

At the heart of the refounding lay a new role for the state. However, there was no inherent need for the modern, administrative state to be associated with social equality. It acquired that association because of the second American left. Without the left, the New Deal state might well have assumed a more nationalistic, intolerant, racist, anti-Semitic and, in a word, fascistic character.

Like analogous states elsewhere, the New Deal demonstrated mass society characteristics – radio, film, monumental architecture, charismatic leadership. Unlike its counterparts, however, such as Nazi Germany, Stalin's Soviet Union and Mussolini's Italy, the New Deal was inflected with the values and meanings created by broad-based social democratic and anticapitalist movements, including those among industrial workers, African-Americans, "illegal" immigrants, and women. The New Deal in general, and Franklin Roosevelt in particular, is often credited with "saving" liberal democracy, meaning that when other nations turned to fascist and communist solutions, the United States held fast to its founding ideals. This is true, but it is not the whole truth. Liberalism survived the Great Depression only by appropriating such leftist attempts at crisis resolution as planning, the socialization of risk, and social democracy, all inflected by the core leftist principle of social equality.

The first two stages in the history of the American left already constituted a tradition. The second American left made this explicit, connecting itself to Puritan reformers, Jacobins, abolitionists, feminists, Christian socialists, and even with the Spartacist Rebellion of ancient Rome. As a result, when the third American crisis erupted in the 1960s, the egalitarian forces of that time were able to situate themselves in relation to a left-wing tradition, hence to call themselves a "New Left."

Of the three case studies in this book, the New Left is the most difficult to comprehend, in part because it is so new, and its historiography just beginning. How, for example, are we to define the New Left, given that it was composed of many diverse movements, including the radical wings of the civil rights and Vietnam War movements, new and unexpected forms of social protest, such as ecology, second-wave feminism ("women's liberation") and Gay Liberation, and new sites of struggle such as schools, prisons and hospitals? In what sense did the New Left confront a crisis comparable to the crises of slavery and industrial capitalism? Finally, what is the legacy of the New Left, especially given the political and even intellectual predominance of the right since the 1960s?

By the New Left I mean what was then called "the movement," the activists of the sixties who intervened in the three great mass movements of the time, civil rights, antiwar, and feminism, and in intervening tried to draw out the continuity between the three movements. In calling itself "new," the New Left sought to distinguish itself from the "old left," that is, the socialists of the New Deal era. The difference lay in the different stages of capitalism from which the two lefts arose. From the "old left" point of view, the emancipation of man from nature depended on building up collective institutions, such as trade unions, and on gaining influence and ultimately control over the state. The old left was able to succeed, to the extent that it did succeed, because capital needed a strong state to help order and rationalize the process of economic growth.

By contrast, the New Left arose not from the accumulation of labor, but from the release of (first world) labor from direct engagement in material production, in other words from the scientific, technological and educational revolution that has produced the wealth of our time. Beginning after World War Two, capital organized itself globally, so that the nation-state, including the United States, underwrote a system of global finance and sought foreign markets. On the one hand, labor became increasingly productive, which was experienced in the sixties under such rubrics as "affluence," automation and "the triple revolution." On the other hand, capital became increasingly mobile, as new forms of "cheap labor" developed globally. The changed geography of production was experienced in the seventies as "deindustrialization," in the eighties and nineties as the global spread of finance and services, and today as an unemployment crisis based on global overcapacity, and fiscal austerity imposed by banks. The disaggregation of market forces that has characterized capitalism since World War Two ultimately generated what Daniel Rodgers has called "the age of fracture."[8]

The crisis that the New Left faced was analogous to the crisis faced by the previous two lefts. Structurally, the 1960s witnessed the culmination of decolonization and the beginning of the end of US global hegemony. Its economy was increasingly centered on service work. Due to the Cold War and the mushrooming post-industrial economy, the dismantling of Jim Crow and the transition to the two-earner family were on the agenda. Likewise, a state-centered, bureaucratically organized industrial behemoth was going to give way to smaller, more diverse and globally mobile capitalist interests. The question facing the country was what the meaning of these changes would be. Would they "disguise exploitation" or advance "equality in people of subordinate status"? The answer proposed by the New Left was a deepened, extended, radicalized sense of equality, tantamount to a third refounding. Thus leftists struggled, in the three movements in which they played a role (civil rights, antiwar, and feminism), to bend the arc of capitalism toward equality.

Almost certainly there would have been a cultural revolution in the 1960s had there never been a New Left. One did not need a left to see that the sixties marked the first full-scale emergence of mass consumer culture, characterized by uninhibited vibrancy and sex appeal, reliance on youth and on racial and sexual subcultures, unprecedented international exchanges in design, music, and film, a rights revolution, and postmodern philosophy. One did not need a left to see that Cold War liberalism had produced a "democratic faith lacking in deeper emotional resources."[9] One did not need a left to see that this lack might encourage a religious awakening, shown not only in the importance of prophetic religion to the civil rights movement, but also in Zen, Indian music, meditation, the Christian search for existential authenticity, and "altered states of consciousness," sometimes based on the use of drugs. Without the New Left one would likely still have had the Beatles, the Grateful Dead, *Hair*, Pop Art, Jimi Hendrix, John F. Kennedy, Marshall McLuhan, Buckminster Fuller, Mary Quant, color TV, jet travel, transistors, and the birth control pill.

One did need a left, however, to break through the iron vise of Cold War thinking, to expose the alliance between Democratic Party liberals and Mississippi segregationists, to grasp the corporate and military control of the universities, to face the shocking sycophancy of American intellectuals in the face of power, to acknowledge the almost incalculable extent to which the government lied to its people, especially concerning war, to grasp the continuity between racism, colonialism, and the war in Vietnam, to see that schools, prisons and doctor's offices were sites of power, to develop critical subfields in every academic discipline, to see sexism as a deep structure of human history, not simply a form of discrimination, and to build ties of solidarity with the poorest people on the planet, and with homosexuals, women, and racial minorities. It was the New Left that ensured that the sixties was not only a period of cultural transformation. The New Left gave the cultural transformation its political meaning: a radical deepening in the promise of equality, in terms both of new subjects, such as gays, and new sites, such as the family.[10] These egalitarian aspirations found charismatic expression in iconic figures of the sixties: Martin Luther King, Che Guevara, Fidel Castro, Herbert Marcuse, Angela Davis, Malcolm X, and Albert Camus.

The New Left constitutes the third great left in American history but differs from the previous two in that it did not provoke a successful transformation of liberalism. On the contrary, what followed the sixties was a turn away from the great American theme of equality in favor of neoliberal "competitiveness," meritocratic "achievement," and "postpartisan" pragmatism. What fractured in Daniel Rodgers' "age of fracture" were the aspirations for large-scale social transformation born in the sixties. Equality was reduced to meritocracy, freedom was reduced to choice, and the critique of bureaucracy gave way to the romance of the market. *Why America Needs a Left* traces this devolution, but it also identifies the promissory note that the New Left left behind, "for future use."

What this book argues, then, is that America needs a left if it is to pull itself out of its much-touted "long-term decline." By decline I do not mean the shift in economic power associated with the inevitable rise of China and India. I do mean the country's moral decline implicit in its abandonment of the project of equality. I mean the pampering of elites and the demonization of the poor that are intrinsic to meritocracy, but anathema to democracy. I mean the transformation of a hegemon into an imperial bully. The only way to reverse this decline is by a revival of the egalitarian traditions – racial equality, social equality, cultural and sexual equality, and equality between the peoples of the world – that have proven indispensable to this country in previous eras of turmoil and difficulty. The possibilities of such a revival, and the hope which is the inevitable forerunner of the left, were palpable in 2008, when Barack Obama emerged as the anti-Bush, anti-establishment and antiwar candidate, and as the person who at the level of image, rhetoric and resonance positioned himself as signaling a revival of the left, albeit one appropriate to a new world. The sense of depression that pervaded much of the country since then reflected the failure of that image to correspond to reality. It was a depression born from a longing for a left, since lifted by the appearance of Occupy Wall Street. Is it possible to build a fourth American left? The materials lie before us, waiting to be stirred into life.

1

Abolitionism and Racial Equality

The abolitionists active in the United States between the 1830s and the 1860s did not think of themselves as a left. Instead, like so many American activists and radicals, they mostly thought of themselves as evangelical Protestants, doing God's work, although one of the leading figures, Ernestine Rose, was Jewish. Nonetheless, by any reasonable historical assessment the abolitionists, or at least their "immediatist" or Garrisonian wing, about whom I will mostly be writing, did constitute an American left. Not only that, they constituted the first American left.

Many of them free blacks, the abolitionists flourished amid an enormous wave of reform movements, Fourierist, Owenite and other utopian and socialist communities, and the huge explosion of democratic self-awareness that characterized Jacksonian America. I have chosen to focus on them, however, because as much as or more than any of their contemporaries they invented so much of the repertoire of the subsequent American left, including nonviolent resistance, democratic agitation, cultural and sexual experimentation, and unremitting attempts to shame the liberal, hypocritical majority. They were among the first to explore the power of a principled minority to upset carefully constructed coalitions, that is to disrupt the control mechanisms built into the new mass parties. Above all they – or at least the more radical currents among them – were focused on the goal of bringing the American people to accept blacks as their fellow countrymen.

For them political equality was inseparable from racial equality, especially in immediate, one-to-one relations, such as the abolition of the "negro pew" in churches, the integration of the elementary schools, and the legitimation of mixed marriages. Once the principle of racial equality was accepted, they believed, the imperative of abolishing slavery would become immediately clear.

The abolitionist focus on equality as the basis of American nationhood may be contrasted to the thinking of the American revolutionaries. No doubt, this question is complex and many histories stress the importance to the American radical tradition of figures like Thomas Paine, the very idea of a right of revolution, and the struggle not just over home rule, but over who should rule at home. Nonetheless, at a basic level, the Revolution of 1776 had the aim of national independence; it was not a crisis in the sense that the Civil War was a crisis. Indeed, it is important to my argument that, while the American Revolution was taken as a model for many later national independence movements, it is regularly contrasted with the movements identified with the left. Thus, Edmund Burke praised the American Revolution because it was based on long established rights of Englishmen, just as he attacked the French Revolution because it was based on abstract principles of universal equality. Friedrich von Gentz, a polemicist of the eighteenth century, wrote: "The American revolution was from beginning to end, on the part of the Americans, a defensive revolution; the French was from beginning to end, in the highest sense of the word, an offensive revolution." By this Gentz meant that the Americans were seeking to protect long-established rights, whereas the French were trying to create a new world. So compelling was this contrast that John Adams, the second President of the United States, translated and published Gentz's pamphlet with the aim of freeing the American Revolution from the "disgraceful imputation of having proceeded from the same principles as the French."[1] In 1955 Russell Kirk, a founder of contemporary neoconservatism, republished Adams's translation as a mass-market paperback.

On the crucial question of slavery, the American Revolution emancipated the slaves in most Northern states, excluded slavery from the Northwest Territory and set an end to the Atlantic slave trade. But otherwise the Constitution aimed to remove the slavery question from national politics, to leave its disposition to the masters, and to allow for racial discrimination in the nonslave states. By contrast, the abolitionists believed that it was impossible to imagine the American nation except on the basis of racial equality. In the service of that end, they were not afraid to offend American patriotism. After the abolition of slavery in the British Empire on August 1, 1833 they reversed the clichéd contrast between British despotism and American freedom by regularly celebrating August 1 as the Black Fourth of July.[2] Neither simply "for" nor "against" their country, they refused to regard the United States as a completed entity. Treating the country instead as a project, they sought to revise America's identity by insisting on the centrality of equality. This, too, set them apart from the revolutionaries of 1776. While independence is an objective fact to be celebrated and memorialized ever after, equality is a project, always in need of improvement and elaboration. In turning equality into the project that Richard Rorty called "achieving our country," the abolitionists helped kick-start the American left.[3]

The story of the American left also begins with the abolitionists because as much as or more than their contemporaries, they invented a new and anomalous American type, the radical who was defined by his or her ideals. Combining "steadfastness of purpose with an almost reckless disregard of self-interest," willing to court martyrdom rather than give in to the majority, the radical relied "on a direct appeal to the moral sense of other people."[4] What the immediatist abolitionists realized was that the American commitment to equality is often so shallow, so compromised, and so easily abandoned in the face of short-term opportunities and practical constraints, that America needs a permanent body of "extremists," risk-takers and scolds. In Michael Walzer's words, American politics needs Saints characterized by an "uncompromising and sustained commitment to a political ideal (which other men called hypocrisy), and by a pattern of rigorous and systematic labor in pursuit of that ideal (which other men called meddlesomeness)."[5] Alexis de Tocqueville, visiting the United States thirty years before the Civil War, was "astonished by the equanimity, indifference, [and] moral carelessness with which Americans managed to live with slavery." The abolitionists did not share that indifference and they made indifference impossible for others, creating the space within which mainstream figures like Lincoln operated.

We also begin with the abolitionists because the Civil War was the country's first and greatest crisis and the left, as I have argued, has a special relationship to crisis. Behind the war lay intensely rapid economic development as well as the growth of nationalism since Independence. Beginning in the 1830s or so, one can observe two different social systems pitted against one another: the North and West were republican, democratic, middle class, and believed in a wide dispersal of property. The South, though diverse, was still dominated by slaveholders convinced that patriarchal, hierarchical dependence was the basis of freedom. A struggle over control of the increasingly important national government precipitated the war. The Union's victory brought not only the end of slavery, but the 14th Amendment to the Constitution, which created national citizenship and guaranteed equality before the law. This outcome, however, proved reconcilable with racial hierarchy, as demonstrated by such elements of America's post–Civil War history as the Black Codes, the disfranchisement of most Southern blacks, the institution of Jim Crow, widespread toleration of lynching, segregation of the armed forces, redlining, employment discrimination, and an almost infinite variety of other discriminations.

Abolitionism left a different legacy. The abolitionists created the model for the subsequent American lefts by insisting on equality as the way to resolve a national crisis. The crisis at issue had two aspects. As a system crisis, the Civil War may be understood in terms of powerful global forces, such as the rise of nationalism, democracy and self-government, forces that were at war with older forms of hierarchy. But as an identity crisis, the war posed the question of what it means to be an American. The abolitionists – black and white – answered that question by inflecting the meaning of American identity with racial equality. In doing so they presumed that white Americans, in spite of their racial prejudices, which white abolitionists knew they shared, believed in equality and could learn to live as coequals with blacks. To be sure, this extreme and minority viewpoint entered the American mainstream only by overcoming intense and pervasive resistance. However, the message was transmuted through the development of a great new mass party, the Republicans, through the terrible ordeal of the war, and through the efforts of many great leaders, including the greatest, Abraham Lincoln.

This, at any rate, is the argument of this chapter, which unfolds in three steps. First, I will show how slavery in the form of "primitive accumulation" was at the center of the national (not just Southern) economy. As such it infected the ideal of political equality, which is central to the republican tradition. Two innovative democratic institutions aimed to keep slavery out of national politics: the new, mass parties, and the cult of the family and "true womanhood." These, however, also became the flashpoints through which abolitionism spread. In the second part I will show how the abolitionists grappled not just with slavery but especially with racial prejudice, which they related to America's foundational and enduring tendency toward violence, to Indian Removal and to what we call today sexism. Finally, I will describe the crisis and the war, emphasizing the relations of the nineteenth-century Republican Party and the abolitionists and indicating both the success and the weakness of the abolitionist attempt to refound America on the basis of racial equality.

Slavery was integral to all aristocratic, patriarchal and paternal societies until the rise of democracy. In Hannah Arendt's words, "All rulership had its original and its most legitimate [sic] source in man's wish to emancipate himself from life's necessity, and men achieved such liberation, by means of violence, by forcing others to bear the burden of life for them."[6] Slavery was enshrined in such core Western documents as the Hebrew and Christian Bibles, the texts of Plato and Aristotle, the preachments of the Catholic Church (which owned many slaves), the Koran (the Muslims spread slavery throughout West Africa and elsewhere), and the great philosophical writings of the seventeenth century, such as those of Thomas Hobbes, for whom the slave was a vanquished warrior who promised absolute obedience in return for his life. Reflecting his or her dependence, the precapitalist slave was typically a member of a patriarchal household or, in the Islamic world, of a *waqf* (religious endowment). So common was such dependence that slavery was sometimes not a distinct status but simply the most extreme form of unfree labor, a category that also included serfdom, servitude, and indenture.

The men and women of the democratic revolutions understood freedom as the opposite of slavery. Just as slavery was rooted in violence and war, so freedom was rooted in the social contract.

Just as slavery was rooted in privation and decline, so freedom was linked to abundance, and to the possibility of avoiding decline. Just as slavery pervaded the inner life, which was marked by sin and dependence, so freedom implied a revolutionary shift toward independence and self-reliance in human psychology. For defenders of slavery, the master had to oversee, guide and educate the bondsman just as the soul had to govern the body; to free or enlightened eyes, however, the slave-owner had put himself in God's place.

Although the American ideal of freedom was based on this contrast, freedom could not emancipate itself so easily from slavery. American slavery was not ancient, patriarchal or aristocratic slavery but the new commercial – even bourgeois – slavery that emerged with early modern capitalism. Sugar, coffee, cotton and cacao from the Caribbean, tobacco, rice and indigo from North America, and gold and silver from South America supplied the basis for the new modern commercial empires – English, French, Dutch, Spanish and Portuguese. Although slavery prospered during the mercantilist era, the plantations were not built by the state but rather by the "new merchants" of seventeenth-century England and Holland, who traded in mass rather than luxury goods. Run out of banks, counting houses and law firms, based on an extensive system of credit and bills of exchange (indispensable for bulk growing of raw materials and long-term exchange), inseparable from shipbuilding, banking, textiles and other key industries, the slave plantations constituted the sinews of commercial capitalism.

As a result, the newly emerging market societies were thoroughly saturated with racial violence. Insofar as slaves had been members of patriarchal households or religious endowments, they had been protected from the most brutal forms of violence, at least in part. On the capitalist plantations, by contrast, they were treated as factors of production: commodities. As a result, their condition worsened dramatically. As David Brion Davis has noted, from the 1440s, when the Portuguese began transporting black slaves to Iberia, to the 1860s, when the illegal slave trade to Cuba came to an end, an estimated 11 million slaves entered the New World. By 1820, however, when 2 million European immigrants had become 12 million, the 11 million Africans had left only 6 million descendants.[7] This almost incomprehensible destruction laid the basis for the first great crisis of American capitalism, a crisis that arose from the fact that the American republic as a whole was deeply entwined with racial slavery.

In theory, America was a "yeoman democracy," resting on a wide distribution of land and property. The English encouraged large-scale emigration to North America, so freehold agriculture developed alongside the plantations. In England inequality based on unequal land tenure had been ingrained for centuries, but in the colonies indentured servants, criminals and propertyless immigrants could attain independence. The result was basic to American republicanism. As Charles Sellers explains:

> Cheap land, virtually free at first, not only elevated the mass but imposed a limit on wealth by making labor expensive. With farm ownership readily attainable, Euro/Americans would not labor for others except briefly and at high wages. A few years of high wages financed enough cheap land to yield a comfort and independence inconceivable to poor Europeans. With wages too high for most farmers to pay, production was limited – no matter how much land they had – by the family labor available. While raising European immigrants to an exhilarating rural well-being, the person/land ratio inhibited further accumulation. The resulting society of roughly equal landowning families was the seedbed of American republicanism.[8]

In practice, though, republicanism coexisted with slavery. Not only did the plantations dominate the rural economy, but they served as forerunners for the factories of the industrial revolution.[9] Paradoxically, the democratic revolutions, by releasing men of property from clerical and royal controls, had thereby freed them to develop a new level of intensive organization reflected in the gang system, "an incessant cycle of planting, weeding and harvesting, and night work in the mill, adding up to eighteen hour days." Planters turned plantations into total environments, bent toward "diligent and systematic behavior aimed at profit maximization." The larger plantations were subject to every advance in scientific management, including "simplification and repetition of tasks," coordination of labor, "precise calibration of labor inputs and subordination to mechanical rhythms," dietary experiments, and smallpox inoculation, even as plantations also relied on the natural economy, with slaves building their own huts and growing their own food.[10]

The invention of the cotton gin in 1793 made both slavery and industry profitable and linked them tightly together. Southern plantations, securing the markets that Santo Domingo (today's Haiti) lost after abolishing slavery, became indispensable to the British textile industry. Begun with the resale of high value Indian manufactured goods, especially calico, the industry switched to importing cotton and manufacturing cloth at home. As a result, it relied on the superprofits of American slavery to provide the capital and on the slaves to provide the cotton. Slave-trade ports such as Bristol, Glasgow and Liverpool became centers of textile production. According to Eric Hobsbawm, "the cotton industry was thus launched, like a glider, by the pull of the colonial trade to which it was attached; a trade which promised not only great, but rapid and above all unpredictable expansion."[11] Fueled by the "insatiable and rocketing demands" of Britain's "satanic" mills, cotton plantations spread into Alabama, Mississippi, and Louisiana.

The result was the American boom out of which mass democracy, the slavery crisis and the first American left would all emerge. Between 1815 and 1825 the amount of baled cotton produced in the South quadrupled. In addition, slavery itself became an industry. Slave values more than tripled between 1800 and 1860. A Texas planter advised his Alabama nephew: "Get as many young negro women as you can. Get as many cows as you can . . . It is the greatest country for increase that I have ever saw in my life."[12] By the time of the Civil War, "a young 'prime field hand' in New Orleans would sell for the equivalent of an expensive car, say a Mercedes-Benz today. American slaves represented more capital than any other asset in the nation, with the exception of land," about three times the amount invested in manufacturing or railroads nationwide. Slave grown cotton was also the nation's leading export, powering the textile-manufacturing revolution in New England, and paying for "American imports of everything from steel to capital."[13]

The cotton explosion fueled the great Westward thrust of the country. As the United States turned toward its internal market, the government cut the minimum acreage of land it would sell from 640 acres to 420 acres, and also cut the price, fueling a huge frontier expansion. The Ohio, Wabash and Mississippi rivers served as "interstate highways." The steamboat made it possible to go *up* the

Mississippi while roads, bridges, steamboats, and canals tied the national market together. The land office became the most important government agency. Meanwhile, the Indian Removal Act of 1830 forced at least 100,000 Chickasaw, Cherokee, Creek and Choctaws out of Georgia, Tennessee, Alabama and Mississippi, driving them to the Oklahoma territories, with enormous loss of life and spirit.

Like the plantations themselves, and like the discrimination against free blacks in the nonslave states, the slave-driven expansion into the frontier forced Americans to confront the issue of racial equality. Clarence King's 1871 *Mountaineering in the Sierra Nevada* describes the funeral of an Indian woman, Sally the Old. As King studied her husband, Buck, watching "with wet eyes that slow-consuming fire burn the ashes of his wife," he knew he was seeing "not a stoical savage, but a despairing husband." Leaving the scene, King's friend asked, "Didn't I tell you Injuns has feelings inside of 'em?" King answered that he was convinced, writing "long after, as I lay awake through many night-hours listening to that shrill death-wail, I felt as if any policy toward the Indians based upon the assumption of their being brutes or devils was nothing short of a blot on this Christian century." But the next morning, when King learned that Buck was drunk, and that he had taken a new wife, he questioned his newfound enlightenment.

Slavery, then, and with slavery racial hierarchy, was embedded in the first stage of American capitalist development, commercial capitalism. The violent appropriation of wealth, slavery, along with Indian removal, was the precondition for economic development that Marx called "primitive accumulation." The key word is violence: primitive accumulation precedes and underlies the superficial equality of contractual and market relations. As the country developed, moreover, its violent underpinnings came to the fore. The result was a twofold crisis: On the one hand, a structural crisis, precipitated by the development of a national market, the struggles over a national bank, the growth of railroads and canals, and the drive for a more coordinated foreign policy; on the other hand, an identity crisis centered on the issue of racial equality. The convergence of these two crises created the political terrain on which abolitionism arose.

The American political order at the time of the Revolution was based on classical republican principles. It was assumed that only men who owned landed property or other secure, customary forms of wealth, including slaves, had the independence and breeding that conduced to virtue. But rapid economic expansion soon produced a new political order, often termed liberal-republicanism, and eventually liberalism. Based on John Locke's idea that "every Man has a Property in his own Person," liberalism valorized work and property as the basis of independence. Tocqueville, visiting America in the 1830s, noted that "not only work itself, but work specifically to gain money" was considered honorable. The aim of work was not wealth but social and economic independence. As one newspaper argued, "every man holds his fortune in his own right arm." Later Abraham Lincoln explained: "it is not the fault of the system" if a man did not rise above the status of wage laborer, either through his own "dependent nature" or through "improvidence, folly, or singular misfortune."[14]

In contrast to classic republicanism, liberalism presupposed the limitation of governmental activity and the guarantee of an unimpeded private sphere. Yet liberalism was also grounded in the market. As a result it required a state, not just for defense, but also to allow for coordination between competing elites, to provide internal improvements such as roads and canals, and to guide finance, typically through a national bank. The growth of an increasingly strong and increasingly democratic government was reflected in the two great political innovations of the Jacksonian period (1828–36): the "second party system" and a new, woman-centered redefinition of the public/private divide.

The second party system is the term historians use for the mass parties (Whig and Democratic) that emerged amid the economic expansion and explosive liberalism of the Jacksonian years. Unlike the first party system, which comprised the elite factions of the 1790s, the Jacksonian parties were mass parties premised on "universal" male suffrage. Aiming to appear as representatives of the whole society, the new parties tended to eschew divisive ideological issues. From this, some have drawn the conclusion that the United States has had no significant left, since it is controversial ideas and values that define the left. But the truth is quite the opposite. The diffuse, nonideological predispositions of the American party system created a special role for small, ideologically driven groups that interrogated the country's identity, rather than seeking to advance particular interests.

The second party system revolved around a strong, charismatic President. It was in relation to such a Presidency that the American left developed its characteristic small-group form. The Jeffersonian and Jacksonian "revolutions" had made the Presidency the center of democratic aspirations. The War of 1812 and the subsequent Indian wars produced "a powerful nationalism, a militant liberal egalitarianism and a charismatic national political figure," namely Andrew Jackson.[15] After the battle of New Orleans (1815), Jackson was portrayed as "the embodiment of transcendent forces – nature, agrarian virtue, the will of the people or God."[16] He portrayed "himself as the tribune of the people against selfish and entrenched leaders. He relied on personal leadership to overcome [obstacles]. He fought conspiratorial enemies who were seeking to overwhelm republican virtue."[17]

After Jackson left the Presidency "the routinization of charisma" set in. There arose "a new breed of politicians, men of humble origin who challenged genteel officeholders by courting voters assiduously in the oral style of rural vernacular."[18] These politicians "substituted the ties of personal loyalty to a leader ... for shared beliefs in policy objectives. They relied heavily on the sentimental bonds which develop among men who have worked as a team in victory and defeat, and on the pragmatic importance of winning."[19] The pragmatic sharing of spoils and other rewards moved to the center of the new liberal order. Although never President, Henry Clay, "the great compromiser" (and Lincoln's personal hero), exemplified this. Clay's "American System" linked protectionism with internal improvements, high tariffs to provide revenue for roads and canals, and transportation appropriations to sop up surplus revenues. The only danger to stability, explained Martin Van Buren, President from 1833 to 1837, was the "clamor" against Southern slavery, which he feared could lead to sectional conflict.[20]

The party system was one of two key institutions that served to hold the country together by avoiding the disruptive issue of slavery. The second was the conception of the family as a "haven in a heartless world." That conception arose as production left the household for the factory and the office. Left to specialize in "social reproduction," the domestic sphere, along with the disestablished churches, acquired a new ethical significance. Beginning in the 1820s, a middle-class ideology of domesticity overflowed "into advice books, home medical manuals, sentimental novels, and [into] the tales, verses and engravings of women's magazines and decorative gift books for the parlor." Written mainly by clergymen and physicians, as well as by women, America's first popular literature was profoundly steeped in gender imagery. Such literature "grounded human relationships in a conception of True Womanhood as weak, selfless, and pure."[21] For example, the educator Catherine Beecher argued that only women were sensitive enough to be teachers and fought to establish schools along with ministries at the country's frontier borders.

The cult of true womanhood complemented the two-party system by bolstering the American sense of national superiority, and by encouraging a sense of the inevitable contamination of political life. In addition, the cult informed and helped shape the codes that have regulated American protest, codes that encouraged genteel leadership, avoidance of conflict, and "uplift" among the oppressed. Finally, the cult of true womanhood helped bind the North and South together, giving both sections of the country a common set of familial assumptions. Thus, Southern slaveholders and their supporters had a patriarchal, romantic and chivalric familial ideology, expressed in dueling and other expressions of male honor, and in the idea that the slaveholder was responsible for all those in "his" household. Northerners rejected dueling but their idea of true womanhood was equally rooted in romantic, chivalric or courtly ideals, and often in an idealized view of the South as well. While North and South might differ on slavery, they agreed on the cult of womanhood. How bad could a slaveholder be if he subscribed to that?

Nevertheless, the institutions created to keep divisive issues like slavery out of politics also made it possible for the abolitionists to function. The second party system reflected the mass explosion of Jacksonian democracy. Not just poorer white men but women and free blacks took to the public sphere as if they owned it. With the shift from classic republicanism to liberal-republicanism, rights – the core of the American liberal tradition, as we shall see – came into prominence. As many abolitionists argued, the antislavery movement was America's greatest "school for rights." The second party system allowed for petitions, lectures, conventions, and the mass production of pamphlets, newspapers and posters, made possible by the newly invented steam press. The number of newspapers in America grew fourfold from 1830 to 1850.

As to the cult of true womanhood, its emphasis on sensitivity, suffering and compassion infused abolitionism with emotional content.[22] Earlier forms of elite abolitionism based on rational argumentation gave way to attempts to stir up mass emotions. To be sure, the cult encouraged women to participate in politics as a redemptive force, reinforcing a gender stereotype. But it encouraged women's activism nevertheless, including the common activism of black and white women, and it also revolutionized the relations of men and women. At the very time that the two sexes were becoming physically separated through the rise of commerce and industry, and the consequent separation between work and the family, they were also becoming psychologically closer and more entangled. The market revolution thus set in motion that tension-ridden but profoundly creative interaction between men and women that has been central to the American left. So explosive were the possibilities opened up by the new mass democracy that within two generations the United States had abolished slavery in a war in which the slaves themselves fought, denied compensation for the slaveholders, and granted citizenship and voting rights to the ex-slaves.[23] This could not have been achieved, however, without the intervention of the abolitionists, operating as the first American left. Their key innovation was what became the characteristic organizational form of American radicalism, the intensely-cathected, ideologically-motivated, uncompromising small group.

The sources of the antislavery tradition are many and varied. They include Enlightenment thinkers such as Montesquieu and Rousseau, Reformation precedents such as the Münster Anabaptists who "made the immediate surrender of personal property a test of faith," Arminian reformers who rejected the doctrine of original sin, maroons, slave rebels, rioters, heretics, army agitators, independent women, urban mobs, strikers, "rural barbarians of the commons" (as Thomas Malthus called them), rural farmers, maritime laborers, peasant rebels, Cossacks, and free thinkers who made up the everyday ranks of the democratic revolutions.[24]

Nevertheless, antislavery took a decisive turn when the French Revolution inspired the slave revolt in Santo Domingo, the "treasure house of eighteenth-century France." The colony had half a million slaves plus thousands of mulattos and freed slaves. It produced half the coffee in the world and exported almost half as much sugar as Jamaica, Cuba, and Brazil combined. As Santo Domingo was literally part of France, its free blacks and mulattos demanded citizenship in 1791, just as their white counterparts in France had the previous year.[25] On April 4, 1792 the French legislative assembly decreed free and equal rights to all free blacks and mulattos in the French colonies, "one of the truly great achievements of the French Revolution," according to David Brion Davis, precipitating the issuance of a general decree of emancipation by one of the black generals, Toussaint L'Ouverture.[26] In February 1794 the National Convention in Paris abolished slavery throughout the French colonies and granted rights of citizenship to all men regardless of color. Robespierre declared, "Let the colonies perish rather than a principle," while the sans-culottes denounced the "aristocracy of the skin."[27] Although in 1802 Napoleon, with British and US encouragement, sought to regain the island and reestablish slavery, and although L'Ouverture was captured and died in France, a slave army effectively ended Napoleon's ambitions for a revived empire in the New World, directly precipitating the Louisiana Purchase.[28]

In the decades following the Haitian Revolution, slavery was abolished everywhere in the world except Cuba, Brazil, and the United States. In 1819 hundreds of Haitian fighters, known as "los franceses," sailed with Simon Bolivar in the invasion that precipitated Latin America's independence from Spain. In return Bolivar promised to extinguish slavery in the lands he was to free.[29] After independence, all the Spanish American republics except Paraguay adopted "free womb" laws, meaning that the children of slaves were freed, and one by one the republics began to abolish slavery. Mexico abolished slavery in 1829, leading many Texans to convert their slaves to indentured servants. After the slave uprising in Jamaica of 1831–2 slavery was abolished in the British Empire. Finally, US slavery was abolished with the Civil War (1861–5).

Eric Williams's 1944 *Capitalism and Slavery* is often considered the first modern attempt to explain the abolition of slavery.[30] In Williams's view, slavery conflicted with industrialization; thus self-interest explains emancipation. Further research demonstrated, however, that slavery was booming and seemed headed for a long life when it was abolished. Accepting the fact that slavery was profitable led to the second great explanation for abolition, that of Howard Drescher, according to which the massive "econocide" of abolition – the destruction of a hugely profitable industry – demonstrated the ability of humanitarian interests to triumph over economic ones. Many contemporary works also ascribe the end of slavery to the apparently inevitable rise of universal human rights. In the 1960s and 1970s, however, an alternative to both views developed in what might be termed the neo-Marxist work of David Brion Davis.

According to Davis, the rise of large-scale industrial capitalism required a moral justification. Antislavery, Davis held, supplied that justification. The abolition of slavery, he writes, "was a highly selective response to labor exploitation. It provided an outlet for demonstrating a Christian concern for human suffering and injustice, yet thereby gave a certain moral insulation to economic activities less visibly dependent on human suffering and injustice."[31] Antislavery thus served as a kind of "ideological supplement" to the emerging wage-labor system. In Davis's summary:

> There was a pressing need felt by both skilled workers and employers to dignify and even ennoble wage labor, which for ages had been regarded with contempt. And what could better dignify and ennoble free labor, and even provide a sense of equality between the man who pays wages and the man who receives them than a common crusade against chattel slavery?

Like any ideology, antislavery was two-sided in its implications. As Davis writes, the "sense of self-worth created by dutiful work" could be cynically manipulated "as a way of disguising exploitation" or it could lead to the recognition of "elements of equality in people of subordinate status."[32] Davis's explanation sets the stage for understanding the "extra" contribution of the abolitionists. Embracing racial equality as the goal of their struggle, the abolitionist movement did not exhaust itself with the end of slavery and the triumph of liberal capitalism. Rather, it left a residue or supplement, by interpreting the abolition of slavery through the lens of equality. That supplement was the seed from which subsequent American lefts germinated.

The special role played by the abolitionists in the genesis of the American left can be better understood if we contrast American abolitionism to British. As in the United States, British antislavery leaders such as William Wilberforce drew on the new evangelical strains (in their case among Anglicans) to moralize reform. In contrast to the United States, however, British antislavery remained under the control of ruling elites, for whom it functioned as a symbol of Britain's moral supremacy, idealism and willingness to forgo material advantage. Focused on the single goal of abolition, British abolitionists tried to build a parliamentary majority, moderating their views to attract votes. Urging that slaveholders be compensated, they cautioned, "though men may be generous with their own property, they should not be so with the property of others."[33] Even so, it took the slave uprising in Jamaica of 1831–2 to bring the matter to a head, exemplifying what Barrington Moore called the contribution of revolution to gradualism.[34] British antislavery signaled the triumph of idealism over materialism. In 1815, at the Congress of Vienna, Britain insisted on an international treaty banning the slave trade, an act that signaled Britain's moral leadership of the international coalition meant to check, if not reverse, the French Revolution.[35] The residue left by British antislavery was Britain's hegemony over the global capitalist system.

David Brion Davis's paradigm explains British antislavery well. Abolitionism served as an "ideological supplement" to the triumph of laissez-faire industrial capitalism. By supporting abolition, Britain's dominant classes were able to identify themselves with what they portrayed as the ethical side of market forces.[36] At the very moment that industrial capitalism was taking root, antislavery seemed to demonstrate that moral values were more important than money. Slavery was abolished under the leadership of a liberal elite and through classic, liberal techniques: compromise, moderation, and deal-making among special interests, all of whom wound up benefiting. Abolition therefore served to demonstrate the essential benignity of capitalism, as well as the efficacy of gradualism in the service of reform.

The British abolition of slavery exemplifies liberalism (and republicanism) without a left. By contrast, the United States exemplifies liberalism with a left. Of course, slavery played a much more direct role in American society than it did in British;

America was a slave society whereas British slavery was colonial. Nonetheless, there was a further difference: the "extremism" of American abolitionism. Through the abolitionists' unrelenting pressure on American public opinion and on the ante-bellum Republican Party, the ideal of racial equality became core to the nation's identity. Because the abolitionists deeply impressed the antislavery struggle with the issue of racial equality, the American Civil War should be considered a refounding of the American nation, not simply the preservation of the union.

By speaking of a "refounding" I mean to contrast two different conceptions of American history. One conception sees the nation as having been founded with the "blessings of liberty" already present, only needing to be extended to new groups such as blacks and women. The idea of refounding is an alternative to this view. It presumes not only that freedom and equality are long-term projects, rather than already present, but also that they entail internal conflict, struggle, and contradiction. The confrontation with slavery was the first moment at which a view of America as crisis-prone and riven by contradictory forces loomed into view. But it was not the last time, to be sure.

Abolitionist sentiment and abolitionist societies could be found in America in the revolutionary period and before. But American abolitionism was profoundly transformed around 1830, with the creation of what is variously called its "modern," "immediatist," or Garrisonian wings. The immediate impetus for the change came from Free Negroes' resistance to the elite American Colonization Society, formed in 1816, which sought to return them to Africa. In his 1829 Appeal to the Colored Citizens of the World, David Walker invoked the Declaration of Independence to denounce the fact that "for too long others have spoken for us." Moreover, Free Negroes constituted the bulk of subscribers to such journals as William Garrison's *The Liberator* (three-quarters of the subscribers during the first year of publication), as well as to African-American newspapers like *Freedom's Journal*.[37] Garrison, the most well known of the white abolitionists, converted from colonization to abolition as a result of his experience of the vibrant black communities of Baltimore and Boston.[38] Free Negro abolitionists brought African-American slave culture, including spirituals, into the abolitionist movement. There, views of the slaves as a

chosen people became mingled with romanticism, transcendental-
ism, utopian socialism and evangelical reform: currents that had
come to see the democratic revolutions of the eighteenth century
as spiritual events, revolutions in human consciousness, aimed at
achieving what Alfred North Whitehead later called "the awakened solidarity of the human race."

Together, Free Negroes and whites founded the American
Anti-Slavery Society in 1833. At its peak in 1838, the Society
had 300,000 members in 2,000 loosely affiliated local chapters.
Extensive though it was, from the start abolitionism had the
character of a sect, meaning that membership was based on conversion, not birth. One converted to abolitionism; one did not
send in a check to an anonymous office. Afterward, one devoted
one's life to the cause. Abolitionists constituted a "blessed community"; frequently abolitionists married other abolitionists, and
they referred to their fellow abolitionists as brothers and sisters,
not fellow citizens. Particularly for whites, joining an abolitionist group meant standing aside from the dominant community.
White abolitionism, writes Sean Wilentz, constituted "an act of
defiance of widely and deeply held social conventions, [courting]
disapproval, ostracism, and even physical attack."[39] Ostracism
was welcomed as a sign of being on the right path, while ordinary
self-interest was rejected. "None know," wrote Wendell Phillips,
"what it is to live, till they redeem life from its seeming monotony
by laying it as a sacrifice on the altar of some great cause."[40] Lydia
Maria Child, an advocate of women's rights and Indian rights,
as well as an abolitionist, reminisced, "mortals were never more
sublimely forgetful of self than were the abolitionists of those early
days."[41] For Angelina Grimké, also a women's rights advocate and
abolitionist, "this is a cause worth dying for."[42]

The Calvinist idea of conversion was central to the abolitionist
commitment: one dies and is reborn; one breaks with one's place
in both society and the family and creates a new identity.[43] A charismatic sect, abolitionism was part of the "benevolent empire" of
evangelical reform, infused with millennial fantasy and a desire
"to 'come out' of a secular world corrupted by market egoism"
and to seek spiritual perfection by purging oneself "of egoistic pos-
sessiveness in relations of sex and property."[44] Just as preachers
like Jonathan Edwards had proclaimed the Great Awakening to
be part of a global revival, so abolitionists saw themselves as part

of a global wave of romantic sentiment, what T. E. Hulme called "spilt religion."[45] No less than the Great Awakening, abolitionism was a global event. But while these sentiments were widespread among the reformers and radicals of the age of Jackson, what distinguished the abolitionists was the relation of blacks and whites.

Free Negroes occupied leading roles in the Garrisonian branch of the abolitionists. White abolitionists cultivated black leadership, actively incorporating escaped slaves and ex-slaves into their organizations, and developing interracial friendships, sexual relations and marriages. Above all, whites were "radicalized by the novel white experience of listening to what blacks were saying."[46] In 1846, for example, the black physician and abolitionist James McCune explained to his white abolitionist friend Gerrit Smith what must be done to convince Americans of "the eternal equality of the Human Race." "Good Government," he said, would help, particularly "Bible Politics." But the "first principle," he insisted, was racial equality. Government, McCune elaborated, was only the "outward sign" of an "inward and spirit-owned conviction." Formal equality meant nothing without a shift in consciousness. "The hearts of the whites must be changed, thoroughly, entirely, permanently changed." Whites had to learn what it was like to be black.[47]

To be sure, the relations of Free Negroes and whites were fraught. Frederick Douglass, an ex-slave, wrote in 1860,

> Consciously or unconsciously, almost every white man approaches a colored man with an air of superiority and condescension ... Each prepares, when brought together, to soften the points of antagonism. The white man tries his hand at being negro, and the negro, to make himself agreeable, plays the white man. The end is, each knows the other only superficially.[48]

William Whipper, a black abolitionist from Pennsylvania, concurred. When white and black abolitionists "meet each other," he wrote, "it is for the most part under a mask, like courtiers, so that it is next to impossible, generally speaking, to divine their real meaning and intent."[49]

Nonetheless, whites sought to learn from blacks in one-to-one relationships. Angelina Grimké pleaded, "You [Free Negroes] must be willing to mingle with us whilst we have the prejudice because it is only by associating with you that we shall be able to overcome it. You must not avoid our society whilst we are in this transition state ... We entreat your aid to help us overcome it." Sarah, her sister, added that the inner barriers between white abolitionists and blacks could only be dissipated by "sitting with them in places of worship, by appearing with them in our streets, by giving them our countenance in steamboats and stages, by visiting them at their homes and encouraging them to visit us, receiving them as we do our white fellow citizens."[50] The abolitionists encouraged racially mixed marriage and early childhood coeducation. Louisa May Alcott, Lydia Maria Child and Anna Dickinson all wrote short stories and novels defending intermarriage. In 1843 abolitionist pressure led Massachusetts to rescind its ban on black/white marriage. A few years later abolitionists successfully integrated the state's elementary schools.[51] "While the word 'white' is on the statute-book of Massachusetts," explained the abolitionist editor Edmund Quincy, "Massachusetts is a slave state."[52]

Breaking with the colonization schema for returning blacks to Africa meant accepting blacks as coequals in a political community. As Gerrit Smith explained,

> Had I commenced with him [the Negro], instead of those who stood entirely aloof from him, I should not have been the victim of the colonization delusions for so long a time; for as soon as I came to commune with him ... and, in a word, to make myself a colored man – I saw how crushing and murderous to all the hopes and happiness of our colored brother is the policy of expelling the colored race from this country.[53]

Ever since the formation of the American republic, many Americans had been trying to get rid of slavery. As Lincoln explained, it dishonored their pride in being a republic; it weakened their self-confidence as a people. But as the example of the Colonization Society shows, getting rid of slavery could mean getting rid of the African-American race. By contrast, the primary goal of the Garrisonian abolitionists was not merely the abolition of slavery, but rather to transform the relations of black and white, both inward and external, and thereby to reestablish the United States on the basis of racial equality.

The Garrisonian group in Boston, which included black women abolitionist leaders such as Sojourner Truth and Harriet Tubman, also pioneered in generalizing from the experience of racial inequality, that is in building what later lefts would call a theory. Thus, they understood nonviolence – central, as we shall see, to the second and third lefts as well – not simply as a tactic but as the ontological grounding of a just society. By the late 1830s, according to Lawrence Friedman,

> a metaphorical view of slavery had . . . become basic to . . . [the Garrisonians'] general orientation. [Garrisonians] perceived black bondage as only the worst example of American reliance on force – of man oppressing his fellow man rather than partaking in mutual love. Oppression of man by man in all its forms, not simply Southern racial bondage, made up the American slave system.

The Boston group also regularly connected women's inequality with racial inequality. As Garrison put it, "Our object is universal emancipation – to redeem women as well as man from a servile to an equal condition."[54]

In stressing the role of violence in establishing the American compact, the abolitionists were grappling with America's history of violent dispossession. Thus, they regularly connected slavery and Indian removal. Benjamin Lundy, a Quaker abolitionist, described the American people as "slave-holding, land-jobbing, and Indian-exterminating 'republicans.'" James G. Birney, the Liberty Party's Presidential candidate, complained that "not content with a war of destruction" against the Native Americans, Americans "traversed the seas, invaded another continent [i.e. Africa] . . . and enslaved their young men and maidens." In 1836 John Quincy Adams opposed the proslavery Texas Rebellion by asking, why do you "an Anglo-Saxon, slaveholding exterminator of Indians . . . hate the Mexican-Spaniard-Indian, emancipator of slaves?" If the United States was dragged into a war, Adams insisted, it would wind up fighting its own internal "fifth column," Indians, Spaniards, Mexicans, and slaves. The South, Adams rightly predicted, would inevitably become "the battle-field upon which the last great conflict must be fought between slavery and emancipation."[55] Such formulations challenged Adamic views of the United States as a pristine Eden, instead bringing out the savagery and dark violence at the core of its history.

The abolitionists also extended their insights into America's foundational violence to engage the theme of sexual equality.

Thus, abolitionism provided the seedbed from which much of the American feminist movement sprang. Enlightenment works like Mary Astell's 1700 "Some Reflections on Marriage," and Montesquieu's 1748 *L'Esprit des lois*, had made analogies between slavery and women's condition, but in the evangelical, romantic context of the early nineteenth century abolitionists added the critical turn toward self-awareness. Abigail Kelley, a Quaker associate of Garrison, observed that in seeking "to strike his chains off we found most surely that we were manacled ourselves."[56] Abolitionism also provided the context in which white and black women forged bonds with one another. Thus, the Boston Female Anti-Slavery Society, cofounded by whites and black in 1834, encouraged white women to seek out "our colored sisters."[57]

Just as the relations of black and white were fraught in the abolitionist movement, so were the relations of women and men. In 1837 abolitionists roundly condemned Angelina Grimké for insisting that women's rights was a coequal cause with the abolition of slavery. Yet the consignment of women to the balcony at the 1840 World Anti-Slavery Convention in London led directly to the first Woman's Rights Convention at Seneca Falls, N.Y., in June 1848. In 1860 Elizabeth Cady Stanton praised the radical wing of the American Anti-Slavery Society as "the only organization on God's footstool where the humanity of women is recognized." Nevertheless, she added, "many a man who advocated equality most eloquently for a Southern plantation could not tolerate it at his own fire-side."

Abolitionists identified the traditional family and private property with the same "reliance on force" that underlay slavery. Stephen Foster, a radical Garrisonian, likened the family to "a little embryo plantation." In several marriages, such as that of Foster and Abigail Kelley, the men cared for the children while the wife traveled and spoke.[58] So many women joined the abolitionist movement that Julie Roy Jeffrey referred to them as a great army. Harriet Taylor Mill called abolitionism "the first collective protest against the aristocracy of sex."[59] Lydia Maria Child wrote that her husband "despised the idea of any distinction in the appropriate spheres of human beings."[60] Like later radicals, too, the abolitionists encouraged lifelong same-sex partnerships, such as that between Sallie Holley and Caroline Putnam. These partnerships are the forerunners of today's gay marriages.

The most important contribution of the abolitionists to feminism lay in encouraging the entry of women into the public sphere, something previously restricted to women preachers. In this regard, as with nonviolence, the Quakers pioneered, as they had long welcomed women's full participation in services. In 1833, at the founding meeting of the American Antislavery Association, Lucretia Mott rose to speak, but then hesitated as she realized she was not at a Quaker meeting. Beriah Green, chair of the convention, beckoned her: "Go on ma'am, go on; we shall be glad to hear you."[61] This incident attained iconic status. Later Angelina Grimké wrote to a friend, "it is wonderful to us how the way has been opened for us to address mixed audiences for most sects here are greatly opposed to public speaking for women . . . but curiosity for us in many & real interest in the [antislavery] cause in others induce the attendance of our meetings."[62] Speaking in public meant the empowerment of women. As Grimké later wrote, "My heart is pained, my womanhood is insulted, my moral being is outraged continually by men who fail to respect women."

By speaking in public, abolitionist women challenged the public–private divide. In probing the meaning of being a free moral agent in the context of republican self-government, they were insisting that women could not be moral persons in the private – meaning domestic and religious – realm alone. When abolitionist leaders urged Angelina Grimké to explain that her interest in women's rights arose from her Quaker beliefs, she rejected the idea. "We do not stand on Quaker ground, but on Bible ground & moral right," she wrote. She explained the distinction in her 1837 "Human Rights Not Founded on Sex," published in *The Liberator*. Woman, she wrote, "was never given to man. She was created, like him, in the image of God." This was shown, she continued, by antislavery, "the high school of morals in our land." Through antislavery:

We are led to examine why human beings have any rights. It is because they are moral beings . . . and as all men have this moral nature, so all men have essentially the same rights. These rights may be plundered from the slave, but they cannot be alienated . . . Now it naturally occurred to me, that if rights were founded in moral being, then the circumstances of sex could not give to man higher rights and responsibilities than to woman . . . My doctrine is that whatever it is morally right for man to do, it is morally right for woman to do.[63]

In defining herself as a completely equal fellow citizen, Grimké was challenging the cult of true womanhood. She was insisting that her moral right as an individual had to be recognized in the political sphere, in the sphere – she does not yet use the word – of citizenship. Thus, it is not surprising that the famous 1881 *History of Women Suffrage*, written by Elizabeth Cady Stanton and others, credited "above all other causes of the 'Woman Suffrage Movement,' the Anti-Slavery struggle in this country."

To conclude: Max Weber, in *The Protestant Ethic and the Spirit of Capitalism*, argued that the cultural revolution that facilitated early capitalism had to pass through what Weber called the "deep spiritual isolation" of the individual. For this reason Weber singled out Calvinism from all the other reformation sects. Referring to predestination, he wrote: "In what was for the man of the age of the Reformation the most important thing in life, his eternal salvation, he was forced to follow his path alone to meet a destiny which had been decreed for him from eternity. No one could help him." The abolitionist appeal was aimed at this deeply personal level. The fact that it was only a small group of black and white Americans who probed their relations to one another at this level of depth and self-consciousness does not mean that the episode was unimportant. On the contrary, it changed the meaning of abolition. One can speculate that slavery would have been abolished without the abolitionists, but without them the idea of racial equality would have been missing. We owe that idea, or at least its inception, to the abolitionists, hence to the American left.

A left can only flourish when it has a dynamic relationship to a mainstream progressive politics. This relationship, not the conflict between left and right, drives history forward during periods of crisis. The abolitionist contribution is unimaginable without the Republican Party, which emerged from a systemic crisis in the two-party system in 1854 and which gained the Presidency in 1860, precipitating secession.

The product of the market revolution, the Republicans were a coalition of Eastern businessmen, Western family farmers, railroad magnates, labor union leaders, German immigrants, and free blacks, united around such slogans as "free soil, free labor and free men." Embracing social mobility and competitive individualism, rejecting "the permanent subordination of any 'rank' in society," unburdened by a proslavery wing, the Republicans developed a coherent antislavery ideology which included positions on trade, immigration, schools, and land.[64] Crucial to the party was its identification with the core – national, cosmopolitan – identity of the country more than with its local and peripheral identities. The only third party in American history that became one of the two dominant parties, the Republicans were the counterpart to British Radicals and Chartists who fought for the suffrage, to French Republicans, and to German and central European Liberals.

While the Republicans were a party, engaged with all the rituals, spectacles, and logrolling that characterizes the two-party system, the abolitionists were a single-issue movement. In examining the relations between the abolitionists and the Republicans, we can observe the template of "left/liberal" politics. These relations unfolded in three phases. In the first phase, 1830–48, the abolitionists agitated to bring the slavery issue forward and in this way helped prepare the way for the Republicans. In the second phase, 1848–58, the crisis that would lead to the refounding of the country on an antislavery basis emerged. Finally, between the Lincoln–Douglas debates of 1858 and Radical Reconstruction (1867), white Americans, especially in the North, accepted the fact that the freed slaves would become fellow citizens, and the ideal of racial equality, not simply the end of slavery, began to enter America's consciousness.

In struggling with and against the Republicans, the abolitionists cultivated the most important political tool wielded by the left, namely agitation. Public speech or action that disrupts existing assumptions, agitation is the distinctive tactic of American radicalism. Although practiced earlier, as in the Boston Tea Party, agitation was transformed during the second party system into a permanent attribute of the new mass politics. The growth of agitation accompanied the expansion of citizenship, but the abolitionists added something unique. At a time when democratic participation was already exploding, they welcomed people of both sexes and races to their fairs, picnics, public meetings, and conventions. This practice, impertinent to some, was itself an example of agitation. As Wendell Phillips explained, "a democracy functions morally only if it has agitators who devote themselves to stirring public opinion . . . Only by being shocking, insistent, and intransigent can an agitator overcome public apathy and inertia, which always favor the status quo."[65]

The aim of agitation was to win the public's heart to one's convictions, not to gain a particular reform. As Lydia Maria Child explained in 1842, "great political changes may be forced by the pressure of external circumstances, without a corresponding change in the moral sentiment of a nation; but in all such cases, the change is worse than useless; the evil reappears, and usually in a more exaggerated form."[66] The insistence on agitation explains the abolitionist acceptance of the slogan "Moderation against sin is an absurdity," discovered by Garrison in a Christian pamphlet in 1831. In the same year Garrison had published the first issue of *The Liberator*, with its famous editorial, "On this subject I do not wish to think, or speak, or write, with moderation . . . I am in earnest – I will not excuse – I will not retreat a single inch – AND I WILL BE HEARD."

In no area was the need to be "shocking, insistent, and intransigent" more important than in the abolitionist challenge to the patriotic ballyhoo of the Jacksonian era. Angelina Grimké described the United States as "rotten at its heart." Frederick Douglass described the Revolution as a "shackles." William Lloyd Garrison burnt the Constitution, calling it a "covenant with hell." "I have no love for America, I have no patriotism. I have no country," Douglass said, anticipating practically the same words spoken more than a century later by Malcolm X.[67] Not really anti-patriotic, these remarks were actually demands that the country reestablish itself on a new basis.

Along with agitation, the abolitionists elaborated the tactics of direct action and civil disobedience. Nonviolent direct action was a way of demonstrating the limits of liberalism when faced with a particularly divisive issue. Almost invariably, direct action led both the authorities and many private citizens to try to suppress free speech. The free speech issue, in turn, was the driving force in gaining support for the movement. For example, in the 1830s the number of antislavery petitions sent to Congress was so large that the House of Representatives voted to table them upon presentation. This notorious "gag rule" exposed the repression

that underlay the second party system, ultimately protecting
slavery.

Nonviolence was not a passive tactic but was rather aimed at
bringing the society's latent violence to the surface. "Antislavery
lecturers were mobbed [by opponents] wherever they put in their
appearance and were recognized," according to Dwight Dumond.[68]
A turning point occurred in 1837 when Elijah Lovejoy, editor of
an antislavery paper in Alton, Illinois, was killed defending his
paper from a mob. "The most significant result of [such] repression was the growing willingness of many Northerners to identify
abolitionism with the rights of freedom of speech and petition,"
writes Aileen Kraditor.[69] As the abolitionists rightly insisted, it
was the effort to keep the issue of slavery out of national politics
that led to the repression of free speech.

Important as nonviolence was, not all abolitionists were committed to it; some sanctioned violence against slavery. The same
year (1831) that Garrison began to publish *The Liberator* witnessed Nat Turner's Rebellion in Virginia, where fifty-five whites
were slain. For Southerners, this was an unparalleled catastrophe,
but Garrison defended the Rebellion. From that point on, the
abolitionists appeared as fanatics to the vast majority of white
Americans. For every convert to the cause, there were hundreds of
Northerners who were repulsed by what the New Hampshire anti-
abolitionist writer Thomas Russell Sullivan called the movement's
"false zeal and political aggression."[70] Nonetheless, by mobilizing the potent image of the Slave Power, the abolitionists were
insisting that racial slavery itself inevitably generated violence.
"We commenced the present struggle to obtain the freedom of the
slave," wrote one, "we are compelled to continue it to preserve
our own."

Shunned by "respectable society" in the North, disowned by
family members, subjected to mob violence, the abolitionists had a
disproportionate influence. In the early nineteenth century, many
Southerners had been critical of slavery. Abolitionism precipitated a monolithic proslavery Southern sentiment, as Southerners
became convinced that their slaves only became resentful when
incited by outsiders. As John C. Calhoun explained in 1837:

[Abolitionist] agitation has produced one happy effect at least; it
has compelled us to the South to look into the nature and character

of this great institution, and to correct many false impressions that even we had entertained in relation to it. Many in the South once believed that it was a moral and political evil; that folly and delusion are gone; we see it now in its true light, and regard it as the most safe and stable basis for free institutions in the world.[71]

Southerners saw abolitionism everywhere. It was Southerners' extreme reaction to their own fear, evident in escalating demands to fully nationalize slavery, manifest in the Fugitive Slave Act and the Dred Scott decision, that led to the creation of the Republican Party and ultimately to the Civil War.

The second phase in the relations between the abolitionists and the liberal mainstream was marked by the birth of the Republican Party. The product of the disintegration of the second party system, the party's founding reflected a conflict within America's governing elites, betokening a genuine structural crisis. Under normal circumstances, elites mediate and compromise interests through the party system, the Congress and the courts. A crisis occurs when the elites cannot agree and the left becomes relevant. That is what happened in the decades leading up to the Civil War, as well as during the New Deal and again, especially during the war in Vietnam, in the 1960s.

During the Polk Presidency (1844–8) the country expanded by two-thirds through the annexation of Texas, the settlement of the Oregon boundary and the seizure of nearly half of Mexico. The discovery of gold in California, the Mormon settlement of Deseret (Utah) and the growth of the "Young America" element in the Democratic Party, which sought the annexation of Cuba, all intensified the expansionist drive. Expansion, James McPherson has explained, "had been the country's lifeblood. So long as the slavery controversy focused on the morality of the institution where it already existed, the two-party system managed to contain the passions it aroused. But when in the 1840s the controversy began to focus on the expansion of slavery into new territories it became irrepressible."[72]

The first demonstration of the potentially explosive effects of expansion occurred during the Missouri controversy (1819–21), a result of the early expansion of slavery into the Southwest and the lower Midwest. John Quincy Adams detected the possibility of a new antislavery alliance, "terrible to the whole Union, but portentously terrible to the South." The Democratic and Whig parties of the 1840s sought to avoid the slavery issue, through ending expansion (the Whigs) or allowing the people of each territory to decide the issue for themselves (the Democrats). In 1844, the two great architects of the two-party system, Henry Clay and Martin Van Buren, wrote letters opposing the immediate annexation of Texas because of the explosive possibilities inherent in the expansion of slavery. Nonetheless, after the introduction of the Wilmot Proviso in 1846, aimed at forbidding slavery in any of the territories conquered from Mexico, the room for compromise narrowed, leading to the formation of the Free Soil Party, forerunner of the Republicans. After 1854 the space for compromise collapsed, as territories in which slavery had formerly been banned were being opened to "popular sovereignty," typically votes by the local territorial legislatures. Noting that collapse, Rufus Choate, a Northern Whig, lamented the passing of an era when "there were no Alleghenies nor Mississippi rivers in our politics."[73]

The crisis provoked by expansion was deepened by the growth of factories, an urban proletariat, urban poverty, and immigration, especially on the part of Irish Catholics. Between 1850 and 1860 the percentage of foreign-born in the northeast United States grew from 15.5 percent to 22 percent. The workforce began to shift from independent "mechanics" to wage laborers, most of the latter foreign born. A new political party, the Know Nothings, erupted based on anti-immigrant and anti-Catholic sentiment. The seminal election of 1854, which gave birth to the Republicans, "seemed to indicate the possible triumph of Know-Nothingism rather than of antislavery. At that juncture there seemed to be a likelihood that the Catholic or immigrant question might replace the slavery question as the focal issue in American political life."[74] Meanwhile, abolitionists tended to be anti-Catholic, partly in response to the papacy of Pius IX (1846–78), which had declared papal infallibility and condemned liberalism, socialism and public education. Like the expansion of slavery, the growth of immigration posed the question of national identity, a question to which the abolitionist insistence on racial equality was crucial.

The crisis provoked by expansion also had an international dimension. The defeat of the French and German revolutions of 1848 and the eruption of nationalist movements in Eastern Europe represented a new stage in the project of self-government, one in which nationalism and social justice vied for preeminence. The 1850s witnessed a global capitalist boom, sparked in part by the California gold rush. Charles A. Dana, a correspondent for the *New York Tribune*, wrote that while the 1789 revolution had destroyed feudalism, the purpose of the 1848 revolution in France was "to destroy the moneyed feudalism and lay the foundations of social liberty."[75] To some extent, abolitionists shared this sentiment, tying slavery to the world of monarchs, emperors and czars. Conservatives responded in kind, calling the abolitionists "atheists, Socialists, Communists, Red republicans, and Jacobins."[76] The survival and meaning of self-government, then, joined with slave expansion and immigration to put the issue of the nation's identity, and not simply the disposition of slavery, into question.

The Republicans were at the center of all three tendencies – territorial expansion, industrialization, and global democratization – that were bringing the North and West into conflict with the South. Appealing to farmers entering the market, to master mechanics becoming capitalist bosses, to manual workers seeking respectability, and to a new class of "white collar" clerks, salesmen, and bookkeepers, the Republicans represented the new idea of the American middle class.[77] As Lincoln later explained, they stood for economic opportunity, which was inseparable from social justice and equality. In his words, aimed at justifying the Civil War,

> This is essentially a People's contest. On the side of the Union, it is a struggle for maintaining in the world, that form, and substance of government, whose leading object is to elevate the condition of men – to lift artificial weights from all shoulders – to clear the paths of laudable pursuit for all – to afford all, an unfettered start, and a fair chance, in the race of life.[78]

This statement, which put the idea of equality at its core, made for common purpose with the abolitionists in the long run. The Republicans believed in expansion, but only tempered by middle-class leadership. In a *New York Tribune* editorial condemning the Mexican War, Horace Greeley explained, "Opposed to the instinct of boundless acquisition stands that of Internal Improvement. A nation cannot simultaneously devote its energies to the absorption of other's territories and the improvement of its own. In a state of war, not law only is silent, but the pioneer's axe, the canal digger's mattock, and the house-builder's trowel."[79]

The first breach between the abolitionists and the Republicans came over the issue of free soil, meaning the forbidding of slavery in the new territories conquered from Mexico. The Garrisonians rejected the free-soil solution. Getting rid of slavery in one part of the country alone, they argued, would effectively serve to legitimize it elsewhere. When free-soil Congressmen were elected, and some sections of the public were willing to listen to them, the moderate wing of the abolitionist movement, along with many Republicans, felt the time had come to adapt the antislavery sentiment to the new situation. The radical wing, on the contrary, believed that agitational methods had awakened Americans to the danger that came from the aggressive slave power, but had not reformed white American's attitudes toward the Negro. Northern whites were likely to support candidates who denounced slave power, especially after the Mexican War had extended slavery's scope, but they were not willing to accept Negro children into their schools or abolish the "negro pew" in their churches. Republicans wanted to define slavery as a distinctly Southern phenomenon. For Frederick Douglass, however, "the whole system, the entire network of American society, is one great falsehood, from beginning to end."[80]

The second breach between the abolitionists and the Republicans came over "Immediatism." Many Republicans, as well as many Democrats, had pointed to the difficulties in the way of emancipation, including difficulties for the ex-slaves. By contrast, the abolitionists demanded "immediate" abolition, meaning abolition immediately begun. As Garrison explained: "We have never said that slavery would be overthrown by a single blow; that it ought to be, we shall always contend."[81] To drop the demand for immediate emancipation because it is unrealizable, as Aileen Kraditor explained,

> would have been to alter the nature of the change for which the abolitionists were agitating. That is, even those who would have gladly accepted gradual and conditional emancipation had to agitate for immediate and unconditional abolition ... because that demand was required by their goal of demonstrating to white Americans that Negroes were their brothers.[82]

Reverend Samuel May, a Unitarian abolitionist, explained: "We must hold fast to that adjective [i.e., immediate]. It expresses the only sound doctrine. . . . Nothing can be done for the improvement of the Slaves until their rights as men are recognized and secured – and when their rights as men are acknowledged, Slavery will be ipso facto abolished."[83] After emancipation, the practical issues of the transition to "freedom" could be dealt with, but to get drawn into discussions now of how emancipation would be handled would be to miss the point.

Abolitionism, by rejecting free-soil politics and insisting on immediate emancipation, became an inflammatory force that disrupted politics as usual, preventing cooperation and coalition-building. It also became an all-purpose symbol. A homestead law was labeled an "ally for Abolition." When Southern Whigs blocked an antislavery candidate in 1852, they explained they did not want "to constitute a tail to the army of abolitionists." Blocking the entry of Nebraska as a free state, Missouri complained it did not want to be surrounded by abolitionists.[84] The emergence of so powerfully negative a symbol had the paradoxical effect of tarring all Northerners by the same brush in the eyes of the South. Earlier, wealthy Northerners had been able to cluck over the evils of slavery while throwing up their hands in mock despair at their inability to do anything about it. But as the mill-owners reassured Southern planters that Garrison represented only a lunatic fringe, their own complicity with slaveholding was thrown into relief.

The influence an intransigent minority can exert on a relatively passive majority showed itself in 1858, during the Lincoln–Douglas debates. Stephen Douglas, the Democratic Senator from Illinois, defended the classical Democratic position of "popular sovereignty," that is, holding elections in the new territories to decide whether or not to allow slavery. Lincoln described himself as caught between "the unreasoning populism of the Democrats, who believed that the majority was always right, and the equally unreasonable moral absolutism of . . . the abolitionists, who appealed to even a higher law than the Constitution." Nevertheless, faced with this choice, Lincoln came down on the side of the latter.[85] While historians differ as to whether Lincoln's focus on the moral character of the slavery issue was tactical or strategic, Lincoln and the abolitionists shared the perception that slavery was a moral issue that went to the heart of American identity.

The first issue in the debates was whether morality had any place at all in politics. For Douglas, the politician's job was not to deal in moral issues. "He would not say that [slavery] was right or that it was wrong, and he professed not to care whether the people of a territory voted slavery up or down." His proposed solution, "popular sovereignty," was left deliberately vague and ambiguous as to its execution. Lincoln, by contrast, called Douglas's popular sovereignty policy a "care not policy" that allowed the proponents of slavery to expand slavery without effective opposition. The only way to stop them was to elect Republicans "whose hearts are in the work – who do care for the result," who "consider slavery a moral, social and political wrong."[86] "If you won't say slavery is wrong," Lincoln added, "you must think slavery is perfectly all right, since you cannot logically say that you 'care not' whether people vote in favor of something that is morally wrong." Broadening the issue, he concluded, "I object to it because it assumes that there CAN be a MORAL RIGHT in the enslaving of one man by another . . . No man is good enough to govern another man, without that other's consent." That, he added, is "the leading principle – the sheet anchor of American Republicanism."[87]

Implicit in Lincoln's response was a second assumption, namely that "numbers should not be looked at as much as right."[88] The "real issue" dividing him from Stephen Douglas, Lincoln elaborated, revolved around

> the two principles that have stood face to face from the beginning of time; and will ever continue to struggle. The one is the common right of humanity and the other the divine right of kings. It is the same principle in whatever shape it develops itself. It is the same spirit that says, "You work and toil and earn bread, and I'll eat it." No matter in what shape it comes, whether from the mouth of a king who seeks to bestride the people of his own nation and live by the fruit of their labor, or from one race of men as an apology for enslaving another race, it is the same tyrannical principle.

The only way to perpetuate slavery, Lincoln continued, was to "blow out the moral lights around us, and extinguish that greatest torch of all which America presents to a benighted world."[89] In practice, popular sovereignty would mean that the issue would be decided on grounds of material interests. Thus Lincoln opposed it, writing in 1854 that popular sovereignty "is founded in the selfishness of man's nature." The opposite of a politics based on material self-interest he explained was "love of justice. These principles are an eternal antagonism."[90]

The crucial point in Lincoln's position, the point that protected the abolitionists even as he criticized them, was his conviction that the irrational, immoderate and implacable force in American life was not abolitionism, but Southern expansion. Beginning with the Fugitive Slave Act, and proceeding through "Bleeding Kansas," the Dred Scott decision, and the provocations of 1859, the South had responded to the abolitionists by holding the country hostage.[91] At Cooper Union in February 1860, Lincoln urged Republicans to make no provocative gestures toward the South. Republicans, he said, should swear to uphold the Constitution, enforce the Fugitive Slave Act, and refrain from interfering with slavery in the states in which it already existed. "They could say all these things . . . and should. But it wouldn't make any difference . . . Republicans could cede all the territories to slavery, and still, that would not be enough for the South. They could thwart all future slave rebellions and the South would still want more. What would satisfy them? Lincoln asked. What would convince them?" "This, and this only: cease to call slavery wrong, and join them in calling it right."[92] And that he could never do, so there was no room for compromise.

Where Lincoln differed from the abolitionists was over the issue of racial equality. Lincoln hated slavery in part because he regarded it as a form of theft. Thus he asserted, "if the Almighty had ever made a set of men that should do all the eating and none of the work, he would have made them with mouths only and no hands." But Lincoln explicitly rejected racial equality. In his 1858 Senate campaign, he said,

I am not, nor ever have been in favor of bringing about in any way the social and political equality of the white and black races (applause) – I am not nor ever have been in favor of making voters or jurors of negroes, nor of qualifying them to hold office, nor to intermarry with white people; and I will say in addition to this that there is a physical difference between the races which I believe will for ever forbid the two races living together on terms of social and political equality.

Where then lay equality? "In the right to eat the bread, without leave of anyone else, which his own hand earns, he is my equal and the equal of Judge Douglas, and the equal of every living man. (Great applause.)"[93] The continued relevance of the abolitionists, then, lay in their dissent from Lincoln's views on the matter of racial equality.

The final contribution of the abolitionists came during the Civil War and Reconstruction. The beginning of the war saw the emergence of many positions among Republicans concerning slavery, including compensated emancipation and colonization. By contrast, the abolitionists and their allies among the Radical Republicans saw the war as an opportunity to refound American society along democratic and egalitarian lines.

The first consequence of the war was to heighten abolitionist influence. "It is hard to realize the wondrous change that has befallen us," wrote Mary Grew to Garrison. Wendell Phillips, who could scarcely have entered Washington without drawing a hostile mob a year earlier, now lectured to packed, respectful audiences. Noting the change, the *Tribune* observed: "It is not often that history observes such violent contrasts in such rapid succession." The *New York Times*, then as now the moderate "paper of record," sent a reporter to cover the Massachusetts Anti-Slavery Society convention. "In years heretofore . . . much fun has been made of these gatherings," conceded the *Times*. "The fact that black and white met socially here, and that with equal freedom men and women addressed the conglomerate audience, have furnished themes for humorous reporters and facetious editors." This, however, was no longer the case. "Peculiar circumstances have given to [abolitionist meetings] an importance that has hitherto not been theirs."[94]

The reason for the change was that the Republicans had become convinced that "the fate of the nation could not be separated from the fate of slavery." "When I say that this rebellion has its source and life in slavery," declared Radical Republican George W. Julian, "I only repeat a simple truism." "I am prepared for one to meet the broad issue of general emancipation," wrote Senator

John Sherman to his brother, the General. The issue, of course, was no longer abstract or hypothetical. The North was meeting the South on the field of battle. General McClellan, Commander in Chief of the Union army, warned Lincoln that the war should not be looking "to the subjugation of the [Southern] people." Radical views on the slavery issue, he counseled, "will rapidly disintegrate our present armies." But Lincoln had concluded that the war could no longer be fought "with rose water." In July 1862 Lincoln replaced McClellan with Henry W. Halleck, who ordered his commanders to "seize enemy property for public use." Lincoln then informed his cabinet of his intention to issue an emancipation proclamation in the areas occupied by the Union, although it took until January 1863 for him to carry this intention through.[95]

The suffering that Americans endured during the war led them to reconsider the abolitionist claim that slavery was not simply a Southern evil, but an American one. A growing sense of national responsibility and moral purpose lay behind Lincoln's famous address at the memorial service for the Battle of Gettysburg, delivered ten months after the Emancipation Proclamation. Seven thousand corpses had lain scattered across the Pennsylvania countryside, along more than 3,000 dead horses and mules, "swollen and blackening in the July heat." "Fathers and brothers wandered battlefields in search of missing relatives. So did wives and mothers dressed in black. Private agents promised to search for missing men in exchange for a percentage of their widows' pensions. Spiritualists made a good living conveying vague but consoling messages from the Other Side." "The war's staggering human cost demanded a new sense of national destiny," writes Drew Faust, "one designed to ensure that lives had been sacrificed for appropriately lofty ends."[96] Refounding the nation on the grounds of liberty and racial equality were just such ends.

To be sure, Lincoln tied the new post-slavery republic to its progenitor. The link was the Declaration of Independence. An obsessive student of the founding documents, Lincoln had come to believe that the Declaration of Independence was more important than the Constitution. The difference was the attitude toward slavery. Even though the Constitution sanctioned slavery where it already existed, he reasoned, the word does not appear in the Constitution. "The thing [slavery] is hid away, in the Constitution, just as an afflicted man hides away a wen or cancer, which he dares not cut out at once, lest he bleed to death."[97] The real purpose of the Constitution, Lincoln concluded, was to protect the Declaration of Independence. The founders "intended to include all men" in a compact of equality: not equal in "color, size, intellect, moral development, or social capacity," but equal in "certain inalienable rights, among which are life, liberty, and the pursuit of happiness."[98]

However, the Declaration of Independence had put forth an abstract, ahistorical conception of equality. It meant that no one held authority over others as a gift of God. Lincoln historicized the Declaration, turning its assertion of universal equality into an ongoing national project, a telos. At Springfield he elaborated, "the assertion that 'all men are created equal' was of no practical use in effecting our separation from Great Britain; and it was placed in the Declaration not for that, but for future use." The Declaration's signers "meant simply to declare the right, so that enforcement of it might follow as fast as circumstances should permit. They meant to set up a standard maxim for free society, which would be familiar to all, and revered by all; constantly looked to, constantly labored for, and even though never perfectly attained, constantly approximated." The War, then, with its terrible death and suffering, was necessary to answer the question of whether "a new nation, conceived in Liberty, and dedicated to the proposition that all men are created equal . . . can long endure."[99]

By this point, Lincoln and other Republicans had transmuted the abolitionist message into a national language that transcended agitation and dissent. To be sure, the core problem of racial equality remained undecided. For every soldier who wrote home "I have no heart in this war if the slaves cannot be free," there were others who wrote, "we must first conquer & then its time enough to talk about the dam'd niggers."[100] Nonetheless, the use of the term "abolition war" to describe the Civil War, which at first had a negative connotation, began to take on a positive one.[101] In 1876 when then ex-President Ulysses S. Grant visited Germany, Chancellor Bismarck remarked to him: "What always seemed so sad to me about your last great war was that you were fighting your own people," adding "but it had to be done . . . you had to save the Union just as we had to save Germany." "Not only save the Union, but destroy slavery," responded Grant. "I suppose, however, the Union was the real sentiment, the dominant sentiment," said the German Chancellor. "In the beginning, yes," Grant responded, "but as soon as slavery fired upon the flag it was felt, we all felt, even those who did not object to slaves, that slavery must be destroyed. We felt that it was a stain to the Union that men should be bought and sold like cattle."

In 1865, when Lincoln delivered his Second Inaugural Address, companies of black soldiers marched in the inaugural parade for the first time in American history. As many as half the audience who heard the address were black.[102] If the number of white Americans who had begun to think in terms of racial equality was still not that large, at least Negroes were no longer a foreign, inassimilable element in American life, as they had been for the Colonization Society, and for many of the abolitionists of the revolutionary era. After the assassination of Lincoln, and the collapse of Andrew Johnson's ultra-conciliationist Presidency, the Radical Republicans briefly controlled Reconstruction policy. Men and women, wrote journalist James Shepherd Pike, "may prattle as they wish about the end of slavery being the end of strife [but] the great difficulty will then but begin! The question is the profound and awful one of race."[103] According to historian George Fredrickson, "The enfranchisement of southern Blacks by the Reconstruction Acts of 1867 inaugurated what may have been the most radical experiment in political democracy attempted anywhere in the nineteenth century."[104] Southern Republicans, black and white, established a public school system, and built railroads and public works. Black political participation was not equaled again until the 1960s. Northern whites and blacks went south to start schools and businesses. The Freedmen's Bureau supplied the template for the later American welfare state. The adoption of sharecropping as an alternative to reconstituted plantations reflected the freedmen's access to the state. Nowhere else, writes Steven Hahn, "were so many servile laborers liberated in one stroke or soon after provided equivalent civil and political rights."[105]

The abolitionist insistence on a radical, egalitarian solution to the slavery crisis had global, as well as national, implications. Any triumph of the "Anglo-Saxon virtues" of moderation, good sense and the spirit of compromise would have been reactionary in the context of the mid nineteenth-century world. Such a compromise would have been the counterpart to Bismarck's celebrated "marriage of iron and rye," that is the alliance of reactionary, urban industrialists with brutal, quasi-feudal planters (the Junkers), the compromise that underlay German unification, industrialization and authoritarianism.[106] What distinguished America was not only the promissory note set down for racial equality, but its willingness to use violence to cripple the planter class, who were never compensated for their losses. The differences between the peaceful but authoritarian German route to a modern economy, and the bloody but progressive American route showed itself during World War Two when the two countries faced off against one another, this time as fascism versus democracy.

When reconciliation between North and South was achieved, the issue of racial equality was again pushed outside of the political arena, in good part through the extralegal violence of the Ku Klux Klan. The abolitionists were discredited, the war described as avoidable, the differences as reconcilable, Reconstruction portrayed as a "disastrous mistake," and slavery remembered "as an unfortunate but benign institution that was damaging for whites morally but helped civilize and Christianize 'African savages.'" The myth of the lost cause, according to which the South had fought for the principle of state's rights, and not for slavery, redeemed Southern honor and came to dominate historical writing. In the late nineteenth century this myth was

> reinforced at countless Memorial Day celebrations, where white Union and Confederate veterans shook hands and recalled their collective heroism, while survivors of the 200,000 black Union soldiers and sailors crucial in helping win the war were not welcome. Woodrow Wilson, the first Southerner elected President after the Civil War, reinforced the same message to the white veterans during the huge 50th reunion at Gettysburg in 1913.[107]

And yet, terrible and protracted as the counterrevolution regarding race was, the abolitionist ideal of racial equality was never eradicated from the national memory. It survived, as subsequent American lefts grasped, as a "promissory note," "for future use."

Meanwhile, the struggle between capital and labor was supplanting the struggle over slavery. Earlier, trade union leaders had appealed to the abolitionists to join forces and condemn the "lords of the loom" (i.e., the mill-owners) along with the "lords of the lash" (the plantation owners), but the abolitionists consistently refused. Rather than link the critique of the slave power to a critique of capital, they contrasted the evils of slavery to the merits of a market system. According to Eric Foner, for labor leaders, slavery was one evil among others; for the abolitionists, any problems labor faced were rooted in slavery. Abolitionists opposed factory owners for their proslavery stance, but not for their treatment of workers.[108]

The abolitionists were right to understand that slavery had to be dealt with before capitalism was addressed, but wrong to fail to see that an exploitative labor system would block racial equality. Once emancipation was achieved, they didn't mount a continuing effort to build the social and economic prerequisites for equality. With the exception of the reformer Wendell Phillips, and the Republican Congressman Thaddeus Stevens, who supported the idea of "forty acres and a mule," the freedmen's need for land, capital, equal education and other resources was ignored. As Garrison claimed, "In a republican government society must, in the nature of things, be full of inequalities. But these can exist without ... even a semblance of oppression."[109] Nonetheless, unleashed by the war, industrial capitalism, far from delivering the producerist democracy that Garrison and other advocates of free labor expected, degraded the ex-slaves by using them as strike-breakers, underpaying them, firing them whenever the profit motive dictated, relegating them to the worst schools and the worst neighborhoods, and denying them political representation.

Garrison's views notwithstanding, there was great continuity between the first left and the second. Karl Marx, who covered the Civil War as a correspondent for the *New York Herald Tribune*, was an enthusiastic supporter of the Northern cause, albeit without recognizing the centrality of racial equality. For Marx, the war was about slavery; he mocked British liberals who viewed it as a tariff or banking conflict. In 1861 he told Engels that while Wall Street would tolerate slaveholders, "self-working farmers" would not. In 1864 he congratulated Abraham Lincoln upon reelection: "If resistance to the Slave Power was the reserved watchword of your first election, the triumphant war cry of your reelection is Death to Slavery." Breaking the power of the slaveholders, Marx believed, would open the way toward the "really revolutionary path" of free, self-owning labor, and eventually socialism. Engels elaborated, "Once slavery, the greatest shackle on the political development of the United States, has been broken, the country is bound to receive an impetus from which it will acquire a different position in world history."[110] This prophecy was in fact to be realized, especially during the Great Depression and World War Two.

2

The Popular Front and Social Equality

For the abolitionists, slavery was the greatest evil; for the socialists, capitalism was the enemy. Not surprisingly, the potential for social democracy reached its high point during the Depression of the 1930s. Like the Civil War, the Depression was a crisis during which the nation's core values were deeply shaken and ultimately rethought. Like the Civil War, the Depression led to the construction of a new social order, centered this time on the ideal of social equality. Rejecting an interpretation of the Depression in terms of recovery alone, the left played a crucial role in this transformation. Out of the death throes of classical or laissez-faire liberalism came a new, socially oriented liberalism, heir to both classical liberalism and the left.

America's second great crisis, analogous to that of the Civil War, did not begin in 1929. Rather, the Great Depression was the last and most intense in a series of depressions that had begun in the 1850s. Recognized as systemic in the 1890s, when such terms as "overproduction" and "glut" entered the language, these depressions were not taken as economic problems per se, but rather as larger illnesses in the body of society. The 1929 Depression was the turning point in a secular crisis, then, just as the Civil War had been. In both cases, Americans sought a new direction; in both cases, too, the left framed the meaning of the new direction. If the first American left helped insure that the abolition of slavery would be imprinted with the ideal of racial equality, the second stamped the ideal of social equality on the modern administrative state.

Previously American liberalism had been associated with a market society and a limited state. Deeply rooted in English Whig suspicions of the monarchy, the liberal tradition held that a large state was dangerous because it could be seized by factions, notably the rich, who would use it for their own ends. From this point of view a limited state grounded in small private property holdings – Jeffersonian individualism – served to protect individuals from "tyranny." A limited state need not, moreover, be weak. Throughout its history, the American state actively solicited immigration, providing many of the immigrants with land, schools, and roads. The early American state was also a military prodigy, engaging in Indian wars, raids against maroon colonies (escaped slaves) and pirates, and border conflicts with England, France, Russia, Spain, and Mexico. What was important from the liberal perspective was that the state not involve itself directly in the production and exchange of goods.

At the turn of the century, however, the rise of the large corporation posed a major challenge to the liberal idea of the state. This was partly because the sheer power of the corporations threatened democratic control and partly because the corporations eroded small private holdings. The result was a widely felt demand for a new type of state that would actively shape economic life in the interest of the overall welfare. Progenitors of the "general welfare state," as it was called, included the Populists, who pioneered the idea of an interventionist state; the Hamiltonian "New Nationalists" of the Theodore Roosevelt era, who championed a powerful, regulatory state; and the Jeffersonian supporters of Woodrow Wilson's "New Freedom", who were antimonopoly and anti-Wall Street. But it was the socialists who gave the emergent welfare state the moral and ethical meaning of social equality. In doing so, they transformed American liberalism and laid down a promise for future realization.

Just as slavery would have been ended without the abolitionists, so the modern administrative state would have been created without the socialists. Such a state was necessary to unify the masses of immigrants, ethnic groups, regions, states, and localities that constitute this vastly heterogeneous, and internally divided continent, heir to the decentralized, self-governing, British imperial system. Such a state was also needed to organize elites, rationalize new forms of knowledge and technology, and provide the planning and research needed to accompany corporate growth. Certainly, such a state would have created centralized, flexible forms of credit, assisted private enterprise in the management of capital, created an infrastructure for investment in the underdeveloped parts of the country (the South and the West), supported trade unions, facilitated corporatist or associationalist cooperation between the state, labor, and capital, and instituted Keynesian spending, all of which the New Deal, which finally created the modern state, did, or tried to do. Above all, such a state was needed to pursue foreign wars. But without the left none of these activities would have been associated with the ideal of social equality. What the socialists and Communists added to all this was not so much the idea of public ownership as the transformation of American democracy via the mobilization of the lower classes. Elaborating the ideal of social equality, both for current and future use, they provided an egalitarian meaning to the otherwise conflicting and particularistic tangle of laws and regulations generated by the modern American state.

I will make this argument in four parts. In the first, I examine the Progressive era (1890–1920), the period of American history during which the problem of the modern American state was first probed. The Progressives proposed a modern state, but their conception was largely an abstract one, based on an idealized model of the middle-class, taxpaying citizen, equating the state with objectivity and rationality, and excluding or marginalizing the bulk of the immigrants and of African-Americans. Debsian socialism, which aimed to mobilize the mass of working people, especially through industrial unions, gave a democratic content to the Progressive idea of the state. If the Debsians grasped the democratic potential of the modern state, World War One demonstrated the latter's close relation to violence, a relation that we discussed in relation to slavery and that we will discuss again in connection to the war in Vietnam. Here we show that the Progressive claim that the state in itself could embody objective criteria and rationality ran aground in the Red Scare, laying the ground for the "disillusion" of the 1920s.

The equation of the modern state with an abstract conception of rationality continued in the early or "planning" phase of the

New Deal, the subject of the second part of the chapter. Planning rested on a huge body of reform and leftist thought, including the Soviet example of the five-year plan and Thorstein Veblen's critique of the "pecuniary interest." Planners welcomed the scientific, technological and managerial revolution that accompanied the corporation but sought an "extramarket" way of thinking to realize its possibilities, which they mostly found in John Dewey's experimental logic. The planned economy was an inspiring ideal. Walter Lippmann told students at the University of California at Berkeley in 1933 that the "ideal of a consciously controlled society" gives us at last "a transcendent purpose." "The purpose to make an ordered life on this planet can, if you embrace it, and let it embrace you, carry you through the years triumphantly." Even so, the second American left emerged as a *critique* of planning, insisting that only an organized working class, including but not restricted to industrial unions, would have the heft to bend market forces to meet popular needs.

The third part of the chapter describes the process of democratic mobilization, the creation of the Congress of Industrial Organizations (CIO) and the "Popular Front," associated with the "second," postplanning, New Deal. The organization of industrial unions fulfilled a long-standing ambition of the second American left, and was accompanied by massive efforts at working-class education, recreation, radio stations, fraternal benefit lodges, cooperative insurance, summer camps, credit services, cooperative housing, day care, public theater, and arts.[1] Overall, these programs are better described as cooperative than statist. They created for the first time a genuine counterweight to business, rooted as they were in the family wage, the ethnic community, and a strong protective government. No less important, the 1930s gave birth to a new social class, organic intellectuals, a class that was temperamentally antibusiness until the defeat of the New Left in the early 1970s. These intellectuals were not so much ideologues or literary revolutionaries as "writers from the working class, the lower class, the immigrant class, the non-literate class, from Western farms and mills – those whose struggle was to survive." Richard Pells writes:

> Many writers and artists hoped to persuade their fellow citizens that the American people could never be adequately fed or clothed or

housed or employed so long as they continued to rely on a capitalist economy, that the United States must break with the liberal tradition both politically and philosophically, that an individualistic and competitive value system had become not only obsolete but inherently destructive to the nation's social and psychic stability, and that the country desperately needed a new literature, a new theatre and a new cinema to bring all these changes about. These ideas led to an intensification of the intellectuals' desire to overcome his historic isolation from public affairs, to make his essays and novels and plays and films more meaningful in the lives of ordinary people, to devise a realistic program and strategy for democratic socialism, [and] to create a new spirit of community and cooperation throughout the land.[2]

Finally, in the fourth and last section, I describe the growth of the left after 1937 when the New Deal came under attack. The left's core insight was that the perpetuation of the New Deal reforms depended on the organization of a working class, not as an interest group or as a lobby, but as the intellectual and moral center around which a politics of inclusion and equality could coalesce. The goal of organizing was not revolution but a democratic society that recognized its capitalist (class-divided) character. At the same time, new forces of democratic mobilization among blacks and women, released by the New Deal, but also critical of it, presaged the New Left.

As we saw, nineteenth-century non-slaveholding American society was republican, meaning that almost the whole of life was organized at a local, self-governing level, in which individuals participated more or less as equals, and in which property ownership was a universal expectation. The corporate revolution, which laid the basis for the first railroads, factories, and steamships, destroyed this way of life. Family-owned businesses gave way first to pools, trusts, "gentlemen's agreements," and holding companies and then to corporations, culminating in the first great merger movement (1897–1904). The corporate form encouraged oligopolistic control (a few firms dominating an industry), which made it possible to dictate prices rather than allowing the market to determine them. It also vested authority in a new class of managers, planners, engineers, and technicians who were able to secure and organize raw materials, the labor process, and sales, with some measure of control and predictability, even becoming free from dependence on banks for financing.

The extension of control was not simply economic. Previously, the market republic had rested on the Lockean garden of "cheap land," or "the frontier." Now, barbed wire, fences, railroad tracks, telegraph poles, stopwatches, and slag heaps of mine debris crisscrossed and punctuated the "great American desert" of the West and Southwest. Not only were the commons destroyed and the bison ground underfoot, but the last Native American tribes, the Pawnee, Apache, Hopi, Zuni, Cherokee, Blackfoot, Crow, Arapaho, Sioux, Osage, Kiowa, Omaha, and Comanche, were driven into reservations. As the West became subject to corporate rationalization, the South sank deeper into underdevelopment, boasting of its "cheap labor," supplying food, textiles and primary products to the Eastern and mid-Western industrial cities, "at once squalid and vibrant," in the words of Christopher Lasch.[3]

Four great social movements responded to the corporate revolution, laying the groundwork for the second American left: the Populists, the labor movement, the Progressives, and the socialists. Each combined defensive aspects, which aimed to restore the Jeffersonian utopia of small producers, with a more far-seeing vision, aimed to address the needs of a modern economy. Let us consider them in turn.

Originating as the Alliance or Cooperative Movement in the more isolated, frontier regions of Texas during the great agricultural depression of the 1880s, Populist cooperatives soon spread into the cotton states as well as into Kentucky and Missouri. Membership quickly grew to as many as 3 million, including the Colored Farmers' Alliance and Cooperative Union which, boasting over 1 million members, was the largest black organization in America until the Garvey movement of the 1920s. An outgrowth of republican ideals, the cooperative idea was to bring together small farmers to buy seed, bags and other necessities and sell their products on a large scale, thus gaining leverage vis-à-vis the railroads and other corporations. The difficulty, however, was that farmers had no credit. As a result, the movement advanced what was called the "sub-treasury plan," according to which the government would establish warehouses and elevators in which farmers could store nonperishable crops, such as cotton, wheat, corn, tobacco, and sugar, and hold them until the price was right.

With their "sub-treasury plan," the Populists effectively invented the modern idea of government intervention into the economy.

Populism's cooperative dimension reflected the communal background of rural America, most of which had until recently been common land, open for hunting, fishing and pasturage, and populated by tiny villages with an ethic of mutual aid. Many Populists accepted the idea that God, as John Locke wrote, "has given the Earth to the Children of Men in common," and that private property was on loan from God.[4] That is why the railroads, with their barbed wire, fencing rights, telephone poles and stock market tickers, were so offensive to them. They responded by insisting that intrinsically public goods – railroads, telephone and telegraph, public lands, and the money supply – be put under democratic, popular control. Toward that end, they mobilized the South and the West against the Northeast, and fostered the cooperation of farmers with laborers, and of blacks with whites.

The second great upheaval came from America's skilled workers and artisans, who largely controlled the nineteenth-century industrial process, and from the growing number of unskilled workers as well. The Knights of Labor, founded in 1869, epitomizes this current. The largest labor organization of its time, the Knights was a sprawling, community-based movement centered on local assemblies, which sought to unite "all producers," excluding only bartenders, whiskey makers, lawyers, doctors, and bankers. Like the Populists, the Knights espoused Jeffersonian ideals, including the ideal of the local community. Far more inclusive than the later American Federation of Labor, they ran candidates for office, and managed to win offices in many local governments. Beyond the Knights, the decades following the Civil War saw what was arguably the most militant labor movement in the history of the world. Between the great Railroad Strike of 1877, "one of the bitterest explosions of class warfare in American history," through the Homestead and Pullman strike of the 1890s, millions of Americans struck, often led by skilled workers or artisans.[5] As immigration occurred, the corporations counterattacked, playing off ethnic groups against one another, mechanizing and creating a network of industrial spies – there were more Pinkerton men than soldiers in late nineteenth-century America – in their effort to destroy craft or skilled worker unions.

Both the Populists and the labor movement were decimated

during the Depression of the 1890s, the first systemic crisis of the new corporate order. Precipitated by a railroad bubble, yet global in scope, the Depression gave rise to a series of unprecedented phenomena: the hobo, armies of unemployed marching across the land, demands for government assistance to veterans of the Civil War, and brutal suppression of strikes, especially the Pullman strike of 1894, aimed at eliminating unionism from the land. At the time, Arthur Hadley, a professor of economics at Yale University, described the Depression as a cyclical, business cycle depression telescoped within "a secular decomposition of competitive capitalism," a depression that could no longer be explained by neoclassical (i.e., market-based) economics alone.[6]

The Depression set the stage for the election of 1896, the turning point from the older, agrarian-based republic to the newer, corporate-organized industrial order. William McKinley's Republican Party, supported by most of the large capitalist interests, presented itself as the workingman's party by virtue of its program of high tariffs, supposed to raise wages, and its symbolic recognition of the new immigrant (Italian, Slavic, Jewish) through political spoils and appointments.[7] The Republicans, who triumphed, were also the party of US imperialism. By contrast, William Jennings Bryan's Democrats represented the pre-immigration agrarian republic, symbolized by the call for "free silver" – that is, freedom from the banker-imposed gold standard – which appealed to the Populists, as well as by opposition to judicial injunctions against strikes, which appealed to the older – "Yankee," Irish or German – skilled workers.

The inability to win strikes during the 1890s also destroyed labor's esprit de corps, which had been symbolized by the term "Knights." In place of the Knights, the American Federation of Labor (AFL) arose. Founded in 1886, the AFL accepted the depoliticizing and rationalizing implications of the new order. "Collective bargaining," a concept largely invented by the AFL, abandoned a republican language for a corporate one. Repudiating the concept of "one big union," the AFL charged heavy dues, so that an adequate fund could support members during a strike, and disciplined the unruly workforce, limiting and controlling work stoppages. The first union movement in American history to survive a depression, the AFL excluded the largest number of workers, namely the unskilled immigrants, deploying such weapons as the union label, the boycott and the closed (i.e., single-union) shop. San Francisco, to cite one example, became a closed-shop town in good part because of the labor movement's anti-Chinese mobilizations. As the abolitionists intuited, racial equality was the key to progress, and racism was the tool of reaction. As the aspirations of labor narrowed in the 1890s, black leaders like Booker T. Washington repudiated the abolitionist legacy of racial equality, writing, "In all things that are purely social we can be as separate as the fingers, yet one as the hand in all things essential to mutual progress." Corporate-organized agriculture originated in Southern disfranchisement, which affected poor whites as well as blacks, and in Jim Crow, the so-called nadir of African-American history.

The destruction of the nineteenth-century republican order, reflected in the collapse of Populism and the Knights, paved the way for the Progressive movement. A complex amalgam, the mainstream of Progressivism aimed to bypass both capital and labor, and found a new politics on the purported neutrality and moral decency of the middle class. In principle, most Progressives accepted the corporate order, opposing only corrupt variants of the corporations, which the muckrakers called "trusts." Most Progressives, however, did not accept the political influence of the black, immigrant and working classes that the corporations brought in their wake. They insisted, rather, that the elites of these classes (the "talented tenth") adopt middle-class, Protestant norms of respectability, domesticity and sexual propriety. Opposing the immigrant-dominated "bosses" and "machines," Progressives advocated independent voting rather than party loyalty, and restriction of the urban franchise to taxpayers. They passed four constitutional amendments: the income tax, direct election of US Senators (formerly elected by state legislatures), Prohibition (repealed in 1933), and women's suffrage, which they expected to strengthen the middle-class vote. Inventing the ethics of objectivity, professionalism and expertise, Progressives sought to destroy the parochial loyalties and traditionalism of nineteenth-century society, rise above political parties, and create a neutral state, above all in regard to the conflict between capital and labor.

Deeply shaped by America's Calvinist heritage, most Progressives shared the classical American preoccupation with individual responsibility, which they assumed was lacking in "dependent" immigrants, from supposedly nondemocratic, largely peasant societies. This made Progressives not only antisocialist but culturally conservative. Thus the Progressives not only attacked "trusts" but also sought to abolish the liquor trade and prostitution, thereby turning the immigrants and ethnics against them. As Richard Hofstadter later argued, what appeared to be forward-looking programs sometimes incorporated rearguard campaigns to restore America to its rural, republican infancy, when it had been "a homogeneous Yankee civilization." This gave many Progressives their moralistic and depoliticizing character. "The misgovernment of the American people," wrote muckraker Lincoln Steffens, "is misgovernment by the American people."

But Progressivism also contained a left wing. The so-called "advanced" Progressives were very close to socialists. Centered around Hull House in Chicago, *Survey* magazine in New York, and within the German, Jewish, Finnish, Cuban and other immigrant communities, the advanced Progressives challenged the middle-class biases of mainstream Progressivism. Advanced Progressivism culminated in the Bull Moose Party, which supported Theodore Roosevelt in the 1912 election. The key thinker behind the party was Herbert Croly, a founder of the *New Republic*, who advocated "a strong national government capable of regulating giant corporations in the public interest, the use of taxation to redistribute wealth, the elevation of labor unions to parity with government and industry, and a general faith in leadership and expertise as the guiding instruments of reform."[8] Taken by many as a step toward "statism," Roosevelt's New Nationalism provoked a strong counterresponse in Woodrow Wilson's "New Freedom," another current of Progressivism. Reflecting the continued pertinence of the republican ideal, Wilson wanted the state to curb the power of "artificially" concentrated "trusts" or "monopolies" and restore the "natural" workings of society, including small-scale competitive commerce, understood in Jeffersonian terms as part of the substructure of a democratic society. Bull Moose Progressives regarded this as a backward step.

The fourth great precursor of the New Deal lay in socialism, which in the US dated to the 1840s. One current of American socialism harked back to the republican ideal of a "cooperative commonwealth," as exemplified by Henry Demarest Lloyd's *Wealth against Commonwealth* (1894), which argued that the monopoly form was inconsistent with republicanism, and which was aimed at Standard Oil. Another current, the Socialist Party of America, founded in 1901, was one of the great democratic pre-Bolshevik Marxist parties in the world.

Like the Progressives, the Socialist Party emerged against the background of the merger movement that swept corporate America between 1897 and 1904. Because the corporations were still engaged in competitive struggle with one another, they bitterly fought any improvement in the workers' conditions. This made it possible to organize a mass socialist party with deep roots in American culture. According to James Weinstein,

> the party's potential lay in its strategy of making socialism vs. capitalism a central question in all of its public activity. By making millions of people aware of capitalism as a class system run by capitalists in their own interests, and by convincing these millions that socialism was necessary for the development of their full human potential . . . the old Socialist Party established the basis for a genuinely revolutionary movement.[9]

Besides electoral activity, the party worked to organize industry-wide (as opposed to craft) unions, for example on the railroads, in mines, textiles, and breweries. The largest of the Socialist newspapers, *The Appeal to Reason* of Girard, Kansas, had a weekly circulation of 761,747, roughly comparable, adjusting for population size, to the circulation of *Newsweek* in its heyday. In 1912 the Socialist Presidential candidate Eugene V. Debs, running against Roosevelt and Wilson, polled 6 percent of the vote, while Socialists held 1,200 offices in 340 cities, including 79 mayoralities. A few years later there were two Socialist Congressmen in Washington DC, Victor Berger from Wisconsin and Meyer London from New York. In 1920, Debs won 3.4 percent of the vote, running from an Atlanta penitentiary, where he had been jailed for antiwar activity.[10]

Sometimes in tandem, sometimes in conflict with the Socialists, the syndicalist Industrial Workers of the World endorsed the goal of "one big union," its largest successes occurring in the mining camps, the lumber and steel industries, and the textile factories, especially among young immigrant women. The IWW – the "Wobblies" – stood for a self-governing producers' society with a minimal state. The movement encouraged the radicalization of an emerging intellectual class associated with the "new paganism" of Greenwich Village. Literary intellectuals such as John Reed and Louise Bryant sensed an "affinity between their own ideal of the emancipated individual, unburdened by the cultural baggage of the past, and the hoboes and migratory workers glorified by the IWW."[11] Espousing an ideal of "self-expression and defiant irresponsibility," this "lyrical left" intermingled sexual radicalism, bohemian freedom, and antibusiness radicalism.

The famous Lawrence and Paterson, Massachusetts strikes of 1912–13 proved a high point. In the Paterson strike Greenwich Village bohemianism commingled with Debsian socialism, immigrant self-affirmation, and Wobbly syndicalism. The strike's mass cultural pageants were taken to mark a new epoch in American creative life because they seemed to offer radical artists and writers a chance to break out of the neglect suffered by earlier writers such as Herman Melville and Mark Twain. In the same year, women suffragists marched with trade unionists in support of the Armory Show, which brought modernism to the United States. The march was a precursor of the Popular Front desire not only to bring all social classes together, but also to integrate modern art and a feminist sensibility into a broader left movement.[12]

War and empire led to the demise of the Progressive era of reform. Instead of the growth of reason, as Progressives supposed, the Great War (World War One) "offered proof of the mobilizing capacities of nationalism" and "the tremendous power of the modern state."[13] The limits of the liberal tradition, when confronted with war and "boundless acquisition," became clear, as they would again in the 1960s. Herbert Croly, exemplar of "advanced" or Bull Moose Progressivism, supported the war, writing in the *New Republic* that it offered Progressives what social justice could not: "the tonic of a serious moral crusade." War, Croly predicted, would provide the means "to imbue the people with a spirit of common purpose sufficiently powerful to win their submission" to the ends of regulation and state-building. America's entry would prove the apotheosis of Progressive reform. John Dewey agreed, arguing that the US would finally come of age, discovering "a national mind, a will as to what to be."[14] "All the slow agonizing waiting for the American community to integrate itself spontaneously into a cooperative commonwealth was ended."[15] Most intellectuals were equally enthusiastic. The "good fight," one later boasted, refuted "the ancient libelous assumption that [intellectuals] constituted an absent-minded third sex."[16] One, however, Randolph Bourne, sarcastically termed America's entry "a war free from any taint of self-seeking," becoming a New Left hero for his critique of Dewey's "pragmatism."

In one respect, though, Croly was right. The war did in fact provide the first occasion for large-scale planning, the key to the first New Deal. With America's entry into the war, the War Industries Board suspended the Sherman Anti-Trust Act, providing a "lubricating consensus" concerning production goals, labor relations, prices, safety regulations and the like.[17] Based on the model of the rationalized, state-managed German economy, the War Industries Board took a giant step toward corporatism: entire industries, even entire economic sectors, were organized and disciplined through the mediation of the government. Later, Franklin Roosevelt nostalgically recalled "the great cooperation of 1917 and 1918," when he was Assistant Secretary of the Navy, citing it as an inspiration for the New Deal.[18] The war began what historian David Kennedy has called "the modern practice of massive informal collusion between government and organized private enterprise."

The war also destroyed the Socialist Party. Two Communist parties formed, precipitating pointless debates over immediate insurrection and initiating the destructive conflicts between Bolshevik-imitating Communists and non-Communist leftists that limited the successes of the second American left. Nonetheless, with the Russian Revolution came the first American use of the term "left" in its political sense (though not yet a book title) as in the 1919 "Manifesto and Program of the Left Wing Section Socialist Party Local Greater New York." Most Progressives had believed that their own class, the middle class, was a "universal class," embodying the values of society as a whole; they saw other classes, "monopolists" and workers, as "special interests." In contrast, the Bolsheviks viewed the poor, the oppressed, and the proletarianized as the true representatives of universal values. As China, India, Africa, and the Middle East moved to the center of Lenin and Trotsky's world picture, Bolshevism brought home the limits of the American liberal (i.e., Progressive) tradition. The workers, as well as the racial and colonial subaltern classes, were the overwhelming majority of society. Their common labor and widespread suffering gave their claims great moral power.

Meanwhile, the war produced vigilantism, censorship of the mails, espionage acts, the "Committee on Public Information," i.e., anti-German propaganda in the schools and movie theaters, the spread of racial violence, and the Red Scare, which led to the deportation of thousands of leftists, anarchists, and even simple critics of the government. In Zeev Sternhell's words,

> [the] war demonstrated the ... facility with which all strata of society could be mobilized in the service of collectivity. [It] showed the importance of unity of command, of authority, of leadership, of moral mobilization, of the education of the masses, and of propaganda as an instrument of power. It showed, above all, the ease with which democratic liberties could be suspended.[19]

In the 1920s, disillusioned postwar writers like Ernest Hemingway (later a representative of the Popular Front) and William Faulkner (later a staunch opponent of the New Deal) struggled to create a new, modernist language to capture the background of violence against which American history was unfolding. At the same time, the Great Depression was brewing. Something of the coming mood can be grasped from the1932 words of the then thirty-two year old president of the University of Chicago, Robert Hutchins, to the Young Democratic Club:

> After attacking us as the younger generation for ten years after the war they caused they are ... preparing to pass on to us, a world wrecked by that colossal blunder and their inability to cope with its consequences. Their stupidity, selfishness and rapacity in the postwar period have matched the criminal lightheartedness with which they sent us into battle.[20]

This was the atmosphere from which emerged the collaboration between liberals and leftists that came to be called the Popular Front.

Americans were accustomed to the business cycle. From hard experience, they knew what to expect: when the price of labor and raw materials and money fell far enough, recovery would begin. Only in 1929 that is not what happened. Instead of hitting bottom, the economy kept falling. Credit dried up; bankruptcies mushroomed; farms were repossessed; unemployment struck a quarter or more of the workforce. Sales of automobiles, the most important American industry, dropped from nearly 4.5 million in 1929 to slightly over 1 million in 1932. To this day there is no scholarly agreement as to the causes, or indeed the nature, of the Great Depression. One thing is clear, however. The Depression was a collective action problem: the labor, materials, factories, and money were all present; only the means of bringing them into relation with one another was absent.

The 1932 election of Franklin Roosevelt reflected the desire for collective action. A landowning aristocrat, Roosevelt was a Patroon, a member of the great Dutch Hudson Valley landowning elite. In line with this heritage, Roosevelt regarded "America as a great estate to be nurtured and cherished," and not as a business.[21] Campaigning in September 1932, he explained that the Presidency is "more than an engineering job, efficient or inefficient. It is preeminently a place of moral leadership. All our great Presidents were leaders of thought at times when certain historic ideas in the life of the nation had to be clarified." The office, he continued, called for

> someone whose interests are not special but general, someone who can understand and treat the country as a whole. For as much as anything it needs to be reaffirmed at this juncture that the United States is one organic entity, that no interest, no class, no section, is either separate or supreme above the interests of all.[22]

Few Presidents understood as Roosevelt did the importance of morale, a Popular Front idea, psychoanalytic in origin, and centered on group or mass psychology. An early episode, his appearance at the 1924 Democratic Convention, a few years after he was stricken with polio, conveys his grasp of the idea. Called from the stage to nominate Al Smith, sweating desperately, he struggled forward. "But when he finally stood at the podium, unable even to wave for fear of falling, head thrown back and shoulders high, in the exaggerated posture that would now become his trademark, the delegates rose to their feet and cheered for three minutes." Something in Roosevelt's struggle to overcome his disability resonated with the American people's struggle to overcome the wound that capitalism had inflicted on them, and to build a new social order and identity, based on social and economic equality.

Roosevelt understood, as did most intellectuals of the time, that the nation was at a historic turning point. In his 1932 Commonwealth Club address he asserted that while the goal of economic growth had been universally accepted in the nineteenth century, when it seemed that "no price was to high to pay for the advantages which we could draw from a finished industrial system," this was no longer the case.

> Our industrial plant is built . . . our last frontier has long since been reached, and there is practically no more free land. More than half of our people do not live on the farms or on lands and cannot derive a living by cultivating their own property. There is no safety valve in the form of a Western prairie to which those thrown out of work by the Eastern economic machines can go for a new start . . . Clearly this calls for a reappraisal of values.[23]

Thus, Roosevelt recognized that the republican ideal was no longer sufficient, that small private property was no longer an adequate basis for citizenship and participation, and that economic expansion under the leadership of the corporations was no alternative.

Although Roosevelt had run as a Progressive, criticizing Herbert Hoover for excessive government spending and promising to balance the budget, his election left the country agitated and excited. Within a few months, politics began "to recover meaning; the battle of programs and ideas began to recover significance." Leftist journals such as the *Nation*, the *New Republic* and *Common Sense* welcomed the new President with common recommendations: control of production, recognition of trade unions, redistribution of income. Such proposals lay behind Roosevelt's bold First New Deal (1933–5). Included here were the Glass–Steagall Act, which sought to separate banking from speculation, and the Agricultural Adjustment Act and National Industrial Recovery Act, which were based on the model of a corporatist, state-centered economic system, and brought together business, labor, and government to set prices, establish national standards, limit production (in agriculture especially) and, in a word, to plan.

Planning, "the panacea of the age," as the economist Lionel Robbins called it, connoted much more than it does today. Its guiding insight was that markets were incapable of coordinating a complex, modern economy in a way that took account of social and even economic needs. The outcome of innumerable, automatic reflexes, markets lacked the element of consciousness or discursive intelligence (i.e., extrabiological feedback) that characterizes politics in the classic sense of the term. The project of planning was aimed at introducing the higher level of conscious awareness or reflection that markets lacked.

Planning rested on the pragmatic revolution of the Progressive era. At the heart of that revolution lay a reinterpretation of Darwin, which argued that learning was at the center of the evolutionary process. John Dewey's 1896 article "The Reflex Arc Concept in Psychology" was a keystone for this idea. In it Dewey argued that human behavior could not be described as a series of separate reflexes, but rather was a flow of coordinated actions. Even if these actions had a certain automaticity, when conflict occurred consciousness intervened and learning took place. Thorstein Veblen, Simon Patten, Rexford Tugwell and others translated Dewey's theory of psychology into a new economics.

The question was, who would do the planning, and by what criteria? This question had been central both for "advanced" or Bull Moose Progressives, such as Walter Lippmann (in his 1914 *Drift and Mastery*), and for the socialists. It was also at the center of the Lippmann–Dewey debate in the 1920s, in which Lippmann had insisted on the priority of technically trained elites, while Dewey argued for dialogue at local and community levels, along lines similar to those envisioned later by the New Left. With Roosevelt's election the question became pressing.

There were at least three possible answers. Planning could be determined by business interests, by state experts, or by a democratic political process that included popular forces. In the event, large corporations mostly wrote the New Deal codes; and even when this was not the case, planning was technocratic and top-down. But the left struggled for the third possibility. Thus planning exemplified the ambiguous nature of American reform. Like the abolition of slavery, the New Deal hovered between "disguising exploitation" and recognizing "elements of equality in people of subordinate status." The second American left sought to resolve the ambiguity of planning in favor of equality by advocating the idea of the working class as the agent of planning.

The idea of the working class as the agent behind planning entered New Deal reform thought through John Chamberlain's 1932 *Farewell to Reform*. According to Chamberlain, planning required not just a democratic citizenry, but also a self-interested social class that could plausibly identify its interests with the interests of society as a whole. Advocates of planning, Chamberlain believed, were deluded to imagine that they could limit the sway of vested interests without such a class. Economists like Veblen, he charged, seemed to believe that "a hierarchy of technical experts [could] oust the high priests of the price and profit system." Such economists lacked a realistic sense of the American power structure. Along similar lines, Chamberlain criticized Dewey for exalting the role of education without recognizing the underlying institutions of domination. "Hoping for the salvation of democracy through primary and secondary education," he wrote, Dewey failed to see that "regeneration of the body politic as a whole must come from . . . outside the public school," in other words from an organized working class.[24]

The emphasis on working-class agency marked a new stage in the history of the American left. Whereas the abolitionists had relied on the actions of intensely committed morally motivated individuals and small groups, the socialists relied on mass mobilization. And whereas the abolitionists intuited the nation's proclivity to violence and expansion, the socialists had a theory of capitalism, classes and the state, however rudimentary. Moreover, the emphasis on agency and mobilization also distinguished leftists from liberals. Liberals sought planning; leftists sought democratic planning. As early as 1934 the *New Republic*, the *Nation*, and *Common Sense* began to criticize the top-down biases of the New Deal, which they connected to its excessive caution. Intellectuals decried the President's "unwillingness to move to the left – to use the crisis as an opportunity for taxing corporate profits, nationalizing the banks, assuming control over transportation and public utilities, and reallocating the country's wealth more equitably."[25] Harold Laski, the British leftist, wrote Supreme Court Justice Felix Frankfurter in 1934, "America can't live half slave and half free . . . control capitalism [i.e., planning] is a contradiction in terms . . . Either you have to go backward to a kind of industrial feudalism," in other words, planning by the big corporations, "or forward to a much greater increase in socialised economic life . . . Roosevelt is standing proof of Lenin's insistence that you cannot make greater reforms unless you have a theory and an end you want to reach."[26]

The attempt to grapple with the dilemmas of planning led the left to socialism. As early as 1931 the critic Edmund Wilson proposed in the *New Republic* to use the demand for planning to "take Communism away from the Communists." The core point of reference, he explained, should be "social control." "We have always talked about the desirability of a planned society," Wilson wrote, "The phrase 'social control' has been our blessed Mesopotamian word. But if this means anything, does it not mean socialism? And should we not make this perfectly plain?"[27] Wilson's conception of socialism was rooted in the thought of Dewey, but it also anticipated the Marxism of the Popular Front.

In the event, all currents of reform and leftist thought centered on the President, who had become the target of an enormous upsurge of populist sentiment, both urban and rural, sentiment that must be distinguished from leftism proper. For example, Father Charles Coughlin's weekly radio program with an audience of 30–40 million, many of them recently arrived Catholic immigrants, rested on the populist critique of the money power. While Coughlin also drew on the rich history of Catholic social justice encyclicals, he appealed to America as a Christian nation. A critic of the First New Deal, he criticized Roosevelt for leaving banking in private hands and nationalizing industry (referring to the National Recovery Administration, NRA), when he should have nationalized the banks and left industry alone.

In addition, agrarian insurgencies with roots in the post-Civil War greenback, farmer-labor and agrarian movements provided more populist pressure. One historian has called Milo Reno's Farmers' Holiday Association, which was centered in the corn belt and urged farmers to withhold their products, "the most aggressive agrarian upheaval of the twentieth century."[28] Finally, Huey Long revived the South's radical legacy. Long's hometown, Winn, Louisiana, had been a center of antislavery, Populism and Debsian socialism. Appealing "not to the resentments of a petty-bourgeoisie . . . but to the egalitarianism of the poor," Long built a movement of 2,700 clubs with 7,500,000 members, most of them unemployed workers and discontented farmers, on a program of radically redistributive taxation.[29] Critically, the movement was not racist. As Long explained, "My father and my mother favored the Union. Why not? They didn't have slaves. They didn't even have decent land. The rich folks had all the good land

and all the slaves – why, their women didn't even comb their own hair."[30]

But it was the labor movement, with its roots in the earlier attempts to organize industry-wide unions, that most directly pressured Roosevelt from the left. Treated as a stepchild by the Progressives, labor had begun to feel at home with the New Deal. The famous clause 7A of the National Recovery Act, which called for union organization to facilitate planning, had given an enormous boost to those seeking to organize industry-wide as opposed to craft unions. Under the slogan "The President wants you to join a union" auto, steel, oil, rubber, and typography unions enjoyed huge membership surges, as did the United Mine Workers (UMW), the Amalgamated Clothing Workers, and the International Ladies Garment Workers Union (ILGWU). While there was support among labor leaders for a third party, there was even more support for party realignment. Many felt that it was time for labor to abandon its role as a lobby group, and instead become the center of a new progressive coalition, based not only on labor's role in the workplace but also on its importance to "the national political community and in the infrastructure of the state."[31] With so much stirring, John Dewey's League for Independent Political Action, the *New Republic* and the *Nation* began discussing possible third parties aimed at the 1936 election.

Threatened with the disintegration of his centrist coalition of 1932, Roosevelt could have moved to the right, scapegoating banks, Jews, and radicals. Instead, while carefully proclaiming himself the opponent of "Communism, Huey Longism, Coughlinism," he moved to the left. His January 1935 annual message to Congress spotlighted the lower classes, discussing the slums, and calling for respect for the laboring man, although not yet for the trade unions. Looking toward the 1936 election, Roosevelt realized "that he would win the greatest response by exploiting the class antagonisms of the Great Depression."[32] Having begun his Presidency with the idea of uniting all classes, he now complained that businessmen had no sense of moral indignation about the sins of other businessmen. As the election drew closer, Roosevelt concluded "that nothing would help him more than to have newspapers, bankers and business aligned against him, for their attacks would only win him more votes." He directed the Democratic National Council to direct its fire not against the Republicans, but against symbols of wealth such as the American Liberty League. By the time of the election, his language had become dramatically antibusiness: "money changers," "economic royalists," "privilege," "malefactors of great wealth." Speaking of the rich, he boasted: they are "unanimous in their hatred of me and I welcome their hatred."

Roosevelt's advisors also encouraged him to move to a more anticapitalist or at least antibanker position. "The time has come to assert the leadership that the country is demanding," they told him. It's the "Eleventh hour," Supreme Court Justice Louis Brandeis added.[33] A month after receiving this advice in 1935 Roosevelt appeared before Congress calling for passage of the Wagner Act, which put the force of the federal government behind unions; the Public Utility Holding Company Act, which subjected the electric industry to regulation, especially by the states; and Social Security, which included not only old age insurance, but unemployment insurance and welfare. In addition, Roosevelt called for "very high taxes" on large incomes, an estate tax since "the transmission from generation to generation of vast fortunes . . . is not consistent with the ideals and sentiments of the American people," a graduated corporate income tax, and taxes on holding companies, all of which, taken together, he called a "wealth" tax. "Our revenue laws have operated in many ways to the unfair advantage of the few, and they have done little to prevent an unjust concentration of wealth and economic power," he explained. The result had been "a deepening sense of unfairness."[34]

The election of 1936 richly rewarded the Democrats. During the 1936 World Series, those watching the baseball game in the expensive boxes had all worn sunflowers, the Republican Party symbol, while the bleachers broke out in wild applause when fans saw the President. Roosevelt got 42 percent of the upper income vote but 76 percent of the lower income vote and 80 percent of the labor vote. A furniture worker from Paris, Texas, wrote: "Now that we have a land Slide and done just what was best for our country . . . I will say . . . you are the one & only President that ever helped a Working Class of People."[35] The transformation of the American Progressive tradition into the party of militant liberalism – a term now signifying social democracy that Roosevelt took over from British Fabians and socialists – was no electoral trick. Secretary of Interior Harold Ickes noted, "I've been hoping ever since 1912 that we'd have political parties divided on real issues. ... I'd like to see all the progressives together and all the conservatives together."[36]

The 1936 Presidential election presaged a new conception of the state. Americans, opined a writer in the journal *Christian Century* after the election, had been "so busy defending a traditional ... concept of freedom from governmental control" that they had forgotten that it was their government, and that they could use it to protect their freedom.[37] Underlying the new conception, though not yet fully articulated, was the ideal of social equality. This ideal did not take the form of an abstract demand for leveling. Rather it took the form of a recognition that the society had changed to such an extent that the lone individual, as Roosevelt explained in a 1934 Fireside chat, was "quite helpless." Only collective security, or what Roosevelt called the "intervention of that organized control we call government," and not the market, could provide a realistic basis for the independence and self-sufficiency that small private property had once provided.[38] This insight, central to the populist, labor, progressive and socialist critiques of the corporate revolution, was also consistent with the egalitarian thrust of abolitionism. Hence the election inspired a large number of letters comparing Roosevelt's task to Lincoln's. "Truly," one began, "there is such a thing as economic slavery." The President, another insisted, should "free us from the slavery that we are in."

Around 1935 the second American left morphed into what was known as the "Popular Front." During this period the idea that American society was best understood in terms of the conflict between capitalists and workers, and that eventually America and other nations would evolve toward some form of democratic socialism became widespread. The significance of this idea was that it inflected the structural transformation then underway with the meaning of social equality. This can be seen in the changed meaning of liberalism. Originally, liberals assumed that the state endangered freedom. Now liberalism conveyed the idea that the state needed to protect workers, farmers, and the poor from the ravages of market capitalism.

The Communists, who invented the phrase "Popular Front," were significant in the ensuing period, but not because of their numbers. Even at its high point, during World War Two, the party had at most 80,000 members. Rather, the Communists gained popularity because they downplayed the idea of revolution in order to support the New Deal. Thus, Steve Nelson recalled how Communist organizers of the Chicago Unemployed Councils "spent the first few weeks agitating against capitalism" until they realized that working-class people were "more concerned with their daily struggles," after which they adopted what Nelson called a "grievance approach," meaning they talked about the grievances, and not about capitalism.[39] In addition, after the Spanish Civil War broke out in 1936, the "Popular Front" meant an alliance of representatives from all social classes against fascism. Spain, France, Chile and China were among the nations with Popular Fronts. The attempt to build broad-based coalitions against fascism in Europe and militarism in Asia signified that the nation, rather than the working class, had become the vehicle of change. Communists, party leader Earl Browder explained, would never "raise the issue of socialism in such a form and manner as to endanger or weaken [national] unity."[40]

The Popular Front reflected the coming of age of American intellectuals as a social class. Earlier intellectuals had been "men of letters" who supported themselves by writing, preaching or lecturing. In contrast, the intellectuals of the thirties were "organic intellectuals," meaning that they worked in the new mass consumption industries, such as advertising or film, or else for the expanding New Deal state. They identified with the working class, often seeing themselves as intellectual workers allied with manual workers against capital. The Popular Front largely consolidated the idea of the intellectual as a critic of power. In 1966 Lionel Trilling wrote, "the importance of the radical movement of the thirties cannot be overestimated. It may be said to have created the American intellectual class as we now know it in its great size and influence."[41] In fact it is impossible to understand twentieth-century American intellectual and cultural history without giving full weight to the painting, sculpture, literature, poetry, theater, film and music, as well as the historical writing and social theory of the Popular Front period, even though most contemporary historians still fail to do so.

Roosevelt's "turn to the left" in 1935 had opened up a new possibility, to which the idea of the Popular Front spoke. This was a new kind of state, which in Europe would have been called a social democratic state, in which business, the churches, the working class, professionals and the poor would actively participate. The creation of such a state could not rest on change in the political realm alone; in addition, the structure of capitalist society would have to be changed. The wave of New Deal reforms that began to be passed in 1935 suggested such a possibility, by protecting the rights of unions to organize, and by guaranteeing collective security for unemployment and old age. Powerful though these reforms were, their meaning was ambiguous. Just as the abolition of slavery could either provide a new means "of disguising exploitation" or could lead to the recognition of "elements of equality in people of subordinate status," so the New Deal reforms could infuse a corporate-dominated order with market dynamism, or could signal a wider democracy.[42] The key to shaping the meaning of a reform was not so much the reform's content as the mobilized presence of the working class in interpreting the reform's meaning and guiding its influence. And that depended on the energies and imagination of the left.

America needed a social democratic state, according to the leftist thought of the time, because it was more a system of estates or orders than a system of classes. What divided the society was not ownership of property or income level, but "insecurity of employment with its consequent disturbance in the rhythms of life," as Robert and Helen Lynd's 1929 *Middletown* insisted.[43] "That word [job] came into my vocabulary," social worker Mary MacDowell had written earlier, "and has since become almost a sacred word . . . It is the word first learned by the immigrant, the children lisp it, and the aged cling to it to the end. A 'steady job' or 'please get me a job' is ever at the front of their minds and at the tips of their tongues."[44] In addition, American society was organized through race and ethnicity as much as through social class. In the Jim Crow South, state-supported lynching enforced the racial code. But the rest of the country also distinguished, albeit informally, old-line "Americans," for example, English, Scotch-Irish, and perhaps Irish and German, from recently arrived immigrants, Southern and Eastern Europeans, Hispanic-Americans, Asian-Americans, and Jews.[45] Native-born "Yankees" tended not to recognize the latter groups as Americans, even after they became citizens. As to blacks, throughout the country they were referred to as "boy," "George," or "Jack."

The Popular Front, in essence, was an effort to turn this system of ranks and orders into a modern, democratic society in which the working class qua working class had a distinct voice. In classical Marxist terms, the Popular Front aimed not to bring about socialism, but simply to complete America's bourgeois revolution (which is why Trotskyists and many other leftists attacked it as essentially conservative). There were two main fronts in this struggle. In the South, the US had a racial state, in that its laws, institutions and ideologies were racially organized. The modern civil rights movement in the South began in Popular Front labor struggles, bookstores, and struggles for basic rights, like the right to demonstrate in public spaces, or to read anti-imperialist literature. The theory of antifascism, which Communists and other Marxists developed to explain the rise of Nazism, encouraged antiracism, as when the African-American *Pittsburgh Courier* asked, "What are Jim Crow laws but fascist laws?" or when Roosevelt in 1938 called the South feudal, adding, "There is little difference between the feudal system and the fascist system. If you believe in one you lean to the other."[46]

At the same time, a bourgeois revolution meant organizing the 23.5 million Southern and Eastern Europeans who had immigrated between the 1880s and 1920s, as well as the several million Southern blacks who had migrated to the North. Both groups worked in the great multiplant manufacturing operations aimed at national and international markets. Building industrial unions was central to the Popular Front, in which unions were conceived of as forms of social and political organization, and not simply as means of negotiating wages and hours.

CIO unions, in this sense, were qualitatively different from the skilled trade unions that had dominated American labor since the founding of the AFL in 1886. The earlier craft unions were largely composed of skilled "Yankee" workers; the industrial unions included a higher proportion of immigrants, and the children of immigrants.[47] The earlier movement was overtly racist; the industrial unions chanted "black and white, unite and fight." The earlier movement tried to convince the middle class of its "respectability"; the industrial union movement was based on the idea that the working class had its own values, superior to those of the middle class. The earlier movement had little connection to intellectuals; industrial unions not only organized "white collar" and other forms of educated labor, but also forged a "cultural front." The earlier movement restricted itself to negotiating and administering contracts; the industrial unions worked closely with the left wing of the New Deal both in government and in the Democratic Party.

The slogan of the new union movement, along with the new labor radio stations, rent strikes, eviction protests, writers' and artists' clubs, unemployed councils, and CIO political action committees that accompanied it, was solidarity. Solidarity, writes Liz Cohen, "was the age-old cry of the labor movements, but it had a very particular significance to the . . . 1930s." The difference lay in the emphasis on the workers' agency. "If any theme prevailed it was the recognition that the workers themselves must change to prevent the kinds of divisions that had doomed similar efforts to organize them in the past."[48] In the Akron, Ohio tire factories, skilled machinists and electricians attended CIO meetings, which were filled with unskilled and semiskilled second-generation immigrants. The skilled workers, Ruth Kenney writes, refused to believe "that their interests were different from the common ordinary rubber worker."[49] "The CIO's effort to create a culture of unity that brought workers of different sexes, races, nationalities, and locales together was so basic to its organizing philosophy that it permeated all CIO union activities . . . on and off the shop floor." Union drives included speakers of different languages, representatives of the different ethnic groups, and meetings that brought together different ethnicities.[50] Perhaps the most powerful expressions of solidarity came from the labor movement's songs, chants, hootenannies, and marches, which supplied a vernacular language and sense of collective rhythm that lasted into the 1960s, when they infused the civil rights and antiwar movements.

Racial equality was crucial to the industrial union movement, which in that sense was building on the abolitionist precedent. Among the Chicago Packinghouse workers, the killing floors of the slaughterhouse where the blacks predominated spawned the most militant unionism. According to one white union member, "I don't care if the union don't do another lick of work raisin' our pay . . . I'll always believe they done the greatest thing in the world getting' everybody who works in the yard together and breakin' up the hate and bad feelings that used to be held against the Negro." For another: "overcoming prejudice didn't mean anyone got invited to somebody's house for Christmas dinner . . . but so far as on the job and in the union . . . we were making a religion of racial unity." A black butcher summarized,

> the white butchers hated the Negroes because they figured they would scab on them when trouble came and then get a good-paying, skilled job besides . . . with the CIO in, all that's like a bad dream gone. Oh, we still have a hard row, but this time the white men are with us and we're with them.[51]

Black/white unity broke down during World War Two, when the availability of jobs and the consequent size of the black migration threatened white advantages, but even the limited cooperation achieved during the thirties was an important advance.

Industrial union organizers aimed at transforming the conditions not only of workers, but also of their families and communities. The early immigrants had mostly been migrant workers, living in boarding houses and working the longest possible hours to send money to their families, or to return to Europe and buy land. When US Steel put up dwellings for immigrants in Gary, Indiana in 1909 the immigrants converted them into boarding houses to save money. Later, as families formed, "children viewed their immigrant fathers as . . . individuals who believed in 'work, work, work, and work.' . . . They always feared the loss of their jobs since they had nothing to fall back on." Union drives transformed communities. The rate of home-buying rose, the crime rate declined; unionization became an alternative to repatriation. Workers explained: "I have got my family here, my woman, and I have five children; and I have that family and I would like to know how a man is going to make a living for himself and his wife and five children on $4.75 a day," and "Why did we strike? We did not have enough money that we could have a standard American living."[52] After union drives, neighborhood park benches were renamed "eight-hour benches," because for the first time men had time to spend with their families.

Because of its focus on family and community, the Communist Party made a special effort to recruit women, and the number of women went from 10 percent of the party membership in 1930 to 50 percent in 1943.[53] But because the party wanted to recruit *middle-class* women, it often appealed to traditional notions of womanhood, which contradicted women's rights. This ambiguity affected union organizing. The CIO supported female unionization unequivocally, including equal pay for equal work, but it did not challenge the sex-typed distinction between men's work and women's work. By 1940 800,000 women had been organized, a 300 percent increase over 1930. In the auto industry, women's average hourly wages rose from 54 cents in 1936 to 65 cents in 1938 as a result of unionization.[54] But by World War Two, women were questioning sex-typed employment distinction, preparing the way for the feminism of the 1960s–1970s.

The culmination of the industrial union drive came with the largely spontaneous but highly disciplined sit-down strikes of 1937, in which nearly 500,000 workers, supported by their communities, occupied factories, packinghouses, foundries, assembly plants, and commercial enterprises. The strikes derived much of their moral power from being nonviolent. The industrialists dreaded damage to their machinery above all else, but the workers damaged nothing. When sit-down strikers took an item from the stock in retail stores like Woolworth, they left the money for it on the register.[55] Equally significant, the federal government refused to use force against the strikers, as previous governments had, and as the government soon would again, in 1941. The La Follette Civil Liberties Committee even called national attention to the use of spies, strikebreakers and private police. Congress enacted a law prohibiting transport of strikebreakers across state lines. In the years that immediately followed, all of the great mass production industries – auto, steel, rubber, oil, chemicals, coal, garment and needle trades, West Coast shipping and newspapers – were unionized, marking "a fundamental, almost revolutionary change in the power relationships of American society."[56]

No change of such magnitude occurs without a constitutional crisis, as we saw in considering the abolition of slavery. For the second left, the crisis occurred with the defeat of Roosevelt's "court-packing" plan. The Supreme Court historically had used the power of judicial review to block reform on grounds of "substantive due process" and "freedom of contract," legal principles that tended to define property rights as untouchable. By 1935 the Court had overturned every aspect of the New Deal, and Roosevelt's plan to reform the Court was widely supported throughout the government. Because the Supreme Court changed course in 1937 and upheld Social Security and the Wagner Act, many have argued that Roosevelt lost the battle but won the war. In fact, the defeat of the plan, according to historian William Leuchtenberg, "helped blunt the most important drive for social reform in American history." Secretary of Agriculture Henry Wallace was more direct. For him, "the whole New Deal went up in smoke" with the Court Fight.[57]

After 1937 the New Deal lost much of its steam but the Popular Front did not. The most consequential discovery of the second American left may have been the idea of democratic mobilization or mass organizing itself. Organizing meant party organizing, whether through the Democratic Party or third parties; it meant organizing powerful blocs like African-Americans, women, Jews, and Native Americans; it meant community organizing, an American innovation that rested on the small group experiences of the first American left; it meant labor and civil rights organizing in the Jim Crow South. Each of these forms of organizing produced its own manuals, schools, training camps, institutes, conferences and bodies of theory, whose influence persisted into the sixties. The goal of organizing was not revolution, except in the imagination of a few militants, but rather a democratic society that recognized its divided character and addressed it through a permanently charged and responsible state.

Popular Front militancy changed the nature of American protest, especially among blacks and immigrants. Most earlier protest was restricted by the ideal of "uplift," an ideology of self-help articulated mainly in racial, ethnic and "middle class specific, rather than in broader, egalitarian social terms." Uplift meant identification with "temperance, thrift, chastity, social purity, patriarchal authority, and the accumulation of wealth."[58] Focusing aspirations on the private depoliticized space of the family, and on the idealization of women, uplift was hegemonic among the teachers, preachers, dentists, undertakers and other "community leaders" of the black world, as well as among the storekeepers, priests, and local politicians of the ethnic communities. The Popular Front repudiated the uplift approach, paving the way for the sixties. In Thomas Bell's 1941 autobiographical novel *Out of This Furnace*, a Slovak steelworker in Braddock, Pennsylvania, reacts to the union organizers: "they didn't talk and act the way the steel towns expected men who were Scotch and Irish and Polish and Italian and Slovak and German and Jew to talk and act." They were "obviously convinced that they were individually as good as any man alive, from the Mill Superintendents up or down." Unlike other immigrants, "they talked – without stumbling over words, uttering them as though they meant something real right there in Braddock – about liberty and justice and freedom of speech."[59]

Instead of deference toward authority, the Popular Front encouraged the sense that citizens had social and economic rights and that these rights were inalienable, just like civil and political rights. Consider the following letter from a recent immigrant, probably Bosnian, Mrs Olga Ferk, written in 1935 to President Roosevelt complaining that she had been mistreated at her relief station, was only $19 behind in her government-subsidized mortgage payments, not three months as accused, and that her son's Civilian Conservation Corps check was always late in arriving. "How long is this rotten condition going to last," Mrs Ferk demanded of the President. "I am at the end of the rope. The rich get richer and the poor can go to H--- that is what it looks like to me . . . Let's have some results." Mrs Ferk's assumption that the national government owed her family relief, a mortgage, and a decent job was unprecedented. A truant officer working in the Black Belt observed an analogous shift. Earlier, being on relief was stigmatized and many blacks demurred out of pride. Now, however, "this attitude had undergone a radical change. These people now demand relief and become indignant when a worker presumes to question their eligibility." Demanding that the Federal government bail out his local relief agency, Thomas Jablonski explained, "We are citizens of the United States, have been paying taxes . . . and are in dire need."[60]

The challenge to the code of deference was especially important to African-American protest. In 1931 the National Association for the Advancement of Colored People (NAACP) forbade any expression of protest against the Scottsboro decision, a railroading of nine Southern black youths who allegedly raped two white women, except for the wearing of an anti-lynching button. This brought the NAACP leadership into conflict with younger militants like Ralph Bunche who believed the old-line organizations were "hopelessly bourgeois in their thinking and living. They pursued goals that evoked admiration from the Negro elite but left the masses of Negroes and their problem of daily bread untouched."[61] Later, in Detroit, Henry Ford worked with the older black community leadership, especially the churches, to provide jobs for black workers. As a result, Ford's River Rouge complex had the largest concentration of black workers in the country, but when the CIO tried to organize Ford, black community leaders opposed the effort. Nevertheless, unionization proceeded, transforming shop floor relations, rolling back the power of the foremen and breaking the company spy system. As a result, the union moved to the center of leadership of the civil rights struggle in the black community. The CIO organization at Ford also moved the national NAACP in a more radical direction. In 1941 its then-leader, Walter White, joined the United Auto Workers' call to support a strike at River Rouge, reversing the NAACP's previous position.[62]

Leftists spoke to the *structural* crisis in American capitalism through popular, democratic mobilization, and aimed to strengthen and solidify the New Deal's commitment to social security and the organization of labor. They spoke to America's *identity* crisis by building a new conception of the American nation, one that put industrial workers, immigrants, farmers, and sharecroppers at its center. While the exaltation of the "yeoman" goes back to Jefferson and Jackson, the Popular Front conception was different in that it foregrounded collective labor rather than small, widely dispersed property. Equally important, artists and writers were central to forging the imagined community of the nation. The Popular Front included a new relation between the artist and the society, one that rejected elitism and esoteric specialization.

The Popular Front artist did not conform to earlier romantic and modernist ideals of rebellious subjectivity. Rather, much of the art of the period has to be seen as a compact with the community. Artists painted murals in small-town post offices; orchestras performed in medium-sized industrial communities; theaters – including black, experimental and children's – dramatized social problems for a newly created public.[63] Popular Front artists adorned the largest public works expansion in American history: "playgrounds and sports fields, public swimming pools and beaches, nature reserves and parks with picnic and camping areas, observation platforms, and outdoor landscapes."[64] They publicized the government's achievements, as at the Tennessee Valley Authority (TVA), which was designed to allow for regular public visits to powerhouses and dams. Since the government paid writers and artists as a job-creating measure, the number or writers and artists expanded exponentially. The earlier idea of the artistic "genius" came into question.

Popular Front efforts to reimagine American identity were based on a valorization of the "common man." Journalistic exposés, historical writing and preservation, the "proletarian" novel, social realist painting, film, and documentary flourished. Social realism produced a great age of photography and reform-minded exposés of chain gangs and poverty among sharecroppers, while also documenting African-American life. This body of work, writes Alfred Kazin, "testified to an extraordinary national self-scrutiny."[65] The "common man" theme also found expression in filmic art, as Charlie Chaplin metamorphosed from the solitary tramp of *The Gold Rush* (1925) to the immigrant of *City Lights* (1931) to the assembly line worker of *Modern Times* (1936) to the Jewish barber in *The Great Dictator* (1940). The Marx Brothers used the immigrant's faulty command of English as a tool against authority: "Go, and never darken my towels again," or "Who are you going to believe, me or your own eyes?" or (defying a lawyer in contract negotiations) "there is no sanity clause."[66]

The social realism of the thirties was based on a reading of class that grasped its subjective dimension. Growing up in poverty, Popular Front writers like Michael Gold, Henry Roth and Tillie Olsen "refracted the concerns of the Depression by writing about their parent's difficult lives."[67] Gold wrote: "I was born in a tenement . . . The sky above the airshafts was all my sky, and the voices of the tenement neighbors in the airshaft were the voices of all my world" or "you should have seen at twilight, after the day's work, one of our pick-and-shovel wops [sic] watering his can of beloved flowers."[68] The interpenetration of class and ethnicity paved the way for the literature of the fifties. Jewish writers, writes Morris Dickstein, were among the first to realize "how much of their identity and affective life they might have to surrender to the bland uniformity of the melting pot."[69] Lionel Trilling wrote, "The discovery . . . of the Jewish situation had the effect of making *society* at last available to my imagination . . . Suddenly it began to be possible – better than that it began to be necessary – to think with categories that were charged with energy and that had the effect of assuring the actuality of the object thought about. One couldn't, for example, think for very long about Jews without perceiving that one was using the category of social class."[70]

Along with Jewish intellectuals, African-American intellectuals were a mainstay of what Michael Denning has called "the cultural front." Black artists and writers like Claude McKay, Countee Cullen, Langston Hughes, Alain Locke, Paul Robeson, and W. E. B. Du Bois began their involvement with the Communist Party because of the party's role in organizing working-class blacks. Almost immediately, however, the appeal of Communism shifted from the critique of capitalism to the project of national cultural revival.[71] "Of all the developments in the Soviet Union," Richard Wright later recalled,

> the way scores of backward peoples had been led to unity on a national scale was what had enthralled me. I had read with awe how the Communists had sent phonetic experts into the vast regions of Russia . . . I had made the first total emotional commitment of my life when I read how the phonetic experts had given these tongueless people, a language, newspapers, institutions. I had read how these forgotten folk had been encouraged to keep their old cultures, to see in their ancient customs meanings and satisfactions as deep as those contained in supposedly superior ways of living.[72]

Complementing the changing vision of American identity, Marxism was revolutionized to take account of race. The two greatest Marxist works of the 1930s, W. E. B. Du Bois's 1936 *Black Reconstruction* and C. L. R. James's 1938 *Black Jacobins*, both argued that racial equality was the precondition for socialist revolution not, as earlier socialists and Communists had claimed, the consequence. As early as 1906 Du Bois had argued that the imposition of the color line on a world scale "transferred the reign of commercial privilege and extraordinary profit from the exploitation of the European working class to the exploitation of backward races under the political domination of Europe." The wars unfolding in the thirties in Spain, Ethiopia, Manchuria and China bore this out. In 1948, James wrote, "The independent Negro movement is able to intervene with terrific force upon the general social and political life of the nation, despite the fact that it is waged under the banner of democratic rights, and is not led necessarily either by the organized labor movement or the Marxist party."[73] Civil rights, James was saying, was the really revolutionary path toward democratization. This was more or less the same line that Marx and Engels had taken in writing about the Civil War almost a hundred years earlier. Ultimately, democracy would lead to socialism, not the other way around.

The Communists' grappling with race, like that of the abolitionists, was deeply personal. The Communists invented the term "white chauvinism." Like the abolitionists, they "made special efforts to recruit blacks to their organizations and to promote them to leadership positions." Who sat where at union meetings, who spoke and in what order, who socialized with whom: these were all subject to self-scrutinizing vigilance. More than any group of that era, the Communists "encouraged interracial dating, sex and marriage, believing that full extirpation of racial prejudice would only be achieved when love and sex freely crossed the color line."[74] Swing music, a blend of African-American and European influences, was explicitly identified with the Popular Front. Benny Goodman began interracial recording in 1933, later integrating his quintet by hiring Lionel Hampton. White musicians like Artie Shaw and Charlie Barnet toured with black artists like Billie Holiday and Lena Horne. Pete Seeger worried that by concentrating on folk music he was not doing justice to jazz.

Overall, the second American left anticipated today's multicultural understanding of American identity. In 1849 Herman Melville wrote: "Settled by the people of all nations . . . We are not a nation, so much as a world."[75] Until the Popular Front period, however, this boast was belied by WASP domination. "The Progressive mind," wrote Richard Hofstadter, had been "a Protestant mind." By contrast, the 1936 election signaled "a social revolution completing the overthrow of the Protestant Republic."[76] The Popular Front, Steve Fraser summarized, "seemed to embody everything . . . that offended the pieties of Middle America: its gaudy cosmopolitanism, its 'Jewishness,' its flirtations with radicalism, its bureaucratic collectivism, its elevation of the new immigrant, its statism, its intellectual arrogance, and its racial egalitarianism."[77] Robert Frank's *The Americans* (1958) expressed the Popular Front's openness to diversity. A collection of photos taken across the whole continent, it included prayer meetings, deserted mining towns, waitresses, crowds, billboards, flags, parades, barber shops, subway cars, highways, buses, out-of-work cowboys, street toughs, abandoned cars, and African-Americans in multiple settings. Published by Grove Press, with an accompanying text by Jack Kerouac, it also became a founding document of the New Left.

The anti-Communist arguments of the 1950s relegated the Popular Front artist to the role of propagandist. In fact, the Popular Front was a key moment in the evolution of the American artist, and in his or her understanding of subjectivity. Consider, in this regard, the career of Edmund Wilson. In 1932 Wilson finished writing *Axel's Castle*, his history of modern poetry, which ends with the cul-de-sac to which avant-garde formalism and symbolism – that is, asocial interiority or subjectivity – had led. As he sent the book to his publisher, he began *To the Finland Station*, his powerful account of the origins of socialism. Wilson was a typical Popular Front intellectual in other respects. Having "grown up in the Big Business era," he wrote, he found the atmosphere of the thirties "not depressing but stimulating. One couldn't help being exhilarated by the sudden unexpected collapse of that stupid, gigantic fraud."[78] "Rather than foreclosing on the intellectual heritage of Bohemia, Greenwich Village, and Paris," then, the Popular Front drew on the antibusiness critique of the previous decade, as well as its pioneering explorations of subjectivity and culture.[79]

The conception of subjectivity at the heart of the Popular Front can be seen in James Agee and Walker Evans's 1941 *Let Us Now Praise Famous Men*, one of the era's greatest achievements. Agee, who called himself "a Communist by sympathy and conviction," insisted that his subjects, "rather than being average or representative types, were each unique: 'a creature which has never in all time existed before and which shall never in all time exist again.'" Thus, his book

did not dramatize its subjects in their social role and show them as "sharecroppers" per se: disputing with their landlord, paying exorbitant prices at the plantation store, nor even (very much) working. Instead it recorded their [concrete, individual] lives: their meals, their traveling to work, their Saturday in town, their worrying about their kin, their posing for pictures, their going to bed and getting up.

According to the historian William Stott, Evans was very careful to protect his subjects' sense of agency, their control over the camera and the photographer, in fact, "he records people when they are most themselves, most in command, as they impose their will on their environment."[80] What we do not learn about, however, is the inner lives of the sharecroppers, their conflicts, their thwarted desires, the duality of their existence, all that psychoanalysis was to bring into prominence in the next decade.

Instead, the Popular Front conception of subjectivity valorized commitment.[81] The decision of the truly free individual for whom a political choice is ultimately an act of salvation – an idea that echoes abolitionism – not only led to Stalinism, but also anticipated postwar existentialism. In André Malraux's *Man's Fate*, a 1934 novel describing the failed Communist uprising against Chiang Kai-shek, Katov, a Japanese Communist, offers his suicide pill to two frightened young militants, about to be burnt alive in a locomotive engine. Malraux's point of view, according to Alfred Kazin, was that of the committed intellectual "who serves the Revolution not in the illusion that man is perfectible, but in order to give value to his knowledge of death."[82] After the outbreak of the Spanish Civil War in 1936, when antifascism became the driving force for the second American left, the ideal became prominent on the left. The Abraham Lincoln Brigade, several thousand volunteers who joined the Republicans in the Spanish Civil War, along with 30,000 other volunteers from throughout the world, exemplified it.

As with the convergence of abolitionism and Republicanism in the nineteenth century, the convergence of leftism and liberalism in the twentieth had an international dimension. After the Depression of 1929 every nation in Europe, including the Soviet Union, moved to the right. By contrast, the United States moved to the left, ultimately inspiring the Popular Fronts in France, Spain, and elsewhere. With the rise of Nazism and of Japanese militarism, Roosevelt, with the help of the left, began to nudge an isolationist country toward war. By 1940–1, the highpoint of Nazi power and the eve of Pearl Harbor, every nation in the world waited for the US entry, which all knew would determine the outcome. While the war involved the US in an alliance with the Soviet Union, which inevitably strengthened Stalin's dictatorship, the alternative would have been far worse. Far from being something new in the world, Nazism, and Japanese expansionism, were based on the older principles of racial and ethnic domination against which, as we saw, the first American left emerged. After the war, US occupations helped democratize Germany and Japan, radically until the Cold War interrupted the process. Thus Marx and Engels's prediction, that the abolition of slavery would launch the US on a democratic path with global consequences, was realized.

To be sure, the Communists' defense of every twist and turn coming out of Stalin's Russia, and their denials of the crimes that were obvious to all, disfigured the second American left. Many leftists, such as John Dewey or Sidney Hook, were passionately anti-Communist, and the Front, broadly conceived, included a vast number of independent Marxists, as well as émigré leftists. What distinguished the second American left, finally, was not that the Communists dominated it, which they did not, but that they were not excluded. Profoundly anti-Communist figures like the labor leader Sidney Hillman understood that exclusion would mean the self-destruction of the left and consistently fought to include Communists in the very parties, conventions, demonstrations, schools, radio stations, and other left activities that Communists sometimes tried to turn to their own purposes. A generation later the New Left's refusal to join liberals in their anti-Communism was decisive for, and definitive of, the third American left. After years of anti-Communist militancy, the pacifist A. J. Muste came to "the deep and much searched conclusion of his soul that he personally would no longer eschew participation in radical activities which contained Communists." "It was an historic moment," wrote Norman Mailer in *The Armies of the Night*, "the New Left was to a degree born of Muste's decision."[83]

Taken in the context of the New Deal state, the Popular Front's reimagining of American identity amounted to a second refounding. Nevertheless, like the first effort, the second was inadequate. For one thing, in spite of the efforts of some leftists, the First New Deal had been complicit with Jim Crow. The Agricultural Adjustment Administration had acquiesced in the eviction of sharecroppers and tenants and the cheating of poorer farmers, often black, as wealthier white farmers administered the program. TVA's model town, Norris, was not just segregated; it was all white. The NRA's wage codes excluded those who worked in agriculture or in domestic service, which meant it excluded three-quarters of all blacks. Blacks referred to NRA as "Negroes Ruined Again" or "Negro Rights Abused." As the black political scientist Ralph Bunche, the first person of color to win the Nobel Peace Prize, wrote, "The New Deal only serves to crystallize those abuses . . . [blacks] have long suffered under laissez-faire capitalism."[84]

Nevertheless, the overall sense of empowerment created during the thirties meant that such oppressions and exclusions could be challenged, and that new paths could be forged in spite of the New Deal's complicity with racial discrimination. Du Bois resigned from the NAACP in 1934, proposing instead black cooperatives based on socialist principles. What was required, he argued, was for blacks to cease patronizing white capitalist enterprises and turn their purchasing power to manufacturing and agricultural businesses owned by Negroes. Far from viewing this as "black capitalism," Du Bois argued that the goal was not for individual blacks to become capitalists, but for the black community to become socialist. "There exists today a chance for the Negroes to organize a cooperative State within their own group," he wrote in 1935. The starting point, however, was to organize within the New Deal: "credit unions, home mortgages, farmers' credit and even industrial capital are available . . . Rail if you will against the race segregation here involved and condoned, but take advantage of it by planting secure centers of Negro cooperative effort and particularly of economic power." Proper use of government resources, he continued, would make it possible for "Negro farmers [to] feed Negro artisans, and Negro technicians [to] build Negro home industries, and Negro thinkers [to] plan this integration of cooperation, while Negro artists dramatize and beautify the struggle."[85]

A. Philip Randolph, the socialist head of the Brotherhood of Sleeping Car Porters, also challenged the New Deal since, as he wrote, it "gave business interests the support of the state," and left Southerners "in the saddle in the Nation's capital." Blacks, he insisted, should not "place their problems for solution down at the feet of their white sympathetic allies, which has been and is the common fashion of the old school of Negro leadership." Instead, he concluded in 1937,

> the task of realizing full citizenship for the Negro people is largely in the hands of the Negro people themselves . . . True liberation can

be acquired and maintained only when the Negro people possess power, and power is the product and flower of organization – organization of the masses, the masses in the mills and mines, on the farms, in the factories.

In 1941 Randolph defied Roosevelt by organizing a March on Washington to protest discrimination in the defense industry. Randolph refused to call "upon our white friends to march with us. There are some things Negroes must do alone." An all-black movement, he added, "helps break down the slavery psychology and inferiority complex in Negroes which comes . . . with Negroes relying on white people for direction and support."[86]

For an example of how the Popular Front liberated black radicalism, consider the life of Anna Arnold Hedgeman. Born in Iowa in 1899, the daughter of a preacher, educator and temperance advocate, Anna Arnold was the first black student at Hamline University in Minnesota, but racial prejudice forced her to find a job teaching at an all-black school in Mississippi, where she developed a "deep hate" for Southern whites. In 1924 she began working for the Springfield, Ohio, Young Women's Christian Association, a magnet for "young, idealistic, church-going women" interested in reform. As a "race woman," Arnold felt she had two responsibilities: to "embody the very virtues that whites believed were inherently lacking in black culture," and to inculcate those virtues into the downtrodden. With the Great Depression, Arnold moved to the Harlem YWCA, where she was moved by the words of Garvey: "No more fear, no more cringing, no more sycophantic begging and pleading." By 1933, when she married, the nationalists had recast their politics under the influence of the Communist Party, the black-led trade unions, and "Don't Buy Where You Can't Work" boycotts. In 1934 she went to work distributing welfare in a black neighborhood in which 55.6 percent of the families received relief. Rejecting the Communists' atheism, but agreeing with their political analysis, she became a militant in the Communist-led National Negro Congress, agitating for black women's economic opportunity and opening communication with other anticolonial struggles such as those of Mohandas Gandhi in India, Kwame Nkrumah in Ghana, and Haile Selassie in Ethiopia. Disturbed by Hedgeman's regular appearance on picket lines, the Y expelled her, but she ended her career as the only woman on the steering council of the 1963 March on Washington for Jobs and Freedom.[87]

The growth of black radicalism rebounded back on the New Deal. After the election of 1936 Roosevelt courted the black vote through patronage, relief, the creation of a "black cabinet" around the President, and the recognition in commissions, studies and speeches of racial inequality as a national problem. Eleanor Roosevelt worked against lynching and the poll tax, while Harold Ickes stipulated that all government contracts in the Public Works Administration hire blacks in proportion to their percentage in the population, and that public housing reserve space both for blacks and for joint black–white occupancy.[88] As we saw, a few years later when the Daughters of the Revolution refused to rent out their hall for a concert by the black soprano Marian Anderson, Eleanor Roosevelt resigned her membership and Ickes arranged for the concert to take place on the steps of the Lincoln Memorial. Meanwhile, the exploits of Jesse Owens, who won four gold medals at the 1936 Olympics in Berlin, and Joe Louis, heavyweight champion from 1937 to 1949, began to "create a national consciousness of the black athlete as an American hero."[89] In 1939 Roosevelt created the Civil Rights division of the Justice Department. By the end of World War Two, civil rights issues had gained national salience. Ten states had created Fair Employment Practice Commissions, several cities had laws against job bias, and in the South black labor was on the verge of an organizing breakthrough.[90] The eruption of McCarthyism after the war not only destroyed the Communists, and turned the labor unions into bastions of reaction, it also destroyed the civil rights breakthroughs of the Popular Front period. It took fifteen years to get back to the consciousness of race that the country had achieved by 1945.

The women's question was also transformed in the later phases of the Popular Front. New Deal women reformers such as Molly Dewson, head of the women's division of the Democratic Party, tended to conform to an earlier uplift model that preached the need to humanize industry or to bring a moral tone to politics. By contrast, the generation of feminists that emerged during and immediately after World War Two broke with the ideal of sentimental womanhood. They criticized the National Industrial Recovery Act, which had sanctioned lower wage rates for women than for men in the same occupations; they criticized social security, which excluded domestic and agricultural jobs, thereby excluding many women; they criticized the Civilian Conservation Camps, which were originally set up for men alone and paid women at half the wage rate when women's camps were added. They criticized the CIO's emphasis on mass production organizing which left many centers of women's work, notably clerical work, unorganized. And they protested the fact that although there were many successful strikes among women workers in the 1930s, women were sent home from the sit-down strikes in order to avoid accusations of sexual promiscuity. As Popular Front institutions politicized the home and the neighborhood, women organized women's councils, neighborhood committees, meat boycotts, rent strikes, and eviction protests.

The true ascendancy of Popular Front feminism occurred during and immediately after the war. The 1940s witnessed the growth of the League of Women Shoppers, the Women's Trade Union League, and the Women's International League of Peace and Freedom. The Jefferson School of Social Science, established in New York City "as an expression of [the] view that Marxism was a legitimate doctrine neglected by the conventional schools," was an early center for courses and research on women.[91] The Congress of American Women, with 250,000 members, was the most important Popular Front organization of progressive women. Founded immediately after World War Two, in part as a reaction to the Nazi emphasis on *Kinder*, *Küche*, and *Kirche*, its leaders were among the founding figures of second wave feminism.[92] Under the influence of the Congress, Communists and other progressive feminists gradually abandoned the position that only working-class women were oppressed and "embraced the idea that women's oppression affected all women, regardless of their class or color."[93] Women in the Congress invented many of the concerns and even the vocabulary later employed by New Left feminism, such as the relation of women's oppression to class, the oppressive division of labor within the household, the "special problems of the Negro woman," and the "triple burden" faced by black women, that is, race, class and gender. As in the case of civil rights, the Congress was red-baited out of existence in 1950.

Betty Friedan was a product of the Popular Front. She came from a highly politicized Popular Front family and attended Smith College where one of her favorite courses was Economics

319 taught by Dorothy Wolff Douglas, a lesbian and socialist activist, who taught her utopian socialism, labor history and socialist thought, and whose research debunked the idea that women worked for "pin money." Friedan spent the summer after her junior year at Highlander Folk School in Tennessee, a Popular Front organization, founded in 1932 as a training ground for American radicals, communitarians and nonviolent activists. During the war, she studied psychology with Erik Erikson at Berkeley at a time when Erikson was seeking to "unreify" (Friedan's word) Freudian categories, that is, situate them socially. In the early 1950s she became a labor journalist for the United Electrical Workers, the most communist of all the CIO unions. Women workers, she wrote in her 1952 pamphlet *UE Fights for Women Workers*, "refuse any longer to be paid or treated as some inferior species by their bosses, or by any male workers who have swallowed the bosses' thinking."[94] After her marriage she lived in Parkway Village in Queens, a typical Popular Front suburb, which boasted a coop nursery, organized reading groups, regular political activity, and sophisticated political discussions. From these experiences she derived her core insight, namely that the most devastating problem women faced was isolation within the home. Nevertheless, her 1963 *The Feminine Mystique*, organized around this insight, did not mention the Popular Front, understandably given the nearly two decades of McCarthyism that had intervened.

Let us conclude. Like slavery, industrial capitalism challenged America's egalitarian republican ideals. While this challenge was apparent in the late nineteenth and early twentieth centuries, precipitating the Populist, Labor, Progressive and Socialist movements, it mushroomed into a full-scale crisis in the Great Depression. The crisis had a structural dimension in that the capitalist system could not go on without fundamental reforms. But it also had an identity dimension, meaning that the reforms had to be inflected with an egalitarian meaning if the country's core identity was to survive and prosper. A second American left appeared in response to the crisis. Just as the abolitionists interpreted the dismantling of slavery through the lens of racial equality, so the leftists of the thirties refracted the New Deal state through the prism of social equality. What the left added to the modern administrative planning state was the insistence on mass democratic mobilization, which reflected the principle of working-class agency. In thus inflecting the structural resolution of the crisis with the ideal of social equality, the left spoke to the crisis – the turning point – provoked by the Depression. Like their predecessors during the Civil War, they undertook a refounding, a deepening of the meaning of American nationhood to include social equality. During World War Two, as the nation turned into a mass consumption society, the idea of economic growth tended to supplant the idea of social equality. This did not mean, however, that the achievements of the second American left were obliterated. Subsequent generations were able to uphold social equality, even as they upheld racial equality, against powerful forces that sought to undermine it.

3

The New Left and Participatory Democracy

Like its predecessors, the New Left emerged at a critical turning point in American history. Viewed from the standpoint of geopolitics, it was the beginning of the end of "the American century," which prefigured a long period of decline or repositioning. Like its predecessors, too, the New Left tried to bend the resulting society in the direction of deepening equality. It did so by intervening in the great social movements that arose during "the long 1960s": civil rights, the antiwar movement, and women's and gay liberation. In each case, the New Left constituted the radical wing of the movement, pushing liberal solutions to their limits and beyond, and attempting to connect the movements to one another, so they formed a coherent challenge to the unraveling order. Of all three lefts, the New Left was at once the most short-lived and the most enduring. If it seemed like an explosive burst of rebellious energy that burnt itself out by the early 1970s, it also set the contours for what remains the left of our day.

The years between World War Two and the 1960s were the high point of American hegemony. At the end of the war the US possessed two-thirds of the world's gold reserves, produced half of the world's manufacturing output, half of its ships, and was by far the world's largest exporter.[1] The men who built the postwar order – almost all of them bankers and Wall Street lawyers – believed that the Depression "had been due largely to the breakdown of the global trading and financial system, and the consequent fragmentation of the world into would-be autarchic national economies or empires." They sought to build an international order centered on a hegemonic nation with the moral authority and military might to enforce stability.[2] As it developed, this order included an international trade and monetary system, but also access to oil and other commodity resources at stable prices. The result was the huge defense spending known as "military Keynesianism," the "invisible government" of the CIA, and a series of wars and interventions mostly aimed at blocking state-centered development in the Third World.[3]

American hegemony over what was then known as "the free world" was the product of the postwar Soviet-American settlement, which created a bipolar world. Beginning in the late fifties this settlement began to crumble. On the one hand, the European recovery – signaled by the creation of the Common Market in 1957 – meant that Western European economies were gaining independence from the US. Japan, similarly, was emerging from US tutelage and becoming an economic rival. On the other hand, following Stalin's death in 1953 the Communist world began to lose its coherence. The Sino-Soviet split and the rise of neutralism, especially in Yugoslavia, were symptoms. Most importantly, a whole host of third world countries, including Egypt, Indonesia, Ghana, the Congo, Guatemala, and Iran, challenged America's global supremacy without becoming Communist; the 1955 Bandung Conference of neutrals offered an alternative to the bipolar settlement. The New Left emerged at this juncture, its very name signaling that it too was moving beyond the Cold War framework.

The New Left also emerged at a turning point in American economic history. Military Keynesianism was industrially based. The US used its global reach to secure markets and raw materials, and to prop up weak trading partners, but the gains of empire were returned to America's domestic economy where they were used to moderate the business cycle, insure relatively high employment, and sustain a social wage through infrastructural spending, provision of services, and income support. The years in which the New Left emerged and flourished, however, saw the beginnings of the shift away from industry and toward finance, consumerism and marketization. The great megaliths of the Keynesian era – automobiles, consumer durables, steel, oil, and electricity – turned into multinational corporations, and began to invest abroad. An economy based on goods production aimed at the masses gave way to one oriented to services tailored to the individual. The end of colonial empires and the rising importance of global trade brought racial, ethnic, and national differences into new prominence. Higher education expanded, just as market forces helped consolidate a generationally specific youth identity, creating the social basis for a new kind of left.

The New Left can scarcely be said to have self-consciously understood the shift that the US went through in the 1960s, since the greater part of the change was not manifest until the following decade, the era of "deindustrialization" when the US went off the gold standard, and neoliberalism began its ascent. But the radical youth of the sixties did grasp that the country was at a turning point. With the benefit of hindsight we can see that the centralized mass production economy of the postwar years was going to develop spontaneous, decentralized forms of self-organization, whether marketized or not. We can also see that the relative global position of the US was going to decline, as the world became increasingly polycentric, if not Asia-centered. But the *meaning* of these changes remained to be decided. Would they deepen the project of bringing "equality to people of subordinate status" or would they serve "as a way of disguising exploitation." As in the previous crises over slavery and industrialization, it fell to the left to articulate the egalitarian alternative.

Let us consider this more carefully. To begin, there were two different ways in which the United States could deal with its declining suzerainty. One was denial, reactive self-assertion and a hollow insistence on an increasingly imaginary moral superiority, all underpinned by a vast expansion of the nation's military capacity. The other possibility – the one urged by the New Left – was that the country would support, albeit critically, the newly emerging and democratizing forces of Asia, Africa and Latin America, which, at that point, often took a revolutionary turn. Domestically, too, there were two possibilities latent in the disintegration of centralized, state-centered Keynesianism and the emergence of new, decentralized forms of self-organization. On the one hand, self-organization could mean marketization and finance-driven neoliberal growth; on the other, it could mean nonmarket forms of local, spontaneous, democratic coordination, such as those championed by the New Left. In the latter case, the country would search for new participatory forms of self-organization, guided by principles of equality and the search for a common good.

Largely originating with students in the universities, including the universities of the Deep South, the New Left was in a good position to shape which direction the country would take, if only because, as noted by Clark Kerr, Chancellor of the University of California at Berkeley, the universities had replaced the automobile as the driving force in the economy. In fact, however, if the New Left can be considered a student movement, it was one that rejected meritocratic competitiveness and technocratic specialization in favor of a larger conception of equality and an extra-academic tradition of critical thought. The most important characteristic of the students was not their role in what some called "the new working class," but rather their ability to identify with those whom Frantz Fanon called "the wretched of the earth." This was important because if the world was going to move to higher and more democratic forms of global organization, the most critical ties that needed to be forged were those between peoples, and not between governments.

Writing of France, Kristin Ross called the New Left's distinctive characteristic "dis-identification," meaning freedom from the imposition of any social roles. May '68, Ross writes,

> had little to do with the social group – students or "youth" – who were its instigators. It had much more to do with the flight from social determinants, with displacements that took people out of their location in society, with a disjunction, that is, between political subjectivity and the social group. What is forgotten when May '68 is forgotten seemed to have less to do with the lost habits of this or that social group, than it did with a shattering of social identity that allowed politics to take place.[4]

This shattering, a phenomenon entirely at odds with the identity politics that erupted in the seventies, underlay the hopes for global solidarity and exchange that animated the New Left. Of course, this capacity for dis-identification was itself grounded in particular social conditions: widespread access to higher education, distance from poverty and material want, and the "wonderful feeling," which followed from the destruction of fascism, "that one was entitled to no less than anyone else, that one could do anything and could be excluded from nothing."[5]

The shattering of social roles, the rejection of externally defined limitations and identities, also underlay the New Left's profound anti-authoritarianism. In the words of Samuel Huntington, who was by no means a supporter,

> the essence of the democratic surge of the 1960s was a general challenge to existing systems of authority, public and private. . . . People no longer felt the same compulsion to obey those whom they had previously considered superior to themselves in age, rank, status, expertise, character, or talents. Within most organizations, discipline eased and differences in status became blurred. . . . More precisely, in American society, authority had been commonly based on organizational position, economic wealth, specialized expertise, legal competence, or electoral representativeness. Authority based on hierarchy, expertise, and wealth all, obviously, ran counter to the democratic and egalitarian temper of the times.[6]

Here, too, the left was struggling to give meaning to a social transformation. Would the anti-authoritarian spirit of the sixties give way to the antinomian consumerism of "flexible network capitalism"? Or would it lead to more egalitarian and more participatory forms of democratic self-organization.

As the radical, political wing of a broad surge of democratic energies, the New Left of the sixties sought to drive events in the direction of a larger and deeper sense of equality, one that spoke to the deep identity of the American people, and not merely to their immediate or short-term concerns. In this regard, the student movement was building on both the errors and the successes of the first two lefts. The first American left, the abolitionists, failed to anticipate how the ideal of racial equality would wither in the absence of a post-emancipation struggle for its social and economic prerequisites. The second left, the socialists and Communists, corrected the first left's error, but failed to anticipate that a people could win social equality and still remain the passive objects of an all-powerful state. The New Left corrected for the second left's error with its idea of participatory democracy, which presupposed an underlying desire for freedom. The great discoveries of the New Left, such as sexism and homophobia, arose from participatory experiences in the demonstrations, meetings or communes of the decade, and from the creation of new subjectivities fostered by those events. These experiences underlay the theoretical achievements of the New Left, which moved toward the insight that capitalism and imperialism were not merely objective structures, but rather were also means of organizing culture and subjectivity. That, at any rate, is the story I will tell here.

My story divides into four parts. The first part describes the crisis that the liberal order faced in the 1950s. The heart of the crisis was another metamorphosis of liberalism. A doctrine of individual freedom, liberalism was originally associated with limits on the state, and then with an activist state intended to pursue the general welfare. After World War Two, however, liberalism was being turned into the instrument of hegemonic control and empire. Fearful of democratic "excesses," whether of the right or left, liberals sought to redefine politics in the apolitical terms of pluralism, modernization and economic growth. The "New Right" mobilized against Cold War liberals by insisting on the priority of individual responsibility and moral content. The New Left emerged from this matrix. While sharing some of the right's critique of the bureaucratic state, it nonetheless linked that critique to the struggle for equality. Thus, the New Left embraced the ideals of racial and social equality advanced by the previous two lefts, while inventing new understandings of equality all its own.

The second stage, which stretches from 1959 to 1965, is the stage of civil rights and its radicalization, a process both hastened and shaped by the Cold War. In this stage, we see the characteristically tense and productive exchange between liberal Presidents and a left that we saw in the cases of Lincoln and the abolitionists, and Roosevelt and the Popular Front. On the one hand, radical students within the civil rights movement drew on long-standing traditions of nonviolent action to create a new kind of protest movement. On the other hand, Presidents Kennedy and Johnson responded to the growing radicalization by attempting to reorient the country in a new, more progressive direction. The death of Kennedy led to perhaps the greatest wave of reform in American history, including civil rights, Medicare and the war on poverty.

The third stage, which began in 1965, was dominated by the war in Vietnam. In this stage the relationship between liberalism and the left ruptured. While the 1960s liberal establishment was willing to move toward racial equality, it was not willing to give up its aspirations to empire. Those aspirations, which were distinct from continental expansion, had begun in 1898 when the American suppression of the Philippine Revolution anticipated the US attempt to suppress the Vietnamese. After the Chinese Communist revolution (1949), the Korean War (1950–3), and the so-called "reverse course" in Japan (the enlistment of Japan into the Cold War), the US reoriented many of its priorities from Europe to Asia. There it stood not just against Communism but also against a whole wave of decolonizing revolutions. As we shall see, the American defeat in Vietnam was the third great turning point in American history, shattering the self-confidence and pride that had followed World War Two, toppling one President (Lyndon Johnson) and, arguably, a second (Richard Nixon), ending the détente with the Soviet Union which had begun in 1962, leaving a long-term residue of mistrust in government, wrecking the Keynesian compromise, and opening the path toward global finance and debt.

The final stage of the New Left comprises the period from 1968 to the mid-1970s. Many historians describe the New Left as coming to an end with the 1968 Democratic Convention, the Weatherman debacle, and the implosion of Students for a Democratic Society (SDS). In fact, the period from 1968 to the mid-1970s was a period of enormous growth and maturation on the left. The period saw the broadening and deepening of the later antiwar movement (the "Mobe"), the flourishing of neo-Marxist social theory and journalism, the development of new and unexpected forms of social protest such as ecology (the first Earth Day took place in 1970), the shift from students to faculty in the university movements (New University Conference was founded in 1968), and the birth of Chicano, Puerto Rican, and Native American liberation movements. Although both feminism and gay rights antedate the sixties, leftism created a revolutionary current in both movements, those of "women's liberation" and "gay liberation."[7] Then, too, the early seventies witnessed the attempt to broaden the New Left from a movement of students and racial minorities to a movement that included rank and file workers, many of whom were women and/or racial minorities who had shared in the anti-authoritarian upheavals of the sixties and were opposed to the war in Vietnam.

At each stage, the New Left was confronted with a social movement much larger than itself, and at each stage it sought to push that movement in a radical-democratic and egalitarian direction. This was the case for the civil rights movement, which faced a choice. On the one hand, it could pursue a "realistic" strategy oriented to achieving de jure formal rights. On the other hand, it could target the underlying power structures and the informal codes that sustained inequality, even after the dismantling of legal apartheid. The antiwar movement faced an analogous choice. On the one hand, it could argue that Vietnam was a "mistake," while failing to challenge the underlying assumptions of US Cold War anti-Communism. On the other hand, it could challenge the liberal Cold War order, seeking to bring the United States into a friendlier relation with a revolutionizing world. Finally, feminism could pursue women's rights in a way that dovetailed with a competitive, individualistic, market-based meritocracy. Or it could mount a comprehensive challenge to the overall division of labor, both paid and unpaid. In each case the New Left sought to push the larger movement in the radical direction. Had it succeeded, it might have created an enduring radical presence in American politics. In the event, however, the New Left did not succeed and the country began to abandon the ideal of equality, and with that much of its moral standing. As a result, the great crisis both in the place of the United States in the world, and in the US economy, that opened up in the 1960s was never resolved, and still awaits resolution today.

In August 1945, a few months after Franklin Roosevelt's death, the United States dropped atomic bombs on Hiroshima and Nagasaki. Even as the dawning of the atomic age brought World War Two's unprecedented human pain and misery to a fiery end, it ushered in new threats.[8] Norman Cousins described "a primitive fear, the fear of the unknown [which] has burst out of the subconscious and into the conscious, filling the mind with primordial apprehensions."[9] H. Stuart Hughes sensed "that the world had suddenly stood still and that life would never be the same again."[10] In the few years that followed, the terrible fate of Bolshevism – purges, famines, gulags – was instrumentalized and politicized through the still little understood outburst of McCarthyism. Rightists excoriated the New Deal's "social planners, and new order advocates" who had undermined "the American way of life."[11] Images of commissars, forced labor, secret police, purge, and sabotage infused the collective unconscious, and perhaps hundreds of thousands lost their jobs.

The traumatic explosion of McCarthyism accompanied the creation of what Daniel Yergin has called the "national security state," "a unified pattern of attitudes, policies and institutions" designed for permanent international conflict of a life and death sort. Even if a postwar conflict between the Soviet Union and the United States was inevitable given the vacuum created by the destruction of the Third Reich, America's Cold War outlook exceeded all rational proportions, assuming the guise of an ideological global crusade combined with severe domestic repression. For many of McCarthy's followers, America's establishment was not a plutocratic oligarchy, but "a liberal elite composed of professors, editors, labor leaders, politicians and, for some, Jews."[12] Fearing a repeat of the anti-intellectual upsurge that characterized the McCarthy period, Cold War liberals such as Louis Hartz, Richard Hofstadter, Arthur Schlesinger Jr, and Reinhold Niebuhr sought, in quite varying ways, to de-ideologize the American liberal tradition, eventually laying the basis for the "pragmatic," technocratic politics against which the New Left rebelled.

The Cold War liberalism that took shape in the fifties condemned "extremism" of both left and right. Both left and right supposedly mobilized "conflicts that involve ultimate schemes of values and that bring fundamental fears and hatreds, rather than negotiable interests into political action."[13] In place of extremism, Cold War liberals espoused the politics of growth and pluralism. The aim of growth was to defuse divisiveness and conflict; economics, so went the theory, was "transpolitical."[14] Pluralist political theorists also condemned the intrusion of morality into politics. Democracy, they argued, required compromise, negotiation and bargaining between groups.[15] President Harry Truman affirmed the new orientation, complaining that many of the people around Roosevelt had been "crackpots and the lunatic fringe." "I want to keep my feet on the ground," Truman opined, "I don't want experiments. The American people have been through a lot of experiments and they want a rest from experiments."[16]

The turn of liberals away from the Popular Front created an opening for a New Right, whose insistence on the individual and moral dimension in politics the New Left shared. The New Right's first step was to repudiate the New Deal. According to Whittaker

Chambers, the New Deal was a "revolution by bookkeeping and lawmaking" that replaced "reverence and awe" with "man's monkeylike amazement at the cleverness of his own inventive brain."[17] Against "social tinkering" the right sought to capture the drama of the individual search for salvation by redeeming such neglected figures as Melville, Dostoevsky, and Faulkner, elaborators of the Augustinian vision of original sin.[18] Ironically, anti-Communist rightists associated the United States, often considered the most superficial of cultures, with renovated ideals of depth and personal freedom, freed of their Christian integument by American democracy, and thereby made available to Jews, who played a leading role among neoconservative intellectuals. As a *Partisan Review* symposium of 1952 put it, "more and more writers have ceased to think of themselves as rebels and exiles. They now believe that their values, if they are to be realized at all, must be realized in America and in relation to the actuality of American life." In the editor's words, "There is a recognition that the kind of democracy which exists in America has an intrinsic and positive value; it is not merely a capitalist myth, but a reality which must be defended against Russian totalitarianism."[19]

Like the New Right, the New Left began with a critique of the New Deal but turned it in an egalitarian and critical direction.[20] An epochal shift in politics and culture underlay this possibility. New Deal politics had been industrial politics; the family had been part of a relatively integrated, work-centered way of life that included the ethnic neighborhood, the church, the ward boss, and even the factory. Oriented toward a deepened commitment to the family, the postwar generation had lowered the age of marriage for both sexes, reduced the divorce rate, and increased the number of children. Between 1945 and 1946 the birth rate in the US leapt by 20 percent and continued to rise until 1957, when over 4 million babies were born in a single year. The baby boomers, as they later came to be called, were the product of a new generation whose attention had shifted to sexuality, the family, and personal life. This made a new politics possible.

As much as any figure of the fifties, C. Wright Mills grasped the magnitude of the shift. Calling what was left of the Popular Front "the remnants of a vast defeat," rejecting the old left's "labor metaphysic," Mills's first book, *The New Men of Power: America's Labor Leaders* (1948), argued that the New Deal had rationalized the conditions of production by introducing bureaucratic controls, rather than socializing them by enhancing workers' autonomy.[21] Behind Mills's critique lay the disfiguring example of the Soviet Union, and the leftist debates over whether 1917 had produced a "degenerated workers' state" or a "bureaucratic collectivist state." In either case, there was broad agreement that statist solutions had failed. By the early sixties, such works as Jane Jacobs's *Death and Life of the Great American Cities* (1961), Rachel Carson's *Silent Spring* (1962), and Ralph Nader's *Unsafe at any Speed* (1965) were also criticizing corporate-inspired regimentation on behalf of freer, more spontaneous, decentralized forms of self-organization.

Rejecting the "labor metaphysic" meant shifting attention from economics to psychology or, in socialist terms, from exploitation to alienation, a perspective evoked in Marx's *Economic and Philosophical Manuscripts*, first translated into English in 1959. According to Mills, if leftists were to understand the reasons for their prior failures, they had to focus on the soul-destroying world of the postindustrial office, the barbiturate- and alcohol-drugged suburbs, the empty, destructive rebellion of the teenager, the fear of doomsday machines, fail-safe devices, and nuclear meltdowns, the omnipresent anxiety concerning world destruction. The theme of alienation also prefigured the clockwork vision of Stanley Kubrick and the paranoid, postmodern worldview of authors like Thomas Pynchon.[22]

Along with the idea of alienation, the fifties witnessed other signs of the coming of the New Left. The rejection of the work ethic, for example by the Beatniks, was especially important. Jack Kerouac's *On the Road* (1957), with the "intense, out-of-focus hurtling across America, the absolute lack of social pretensions, the seeking of something somehow important, somewhere, the experimentation with life and the gobbling of books, the betrayals and loyalties, the tenderness, the raw sincerity, all these showed an American youth different from any before."[23] Another harbinger lay in identification with black "hipsters" as expressed in jazz, the use of drugs, especially marijuana, and clothing styles. The "hipster's laissez-faire attitude toward work and privileging of leisure and pleasure" was prophetic.[24] In Morris Dickstein's words, "The White Negro" (1957), Norman Mailer's psychopathic hero, was "a bomb that explodes beneath the bland surface of the fifties, constructed out of all its repressed violence and rebelliousness, composed of longings for personal autonomy and extreme experience that could not be satisfied by respectability, domesticity, maturity and competitive success."[25]

It was especially in popular music, beginning in 1952 when Alan Freed hosted the first rock and roll concert, that the demotic and antinomian currents out of which the New Left grew, and against which it contended, first erupted. The reason is not only that music appeals directly to the emotions, but also that it was the language of Black America, the only place the Negro has been able to tell his story, according to James Baldwin. Previously African-American music – spirituals, blues and gospel – had been kept separate from pop music. This changed in the fifties, culminating in 1960 when Berry Gordy released "Bad Girl" by the Miracles, the first record with the Motown label. By the early sixties, rhythm and blues was being combined with other traditions, for example, folk music, still then a living bridge between the old left and the new.[26] The explosive entry of rhythm and blues created a new intimacy between the performer and the audience, and a new expression of sexuality in the pre-teen and largely female audiences.

Alongside the gathering energies of mass culture, artistic and intellectual vanguards anticipated the new era. Herbert Marcuse's psychoanalytic *Eros and Civilization* (1955) and Norman O. Brown's *Life against Death* (1959) criticized the "pseudo-individuation" of the Cold War liberal "maturity ethic," and portrayed the artist, the mystic and the homosexual as the charismatic dramatis personae of a new society. The new art was postindividualist, antihierarchical and participatory. In Bebop, no single instrumentalist or harmonic structure established dominance; in postmodern dance no part of the body was privileged; in 1953 Robert Rauschenberg erased a Willem de Kooning drawing, thus dethroning the modernist artwork; in postmodern literature, conversation was taken as the model for democratic participation ("We thought of ourselves as in the spirit of the true left," remarked avant-garde novelist Ron Sukenick).[27] The experimental theater, happenings, and street theater of the late fifties were all democratic, participatory and antihierarchical, anticipating the sit-ins, teach-ins, and marches against the war that were soon to erupt.

John F. Kennedy, elected in 1960, the youngest American President ever, evinced the rising optimism. On the surface,

Kennedy's administration marked the triumph of that "muscular," "pragmatic" Keynesianism that would ramp up the Cold War and "get the country moving again." Underneath the surface, however, a generational revolution was gathering force. Fueled by Sputnik era anxiety, Kennedy symbolized youth, brains and sex appeal: a political leader who might release the underground energies of the fifties. As one reporter wrote "We seemed about to enter an Olympian age in this country, brains and intellect harnessed to great force, the better to define a common good."[28]

Several factors gave the young people coming of age during the Kennedy Presidency their strong generational sense. To begin with the idea of a generational revolt – New Left, New Right – was in the air, in part reflecting the Freudian influence. In addition, the fifties saw the launching of a Cold War fueled revolution in higher education. Student enrollments went from 2.8 million in 1955 to 9 million in 1970, and for the first time university students circulated internationally. Advertisers also tapped the vast purchasing power of the student cohort, beginning in the early 1950s with the Davy Crockett fad, followed by blue jeans, rock music, and recreational drugs. Finally, the acceleration of technological change precipitated and deepened the "generation gap," giving the young a sense of their difference from their seemingly slow-witted predecessors.

Kennedy came to power on a Cold War program, but the world was moving in a different direction. As we saw, after the death of Stalin in 1953 Communism began to "thaw." In 1956 Palmiro Togliatti coined the term "polycentrism" to describe the increasing independence of Communist parties. The biggest change occurred in Western Europe, where by the late fifties a substantial domestic opposition "believed that the Cold War had ended with Stalin's death, that defense spending could be substantially reduced, and that the Cold War was a convenient myth dreamed up by the military-industrial complex." The changed mood in France, where the term "nouvelle gauche" originated, was symptomatic. In the immediate aftermath of World War Two "everything seemed destined for failure in a country torn and disoriented, convinced that its future did not depend on itself." By 1958 in contrast, when De Gaulle returned to power with the promise of ending the war in Algeria, there was hope everywhere.[29]

The Sino-Soviet split, which began in the late fifties, hastened the thaw, even as it encouraged third world militancy. Earlier

Khrushchev had heard Stalin warn that his successors "wouldn't be able to stand up to the imperialists, that the first time we came into personal contact with them we wouldn't be able to defend our interests, and they would simply smash us." After 1957 he heard the same warnings from the Chinese.[30] As Khrushchev toyed with the possibilities of a rapprochement with the United States, tens of thousands marched against nuclear weapons in Turkey, Japan, South Korea, and Aldermaston, England, where the British use of the term "New Left" originated in 1959. In March 1960 the Sharpeville Massacre led to armed resistance to apartheid in South Africa. Following the Greensboro, North Carolina sit-ins by one month, the decision of the African National Congress to engage in armed struggle suggested the global character of the struggle against racism.

Once again C. Wright Mills was prescient. His 1960 "Letter to the New Left" emphasized the importance of new, largely third world, insurgencies.[31] Cuba was especially important. H. L. Matthews, the *New York Times* reporter who had covered the Spanish Civil War, interviewed Castro in 1957. Two years later the Cuban revolution broke out, based not on working classes but on peasants. As Castro barnstormed the United States in 1960, black militants created Fair Play for Cuba.[32] Boxing champion Joe Louis asked, "where else can an American Negro go for a winter vacation," referencing the segregated South.[33] In September 1960 while attending a United Nations General Assembly session, Castro and the Cuban delegation left midtown Manhattan and moved to Harlem's Theresa Hotel where Malcolm X greeted them. The highly publicized discussions that followed concerned the status of the embattled Congolese prime minister, Patrice Lumumba, whose country supplied 95 percent of all US uranium. In the same year, C. Wright Mills's *Listen, Yankee* sold 400,000 copies, more than any of his other books. In 1960 Mills was set to participate in a televised debate over Cuba with Adolf Berle, a Cold War liberal who later served in the Kennedy administration. Mills's preparation for this debate, and the anxiety surrounding it, led to the heart attack that would impair him until his death in 1962.

In general, then, the background milieu from which the New Left emerged was pregnant with possibilities. An avant-garde consciousness, a burgeoning mass culture, and a generational consciousness were converging, all within an opening, fluid international order. Nonetheless, the precipitating event giving birth to the New Left came from the civil rights movement, to which we now turn.

In the United States, political theorist Judith N. Shklar has written, "the struggle between master and slave [has been] not a meta-historical Hegelian image, but a daily fact." The overwhelming importance of slavery, Shklar continued, has given the American liberal tradition its distinctive character: an emphasis on rights guaranteed by a powerful Supreme Court and protected by government.[34] After World War Two, this tradition found expression in the demand for an end to racial segregation and discrimination, both de jure and de facto, a demand that helped launch what was later termed the "rights revolution."

Although the demand for equal rights began with the abolition of slavery, it took on new meaning during the Cold War. Equal rights played the same role for the US global empire that antislavery played for the post-Napoleonic British Empire; it allowed the US to occupy the high moral ground. Even during World War Two, at the newly dug graves at the Battle of Iwo Jima, Rabbi Roland B. Gittelsohn delivered the following eulogy: "Here lie officers and men, Negroes and whites, rich and poor together. Here no man prefers another because of his faith, or despises him because of his color . . . Among these men there is no discrimination, no prejudice, no hatred. Theirs is the highest and purest democracy."[35] The revelations concerning the Holocaust at the end of the war gave added force to the idea that the war was fought to abolish discrimination and prejudice, and not to secure a global trading system.

The powerful wave of decolonization that followed World War Two insured that racial equality would become fundamental to US Cold War policy. When Secretary of State James F. Byrnes protested the Soviet denial of voting rights in the Balkans, the Soviets responded that Negroes in Byrnes's own state of South Carolina were denied the same right. Robert Cushman, a member of the President's Committee on Civil Rights, wrote in 1948, "It is unpleasant to have the Russians publicize our continuing lynchings, our Jim Crow statutes and customs, our anti-Semitic discriminations and our witch-hunts, but is it undeserved?" By 1956, the

Voice of America was sending Louis Armstrong to the Gold Coast and Dizzy Gillespie, with an interracial orchestra, to the Middle East. "We are expected to be the model," Secretary of State Dean Rusk later explained. Decolonization, Rusk continued, is

> one of the epochal developments of our time. The vast majority of these newly independent peoples are nonwhite, and they are determined to eradicate every vestige of the notion that the white race is superior . . . In their efforts to enhance their influence among the nonwhite peoples and to alienate them from us, the Communists clearly regard racial discrimination in the United States as one of their most valuable assets.[36]

In supporting civil rights, of course, the government was not merely responding to international pressures. Membership in the NAACP had grown ninefold between 1940 and 1946.[37] In 1944 the Supreme Court banned the white primary; in 1946 it ruled against segregated public interstate transportation; in 1948 it banned racially prescriptive property covenants. In the same year President Truman called for the desegregation of the armed forces. In 1948 the Democratic Party adopted a civil rights plank, precipitating the "Dixiecrat" revolt. Chester Bowles wrote to Hubert Humphrey:

> I think the Civil Rights [plank] is the single most important victory that has been won in a Democratic Convention in many years. In the past, the Democratic Party has been more or less of a hodge-podge of big-city organizations, southern reactionaries, and northern liberals held together by the leadership of a Wilson or Roosevelt. At Philadelphia . . . we laid the groundwork for a Democratic Party based on liberal principles.[38]

In the growing impetus toward civil rights during the 1950s we have an example of the liberal tradition pushed to its highest and finest potentiality. Alongside its emphasis on material security, the New Deal had generated a "second Bill of Rights," a series of judicial decisions promoted by New Deal lawyers that made most of the original Bill of Rights enforceable against state laws. As a result, the nature of jurisprudence had shifted from an emphasis on the relative jurisdiction of state and federal governments to an emphasis on the obligations of government to guarantee

the rights of individuals. This "rights revolution" culminated in
Brown v Board of Education (1954). In that and other cases, the
Warren Court advanced the view that individuals could claim
rights against the state as a mode of social change, thus effectively
nationalizing the Bill of Rights.[39]

Considered historically, ending racial discrimination seems
inevitable, just as the abolition of slavery seems inevitable, and the
creation of a modern administrative state seems inevitable. As in
the previous cases, however, the meaning of the reform was inde-
terminate. Segregation could have ended in an impersonal, administrative (top-down), and formal or meritocratic way, or it could
have ended with the profound interactions between the races
pioneered by the abolitionists, with the extension of civil rights
to social and economic rights, as pioneered by the socialists, and
with the participation of the poor in their own liberation, as pioneered by the New Left. Because of this indeterminacy, America
has needed a left.

The indeterminacy of desegregation reflected the multiple meanings of rights. Before the Civil War the slave-owners had insisted
on their right to do what they wanted with their slaves. Later, the
same rights that empowered blacks to sue for racial integration
could empower whites who called for the integrity of neighborhood schools, or for the protection of private, though discrimi-
natory, housing markets. Thus the struggle for rights involved
more than an effort to gain and implement them. It also entailed
a struggle over their meaning. Would rights signify equality, or
would they be bent to defend privilege? Equally important, the
struggle for rights was a struggle to change the moral consciousness, both of the activist and of the wider society. This had been
clear in all indigenous radical traditions, such as those of the
nonviolent conscientious objector and the moral witness, and it
came to the fore again in 1955 when Rosa Parks refused to vacate
her seat on a Montgomery, Alabama bus, leading to the spread
of direct action throughout the South. The four students from
the Agricultural and Technical College in Greensboro, North
Carolina who ordered coffee at the segregated Woolworth's
lunch counter on February 1, 1960 went still further. Their sit-ins
uncovered and began to crack the family-based racial and sexual
code that had governed the American struggle for rights since the
emergence of the second party system. The effect was to push the

meaning of the civil rights revolution in the direction of deepening equality.

Recall that the structure governing the expression of protest in America had emerged to keep the slavery issue out of politics. Resting on a distinction between public and private, this structure had profound but differing implications for blacks and for white women, the two great social groups whose condition would be revolutionized during the sixties. Whereas blacks were degraded and associated with the profane, white women had been desexualized and placed on a pedestal, but in a way that denied them full citizenship, and infantilized them psychologically. Black culture, including the black family, was degraded all the more to idealize the "American," that is, white, family, and above all to purify the white woman. The abolitionists had grappled with this version of the public/private division in the form of the cult of true womanhood and the socialists grappled with it in their rejection of "uplift." In the civil rights struggles of the late fifties the same code governing protest reemerged. This code regulated not only black/white relations, but protest in general. Especially in the South, grievances had to be expressed in such a way that "complaints" affirmed the dominant code even as they seemed to question it.

The great African-American writers of the fifties, such as Richard Wright, Ralph Ellison, and James Baldwin, had struggled to develop a way to express protest that did not affirm the preexisting codes of power. Growing up in the South, Wright consciously negated every message that society directed at him.[40] "In what other way had the South allowed me to be natural, to be real, to be myself except in rejection, rebellion, and aggression?" he asked in his path-breaking autobiography *Black Boy*.[41] The students who sat in in 1960 found an answer to this question. Greensboro had always been a center of racial progress. Nonetheless, white leaders "exerted ultimate control by shaping the pattern of dialogue between the races, dictating the terms of exchange," the "ground rules for racial interaction." The key, in the mind of North Carolina progressives of both races, was "that conflict is inherently bad, that disagreement means personal dislike, and that consensus offers the only way to preserve a genteel and civilized way of life."[42] Known as "the Gateway City" and embodying North Carolina's "progressive mystique," Greensboro developed a response to the 1954 school desegregation decision that offered both black and white "moderates" voluntary segregation. This response governed the whole range of desegregation questions. "Justice for blacks would remain contingent upon prior consensus among whites."

According to historian William Chafe,

> As long as the amenities were observed and Negroes conducted themselves appropriately, it was assumed by whites that an equitable solution could be found to any dilemma. Yet the boundaries set by correct behavior or the "amenities" ruled out the possibility that white leaders could hear the full depth of black disaffection. Conversely, devotion to proper social forms caused whites to reject as unrepresentative any black who failed to obey the ground rules of "correct" behavior ... The fundamental contribution of the sit-ins was to provide a new form through which protest could be expressed. The very act of sitting-in circumvented those forms of fraudulent communication and self-deception through which whites had historically denied black self-assertion. The sit-ins represented a new language ... In an almost visceral way, the sit-ins expressed the dissatisfaction and anger of the black community toward white indifference.[43]

Here was the true birth of the New Left. "I probably felt better that day than I've ever felt in my life. I felt as though I had gained my manhood ... and not only gained it, but ... developed quite a lot of respect for it," wrote one black student. "When you start growing up your environment expands and you start observing what's going on. Then you talk about it at home," said another. After the sit-ins young blacks began to insist that blacks seize control of their own lives, define their own rules, compose their own agendas, shape their own culture, language and institutions. The vehicle for achieving this power was community organization. Although similar ideas pervaded the New Left's commitment to participatory democracy, there was a crucial difference. The civil rights movement was not simply a movement for rights, but also aimed at destroying a racially organized state, namely the Jim Crow South. Thus the civil rights movement was "the expression of a group struggling collectively for its rights as a people and not merely as individual Christian believers or American citizens."[44] This gave black power a different valence than the other movements of the sixties such as the student movement, the antiwar movement, and the women's movement. Creating a base of operations independent of white control, what would soon be called "black power" was an expression of the specific situation of American blacks, and not the forerunner of identity politics, as it is often described.

The role of Martin Luther King, who struggled to bridge the gap between the liberal mainstream and the student radicals, can be understood if we consider three aspects of the civil rights movement, which correspond to three moments in the history of the left. In its first aspect, the civil rights movement was an anti-racist revolution in the sense pioneered by the abolitionists, one centered on political equality in the context of the nation. The many references to the Hebrew Bible, as in the spirituals, and to the prophetic tradition reflect King's vision that a nation can have a moral destiny.[45] In its second aspect the civil rights movement was a struggle for social equality in the sense pioneered by the socialists. Since the decline of the New Left the knowledge that King was a man of the Popular Front, a committed socialist since his student days, and a fan of Reinhold Niebuhr's *Moral Man and Immoral Society* (1932), which argued that the unequal distribution of wealth was the root of social injustice, has been forgotten. Yet King's first book, *Stride toward Freedom* (1958), outlined the hope for a labor–Negro alliance.[46] "The gospel of Jesus is a social gospel," King had preached at Montgomery, adding that the black community should emulate the workers of the thirties who, even though "trampled over by capitalist power," nonetheless resisted. In that sense King was in the tradition of the second American left. But the civil rights movement had a third aspect: it was a struggle for equal participation in democratic self-activity. It was in regard to this aspect that King found himself at odds with an unfolding movement.

The black student movement, signaled by the sit-ins, was a critique of King from the New Left perspective.[47] The issue was the deepening of participation. To Ella Baker, one of the founders of SNCC, the Student Nonviolent Coordinating Committee, King's cultivation of a charismatic public image far from the fields of grassroots direct action seemed plain wrong. As a child in rural North Carolina, Baker had been deeply impressed with how local people shared their labor, their food, and their lives, thereby discovering "their own value, and their strengths." In 1930s Harlem she learned from a wide "spectrum of radical thinking [that] the dense, impersonal, and obscenely unequal city desperately needed community institutions dedicated to the wider brotherhood." In the April 1960 Raleigh, North Carolina conference at which SNCC was launched she praised students for their determination to avoid "struggles for personal leadership," instead rotating leadership within small groups, so that the movement would not stagnate "when the prophetic leader turns out to have heavy feet of clay."[48]

Participation implied a deepening not only of the ideal of equality, but also of the meaning of freedom. The idea that emancipation was not the endpoint of the struggle for freedom but rather its start was central to the Exodus story to which the Prophetic tradition regularly referred. Thus, SNCC activists Charles Sherrod and Bob Moses "stressed the importance of eliminating black fears that had resulted from a history of enduring violent racial oppression." According to Moses, "You dig into yourself and the community to wage psychological warfare . . . you combat your own fears about beatings, shootings and possible mob violence."[49] SNCC was suffused with the view that freedom was a struggle, not something given, and that freedom required participation with others, and could not be reduced to individual "choice."

Reflecting the struggle to achieve self-determination collectively, SNCC workers criticized the headline-catching but episodic protests centered on King, and strove passionately to retain control of SNCC's media image. SNCC communications secretary Mary King wrote, "SNCC workers have learned that if our story is to be told, we will have to write it and photograph it and disseminate it ourselves," especially given that its protests "went largely unwitnessed by those outside of the communities in which they took place." It was not enough to overcome what SNCC leader James Forman called the national press "whiteout" of movement activities. The stress on self-determination was evident in the first SNCC recruiting and fund-raising photo, of three students, two male, one female, in a posture of prayer, but without any sense of submission or religiosity. The photograph radiated SNCC's new sense of leadership, not that of a charismatic figure, but that of ordinary people gaining control of their lives.[50]

The radical wing of the Southern civil rights movement had an explosive effect on students and young people throughout the country. The almost mystical appeal of early SNCC is suggested by a communication from Bob Moses in 1961: "This is Mississippi, the middle of the iceberg. Hollis is leading off with his tenor, 'Michael row the boat ashore, Alleluia . . . Mississippi is the next to go, Alleluia.' This is a tremor in the middle of the iceberg."[51] The existential confrontation with what was perceived as evil was central to the new politics. Casey Hayden, who came out of Texas Christian activism, said, "I cannot say to a person who suffers injustice, 'Wait.' Perhaps you can. I can't. And having decided that I cannot urge caution, I must stand with him. If I had known that not a single lunch counter would open as a result of my action, I could not have done differently." Nonviolence, Hayden explained, also affected the activist:

> [It] took one out of the role of victim and put her in total command of her life. By acting in this clear, pure way, in which the act itself was of equal value to its outcome, and by risking all for it, we were broken open, released from old and lesser definitions of ourselves in terms of race, sex, class, into the larger self of the Beloved Community. This was freedom as an inside job, not as external to myself, but as created, on the spot and in the moment, by our actions. This was ideology turned inside out.[52]

Similar testimonials run through the early New Left. The early student heroes were "Robert Moses walking alone in Mississippi, Fidel Castro in the Sierra Maestra Mountains . . . and Mills, the lonely rebel fighting complacency in academe."[53] For Sue Thrasher, it was at a Nashville civil rights meeting that she first "heard black people speak about themselves."[54] Civil rights demonstrations were the "first time I got any real inkling about the costs and the pain of segregation." For Bob Zellner, a Southern white civil rights worker, SNCC workers

> lived on a fuller level of feeling than any people I'd ever seen, partly because they were making modern history in a very personal way, and partly because by risking death they came to know the value of living each moment to the fullest. . . . Here were the models of charismatic commitment I was seeking – I wanted to live like them.[55]

Student activist Mario Savio explained, "My reasons were selfish. I wasn't really alive. My life, my middle class life, had no place in society, nor it in me . . . I needed some way to pinch myself, to assure myself that I was alive."[56] "Last summer I went to Mississippi to join the struggle there for civil rights. This fall I am engaged in another phase of the same struggle, this time in Berkeley."[57]

Northern students who had participated and supported SNCC founded Students for a Democratic Society in 1962. The goal of the organization, the Port Huron statement explained, was "to democratize the structure of modern society," to create "a society in which everyone vitally affected by a social decision, regardless of its sphere, would have voice in that decision and a hand in its administration." This idea, participatory democracy, was the third American left's reformulation of the ideal of equality.[58] In the early years of SDS, according to Tom Hayden, "spontaneity and local initiative were invested with such mystical significance that any sign of bureaucracy, or delegating of authority to older groups, was profoundly suspect."[59] Later, women and others complained of being unheard at meetings. Yet, according to Barbara Haber, "much care was expended to encourage reticent members to express their views. Ideas and questions were responded to without condescension or acrimony."[60] By the fall of 1962 SDS had twenty chapters, and was sending out 10,000 copies of its newspaper. SDSers were convinced in a way that seems foreign today that change had to come from the poor and the excluded.

As a student movement formed, civil rights became the object of countless demonstrations, sit-ins and marches. As these mushroomed, liberals, university presidents, politicians and social scientists complained that "the students would not play by the rules." By this they meant the pluralist mechanisms and procedures of protest, such as the formulation of clear "demands," compromise and bargaining. Some blamed the students' unrealistic idealism on what Edward Shils called their desire for a "totality of undifferentiated perfection," while others claimed the students were manipulative. In fact, as the sit-in protesters intuitively recognized, liberal proceduralism was organized to maintain the status quo and only a continuous, activist challenge to authority could change society. A critically important part of this recognition was that the process of questioning and examination had to be directed inwardly, against hierarchy in the radical movement itself.[61] Another part was what Wini Breines has called the "prefigurative politics" of participatory democracy. In Breines's summary,

> The effort to build community, to create and prefigure in lived action and behavior the desired society, the emphasis on means and not ends, the spontaneous and utopian experiments that developed in the midst of action while working toward the ultimate goal of a free and democratic society were among the [New Left's] most important contributions.[62]

The combination of a powerful liberal, rights-centered tradition and a boundary-breaking radical movement set in motion the dramatic breakthrough we call the Civil Rights Revolution. To be sure, this relationship was fraught. Democratic Party political operatives were impatient with the exploding new student forces. Al Lowenstein

> could not understand why a group of SNCC leaders in the room couldn't decide right then and there what to do . . . But people said we've got to talk about it . . . The people who are suffering, the people on the bottom, have something to say . . . not as a lawyer, not as an expert economist, but they do know what they need.[63]

In fact, SNCC militancy forced the confrontation between Southern segregationists and the Kennedy administration. "In a federal system," Burke Marshall, the head of the Civil Rights Division, explained, rights are "individual and personal, to be asserted by private citizens as they choose, in court, speaking through their chosen counsel."[64] Nonviolent direct action and community mobilization transgressed this understanding of rights. The Birmingham, Alabama direct action campaign that began in the spring of 1963 inspired 758 demonstrations in 11 Southern states and 13,786 arrests, amounting to an insurgency. The freedom struggle, Herbert Hill wrote, seemed to be "taking a revolutionary turn." "We do not shrink from the use of the term 'revolution,'" editorialized the normally moderate *Afro-American* in June 1963, "for how else can the social upheaval that has shaken our nation be honestly described."[65]

Ending segregation was one moment in this larger revolution. In 1962 Michael Harrington had published *The Other America*. The book came to President Kennedy's attention through a review by

Dwight MacDonald in the *New Yorker*. In it Harrington demonstrated that the New Deal had not fully succeeded in creating an employed, housed, educated and healthy working class. Not just blacks, but many whites, not just in Appalachia or the Deep South but in the Northern cities, lived as an "invisible nation" of the poor, according to Harrington.

Harrington's book planted the seeds for the War on Poverty. At the August 1963 March on Washington for Jobs and Freedom, with 250,000 people attending, King announced that the nation's founders had offered a "promissory note." "We refuse to believe there are insufficient funds in the great vaults" of this nation, he added.[66] The next month SDS founded the Economic Research and Action Project (ERAP), which had SDS organizers moving into urban slums in an attempt to build "an interracial movement of the poor." According to Andrew Kopkind, ERAP workers "are not down there for a visit . . . They are part of the slums, a kind of lay brotherhood, worker-priests, except that they have no dogma to sell."[67]

Civil rights implied a social revolution, not simply a rights revolution. For blacks, the point of gaining the right to vote, to demonstrate, and to have access to the state was to use their power to transform their conditions. Breaking the back of the white segregationist Democratic Party was only a first step. The explosive militancy of the movement made Kennedy fear he would lose the Democratic vote in the Deep South and his ill-fated 1963 trip to Texas was an attempt to repair some of the damage. His assassination was the occasion for deepening the nation's commitment to equality. "No memorial or oration or eulogy could more eloquently honor President Kennedy's memory than the earliest possible passage of the civil rights bill for which he fought so long," Johnson stated.[68] Mississippi Freedom Summer, with 800 volunteers from throughout the country, brought the light of the national media, and of the federal government, into Mississippi. Medicare, the Voting Rights Act, and the War on Poverty followed.[69]

The eighteen months that followed Kennedy's assassination proved to be the apotheosis of liberal idealism. Johnson announced the goal of the Great Society in 1964. According to historian Robert Dallek, Johnson's "idea of the presidency was picking up where FDR's New Deal left off."[70] "Whereas FDR had been preoccupied with material security LBJ was focused . . . on social empowerment." Thus the War on Poverty called for "maximum feasible participation" of the poor.[71] According to SDSer Richard Flacks, participatory democracy was not just "another code word for socialism, it meant redefining the socialist tradition in terms of the democratic content in it. It meant extending principles of democracy from the political sphere into other institutions, like industry, like the university."[72] Now this had become government policy as well.

"These are the most hopeful times since Christ was born," Johnson stated as he lit the White House Christmas tree in December 1964. Working closely with Senate Minority Leader Everett McKinley Dirksen, Johnson appeared before Congress on March 15, 1965 to appeal for a Voting Rights Bill. "Should we defeat every enemy," he told a cheering Congress, "should we double our wealth and conquer the stars" and still deny equal rights to Negro Americans, "we will have failed as a people and as a nation." Not just Negroes but all of us, he exhorted, must work to "overcome the crippling legacy of bigotry and injustice. And . . . We shall . . . overcome." Three months later in a speech at Howard University, Johnson called for the "next and more profound stage of civil rights . . . not just equality as a right and a theory but equality as a fact and as a result." Asked how the country could afford it, Johnson responded, "We're the richest country in the world, the most powerful. We can do it all."

Why did the country fail to carry through on this hopeful moment? One explanation is that Americans will support equality before the law, as in the Civil Rights Act, but not redistribution, as in the Great Society. Argued most cogently in Thomas and Mary Edsall's *Chain Reaction*, the heart of the explanation is the phenomenon of "white flight" and "white backlash." According to Daniel Patrick Moynihan, the Watts uprising, which took place five days after the signing of the Voting Rights Act, shattered the "image of non-violent suffering." The immigrant Jewish glove manufacturer in Philip Roth's *American Pastoral* expressed the deep antagonism that some Americans experienced in response to the uprisings: "I built this with my hands! With my blood! They think somebody gave it to me? Who? Who gave it to me? Who gave me anything, ever? Nobody!"[73]

There is much evidence to support the Edsalls' explanation. The three years after Watts witnessed regular summer uprisings, leaving 225 people dead, 4,000 wounded, and $112 billion property damage. According to Doris Kearns, "after the riots, the media described America in very different terms. It was as if overnight an innocent child had become a middle aged man, as if within months the soul of America had passed from childlike mirth and unreasoning optimism to deep dejection." In 1964 "only 34% of the American people believed Negroes were trying to move too fast," by 1966 the figure had risen to 85%.[74] In September 1966 an open housing bill was killed in Congress. Soon, "virtually every important element of Lyndon Johnson's Great Society . . . had come to seem part of a program of aid and comfort for the black minority, rather than an effort to lift Americans of every race onto a higher social and economic plane."[75] In 1966 the Republicans gained forty-seven House seats and three Senate seats, and elected eight new governors, including Ronald Reagan. Kevin Phillips described the election as the "repudiation visited upon the Democratic Party for its ambitious social programming, and inability to handle the urban and Negro revolutions."

It is certainly the case that moving in the direction of substantive equality would have entailed intense internal struggle, conflict and upheaval. It is also the case that some civil rights reforms, such as busing, seem to many today to have been misguided. Nevertheless, the country had moved toward substantive equality twice before: during the Civil War, when the largest source of capital stock in the country was abolished without compensation, and during the New Deal, when wealth and political power were again redistributed, and liberalism redefined in egalitarian terms. In both cases, the entire country benefited from a reorientation based on egalitarian principles. Why not this time? The answer is no doubt complicated, but the growing strength of the right during the sixties, culminating in the election of Richard Nixon in 1968, was not simply, and probably not even primarily, a response to "riots" and other excesses. What lay behind the Democratic Party's collapse, and prevented the country from moving in a genuinely progressive direction, was the war in Vietnam. To say that, however, is not to point simply to an event, but rather to a proclivity toward violence that runs very deep in the American liberal tradition, and that underlies the third great crisis in American history, following those of slavery and industrial capitalism, the one we are living through today.

The second stage in the evolution of the New Left came with its participation in the antiwar movement. Emerging in the context of the civil rights explosion and helping to precipitate feminism and gay liberation, the Vietnam War was America's third transformative moment. Politically, the war was "the point at which trust in government ended and skepticism began," leading more or less directly to Watergate but also pointing toward the anti-government ideology that wrecked the welfare state and degraded much subsequent politics. Economically, the Vietnam War ended the "golden age of capitalism," sparked the economic crisis that took the country off the gold standard, precipitated its turn from industry to finance, and created the inflation that helped discredit Keynesianism. Above all, the war set off the long-term decline of the American liberal tradition, ravaging "popular faith in government, and scorch[ing] the earth from which the liberal agenda had sprung."[76]

Just as the Civil War is best understood as the tipping point in a long-standing structural crisis, namely slavery, and just as the Great Depression was the tipping point in the conflict between capital and labor, so Vietnam was the tipping point in the conflict between the nation's republican character and its role as an empire. Ancient Rome supplied the cautionary example. Having begun as a republic, Rome increasingly turned to imperial methods, eviscerating its own freedoms, turning its forums over to bread and circus, concentrating power and wealth in private villas and latifundia, while public agorae, temples and monuments languished. In the eighteenth century the American nation had been founded on the premise that, because of its "free land," America could avoid the fate of Rome. But in 1898 when the United States became a formal empire through the acquisition of the Philippines, Senator Carl Schurz, a refugee from the German democratic revolution of 1848, warned that a democracy cannot "play the king over subject populations without creating in itself dangerous ways of thinking and habits of action." As Schurz spoke, he was watching American troops introduce surveillance, torture, extraconstitutional prisons and other police-state tactics into the Philippines, where the population had risen up against the American invasion.

The war in Vietnam was no accident. The 1898 Open Door notes, which laid the foundation of twentieth-century American foreign policy, were written in response to the collapse of China. Likewise, the National Security Council's NSC-68 (1950), one of the most pivotal policy documents in American history, situated the need for a military buildup in the context of the disintegration of the European empires. The American intervention supporting French rule over Indochina began in the same year. After his humiliating 1961 confrontation with Khrushchev, Kennedy told James Reston, "now we have a problem in trying to make our power credible, and Vietnam looks like the place."[77] As McGeorge Bundy explained in a crucial memo of March 21, 1965, the "cardinal" principle of the Vietnamese intervention was for the United States

> not to be a Paper Tiger. Not to have it thought that when we commit ourselves we really mean no major risk. This means essentially a willingness to fight China if necessary. . . . The conclusion I draw from this is that it is to our advantage to frame our posture toward our military program so that we have a right to go anywhere (and will if sufficiently provoked).[78]

The decision to intervene exemplified the Cold War liberal mentality in that every effort was made to exclude democratic participation. As Lyndon Johnson explained to Doris Kearns, "The biggest danger to American stability is the politics of principle, which brings out the masses in irrational fights for unlimited goals, for once the masses begin to move, then the whole thing begins to explode."[79] Dean Rusk elaborated, "We made a deliberate decision not to stir up war fever among the American people [over Vietnam] . . . We felt that in a nuclear world its just too dangerous for an entire people to become too angry. That might push the situation beyond the point of no return."[80] The supposedly hard-edged technology and science encouraged killing at a distance. General William Westmoreland, the US Army commander between 1964 and 1968, foresaw "an entirely new battlefield concept, the automated battlefield."[81] Nor did a technocratic war machine exclude idealism, as captured in Graham Greene's *The Quiet American*:

Perhaps only ten days ago he had been walking back across the Commons in Boston, his arms full of the books he had been reading in advance on the Far East and the problems of China. He didn't even hear what I said: he was absorbed already in the dilemmas of Democracy and the responsibilities of the West: he was determined ... to do good, not to any individual person but to a country, a continent, a world.

The sensibility of the sixties was formed in direct opposition to that of Rusk, Westmoreland, and Greene's protagonist. It supposed that behind the cold and rationalistic facade of the liberal's war machine lay not only the interests of capital, nor only those of an American power elite, but also powerful human passions, such as sexuality, aggression and greed. This sensibility expressed itself in a variety of ways, many of which were only half-formed, including anti-technological manifestos like Charles Reich's *The Greening of America*, rejections of rational and technological modernity, as in the hippie lifestyle, and powerful outbursts against the technological imperviousness of the system, as in Mario Savio's "There's a time when the operation of the machine becomes so odious – makes you so sick at heart – that you can't take part." Herbert Marcuse's *One-Dimensional Man* was centered on the problem of locating an oppositional moment in a positivistic, technological society. Stanley Kubrick's *Dr. Strangelove* portrayed the catastrophic consequences of totalizing reason. Savio's outburst, Marcuse's book, and Kubrick's film all date from 1964, the same year as the Gulf of Tonkin Resolution, which made possible the vast, seemingly inevitable expansion of the war in Vietnam.

The antiwar movement was based on the same sixties sensibility but like the civil rights movement, the antiwar movement was not itself a left. It included a great range of positions, including pacifist objections to all wars, calls for negotiations, halts to the bombing, or immediate withdrawal, and hopes for a Vietminh (NLF) victory. Like the civil rights movement, too, the antiwar movement had its roots in preexisting traditions of nonviolence, such as the War Resistors League, a pacifist organization formed in 1923. But there clearly was a left within the antiwar movement, just as there had been a left within the civil rights movement. Indeed, it is impossible to understand the antiwar movement without recognizing the role of the left.

The first contribution of the left to the antiwar movement came from its rejection of anti-Communism. Anti-Communism – the core of the liberal faith – had little or nothing to do with the merits or demerits of Communist regimes, but rather was a worldview that justified American interventions, on the one hand, and worked to suppress criticism of American institutions, on the other. The New Left's challenge to anti-Communism was analogous to the Greensboro student sit-ins: it was a refusal to accept the dominant code, which governed what and how one should protest, characterizing any "excess" as "Communist." The historian H. Stuart Hughes grasped the significance of this issue in a 1960 article. McCarthyism, Hughes wrote, had destroyed not just the Communist Party, but civil society in general.

> For a whole decade, school teachers and college professors denied their students the long-sanctioned right of the young to seek their own path and learn from their own errors. . . . Suddenly in the spring of 1960, I realized with a shock that a new student generation had sprung into life. In the widespread demonstrations against racial segregation a new age group had won its spurs. . . . The fact that its energies turned toward activities on behalf of peace suggested that its concern for racial equality formed part of a wider protest . . . Impatient with ideological rhetoric, [the students] find almost incomprehensible the pro-Communist and anti-Communist polemics that shook the American Left in the decades from 1917 to 1948. Basically, I think this is a good thing. I shall be quite happy to see the young people take leadership from us and direct the new radicalism of America into courses we would never have imagined.

Hughes called his article "Why We Had No Dreyfus Case." Referring to the ease with which American liberals had scuttled their commitment to civil liberties during the McCarthy era, Hughes voiced the hope "that when [the New Leftists] are confronted with their Dreyfus case they will rise to the challenge better than we did in the years of our country's supreme moral crisis."[82]

The question of anti-Communism threatened to derail the first national march against the war, called by SDS in April 1965. Imposing liberal figures, such as Bayard Rustin, Irving Howe and Michael Harrington, insisted that Communists be banned from participating. In what would prove to be a historically consequential decision, SDS refused. Thus, Communists marched under their own banners for the first time since the McCarthy era. An unprecedented 25,000 people came to the march. For economist Douglas Dowd, who lived through the absence of protest during the Korean War, "it was as though spring had arrived after a very, very long fucking winter."[83]

At that march and the following one, SDS supplied the beginnings of an analysis of the war; in two speeches given by two SDS presidents the war was presented as the product of liberalism. In April 1965, Paul Potter asked, "What kind of system is it that allows good men to make those kinds of decisions? . . . We must name that system. We must name it, describe it, analyze it, understand it and change it." In November 1965 Carl Oglesby stated, "The original commitment in Vietnam was made by President Truman, a mainstream liberal. It was seconded by President Eisenhower, a moderate liberal. It was intensified by the late President Kennedy, a flaming liberal. . . . They are not moral monsters. They are all honorable men. They are all liberals."

The liberals who created the war, "the best and the brightest," mostly students of management and engineering, were the products of McCarthyism. Their great fear was populism, with its supposedly emotive character. As an alternative to all forms of mass politics, including Communism, they subscribed to a technocratic modernization theory, according to which inevitable laws of development would bring unenlightened people toward pluralism and the politics of growth. Inequality was central to their outlook. Just as nineteenth-century imperialism was based on a social Darwinian vision according to which colonialism would help "prepare" "backward peoples" for freedom, so modernization theory was premised on the belief that the "stages of economic growth" would turn peasantries into modern consumer societies. Communism, the theory held, was a disease of development.

Against the modernization paradigm, the students who flocked to the antiwar movement were taught by a new, post–New Deal generation of professors, for the most part the children of immigrants, often Jewish, though not yet female, or black, in large numbers. Probably no discipline was more important in presenting an alternative to the modernization outlook than American history. According to the younger historians, Reconstruction was not, as the historical mainstream had portrayed it, a "tragic era," but rather the high point of nineteenth-century democracy. The abolitionists were not neurotic malcontents but heroes. The age of the democratic revolutions was an age of emancipation, beginning with the slave revolt in Haiti. The United States had always been an expansionist nation, preying on its weaker neighbors, whether the Native Americans or the decrepit European empires on its borders. Rather than a succession of expanding new opportunities, each American frontier was a new evasion of the responsibility to refound the nation. Antibusiness populism, not technocratic liberalism, should be seen as the heart of the American democratic tradition. Leftism, not liberalism, was the proper response to the turning point of the sixties.

In contrast to the administration's insistence on "expertise" and secret, backstage knowledge, the academic antiwar movement created a new public sphere, beginning with the first teach-in, held at an all-night session at the University of Michigan in March, 1965. According to anthropologist Marshall Sahlins, "Facts were demanded and assumptions were exposed ... On that night, people who really cared talked of things that really mattered."[84] "The stroke of genius in Michigan put the teach-in on the agenda in the whole academic community," wrote Carl Oglesby. The grandest was at the University of California, Berkeley; it lasted forty-six hours, 30,000 people participated. Isaac Deutscher, who visited the school later, compared the atmosphere to ancient Greece. Quite possibly, the teach-ins, in which participation was not restricted by race, gender or supposed expertise, were the largest and most probing public democratic debate in the whole of American history.

Through the teach-ins, many professors and students came to reject the view of the university as an ivory tower, the sacrosanct guardian of knowledge. Normally hierarchical relations between students and professors shifted, as students challenged their teachers, and teachers challenged administrators. The radicals attacked the collaboration with the military of the anthropology, economics, political science, and natural science disciplines. They exposed Project Camelot, an attempt by the US Army to explain the causes of "violent social action," that is, revolution. Chile was intended to be the first case study but protests led to the program's cancellation. The anthropologist Eric Wolf blew the whistle on counter-insurgency research in Thailand. Perhaps the army didn't really need the university, however, as it relied on the Rand Corporation for research on the NLF in Vietnam, and Rand consistently told the army what it wanted to hear, namely that the NLF was on the verge of cracking.

After the teach-ins and antiwar demonstrations began, the atmosphere of the country shifted. According to Tom Wicker, "no one writing in the press or speaking on campus escaped challenge, argument, confrontation – not only about the war itself but about American institutions and assumptions generally."[85] "Objectivity," the ideal of both academics and journalists, became a term of scorn. According to Michael Schudson, "objectivity in journalism, regarded as an antidote to bias, came to be looked on as the most insidious bias of all. For 'objective' reporting reproduced a vision of social reality which refused to examine the basic structures of power and privilege." The critique of objectivity rested on the view that knowledge was situated, and that the decontextualized character of modern reporting and of social science prevented the true situation from being revealed.

The critique of objectivity was part of the New Left's deepening conception of equality. Against modernization theorists, New Leftists argued that urban planning was not in the interest of the poor, that psychiatrists invented many forms of mental illness, that the courts promoted injustice, and that the schools were the training grounds for the corporations. Intellectuals were dubbed "the new mandarins," unless they "spoke truth to power." The idea of a "culture of poverty," whether in the American slums or in third world countries, came under attack. What Lionel Trilling called "adversary culture," having the "clear purpose of detaching the reader from the habits of thought and feeling that the larger culture imposes, of giving him a ground and vantage point from which to judge and condemn," became more general. Even John Dewey, the originator of participatory democracy, lost his sacrosanct status because of his uncritical ("pragmatic") support for America's entry into World War One.

The critique of objectivity extended into the war zone itself. According to Michael Herr, "Nothing so horrible ever happened upcountry that it was beyond language fix and press relations." False numbers of "kills," fabricated battle-reports, and media self-censorship combined to create an "Orwellian language of euphemism and disguise."[86] Because of what Wicker called the "powerful impulse" provided by the students, the army lost control of this language. As early as September 5, 1965 the *New York Times* described "a woman who has both arms burned off by napalm and her eyelids so badly burned that she cannot close them. When it is time for her to sleep her family puts a blanket over head. The woman had two of her children killed in the air-strike that maimed her."[87] A turning point occurred in 1966 when Harrison Salisbury visited Hanoi and reported the bombing of civilians, which the Pentagon had denied. In 1971 The *New York Times* published the Pentagon Papers, an encyclopedic internal history of the American involvement, prepared by a Department of Defense task force, which demonstrated that the administration had, according to the paper, "systematically lied, not only to the public but also to Congress, about a subject of transcendent national interest and significance."

Just as the abolitionists had tried to make Americans feel the reality of slavery, and just as the Popular Front activists had tried to make the lives of sharecroppers and unemployed workers vivid, so the antiwar activists sought to make Americans feel the horrors they were inflicting on the people of Vietnam. Here they followed the pioneering example of the philosopher William James, who passionately opposed the American war against the Filipinos, while insisting that the very scale and anonymity of the modern corporate-state made it difficult to penetrate to the vital human dimension.[88] In the case of Vietnam, science-based "expertise" created an illusion of logic and inevitability. The antiwar movement sought to puncture that illusion and release what James called "the invisible molecular moral forces that work from individual to individual."[89] Thus the *New Yorker* published a report by Gloria Emerson of a nineteen-year-old soldier with bloody, bent legs. The nurse and orderly began "to prepare him for surgery. They worked very hard, but something went wrong. The boy tried to rise up and push them away, making a noise I had never heard from a man: a long and hoarse shriek." The doctors took off both legs above the knees. Emerson had desperately tried to gain some time for him, to get a second opinion, but there were no second opinions. Later she saw the doctor who had performed the surgery, drinking a Coca-Cola. She asked if the boy had been in shock and why they had not waited. "He wasn't in shock, he was just frightened to death," the doctor explained.[90]

One result of the effort to communicate the incommunicable was the "new journalism," which sought "to break the glass between the reader and the world he lives in."[91] Nonfiction novels about killings (Truman Capote), hippies (Joan Didion), and political marches (Norman Mailer) are examples of works that reported "events from the inside out."[92] Meanwhile, as in Camus's *The Plague*, "Americans were going about business as usual while denying the persistence of pervasive and threatening evils." For Gloria Emerson, "Getting back [from Vietnam] was not good." One "woman asked me what I had worn to officer's dances; the question did not make me smile." TV host Barbara Walters gave advice on how to talk to the veterans: "Keep the discussion generalized . . . Ask about the heat, the dampness, the housing." "What is your methodology," a professor at the Massachusetts Institute of Technology demanded when Emerson said she was writing a book on what the war had done to Americans. "You will never regret the experience," a lady said to Emerson, as they both waited to have their hair cut at a shop on 62nd Street. "It's a once-in-a-lifetime chance."[93]

A turning point in the fight to "bring the war home" was Thich Quang Duc's self-immolation. The event was later described by Judith Thurman in an article concerning the visual artist Marina Abramovic:

> Half a world away, on a street in Saigon, Thich Quang Duc, a sixty-six year old monk, folded his legs in the lotus position and immolated himself to protest the persecution of Buddhists by the Diem regime. His death was photographed by Malcolm Browne, and reported by David Halberstam, who was, he wrote, "too shocked to cry" as the flames consumed the body. Self-martyrdom as a public spectacle had precedents in Asian culture, but Thich's composure, as he lit the match and sat serenely for ten minutes of agony, rocked the West and burrowed into its collective dream life.

"No news picture in history has generated as much emotion around the world," President Kennedy said. Abramovic never forgot that "terrible image of devotion to a cause," which created the art of ordeal, she explained.[94] The next year draft card burning began, followed by the burning of draft records, and other forms of symbolic immolation. In November 1965, Norman Morrison, a thirty-two year old Quaker, burnt himself alive just outside of

Secretary of Defense Robert McNamara's office. McNamara called it a personal tragedy for himself, while the North Vietnamese greeted American visitors with a song to Morrison, who became a national hero in Vietnam. In 1968 Philip and Daniel Berrigan, two Catholic priests, poured home-made napalm over a draft board's records, explaining they were burning paper instead of children.

Eventually eight American antiwar activists burnt themselves alive to protest the war. In addition to Norman Morrison, they were Alice Herz, Roger A. LaPorte, Hiroko Hayaski, Florence Beaumont, Erik Thoen, Ronald Brazee, and George Winne. The general idea was that Americans would not be "good Germans." According to Steven Cohen, "I cared so deeply about Vietnam because I am Jewish and I cannot forget the Holocaust . . . If your country is doing something wrong, you've got to try to change it."[95] People became obsessed. They kept files of clippings. They kept mimeograph machines in their downstairs halls near their kitchens. Relationships broke up because one or the other person was so overcome by the war.[96] High school students started underground newspapers. Everywhere people flashed the V peace sign. Rabbis intoned, "in every generation, every human being must look upon herself, himself, as if we ourselves had gone forth from Vietnam." The idea of the "movement," far transcending SDS, captured the imagination of a generation: antiwar activists could go anywhere in the United States, find a place to stay, food to eat, and actions to join. Protest, one activist recalled, "was like breathing or like feeding your children. We didn't think there was any alternative."[97]

In some cases, protest turned to resistance, leading formerly sympathetic observers like Hannah Arendt to condemn the New Left.[98] In December 1965 Tom Hayden, Herbert Aptheker and Staughton Lynd visited Hanoi, proclaiming, "We are all Viet Cong." Draft resistance mushroomed; elasticized armbands supported "The Presidio Twenty Seven, the Chicago Seven, the Boston Five, the Harrisburg Seven, the Camden Twenty Eight."[99] In October 1967 3,000 protesters surrounded the induction center in Oakland, California, urging draftees not to register.[100] After 1968 dozens if not hundreds of collectives committed bombings, arson, and other destructions of military and war-related property. Historian Kirkpatrick Sale estimates 2,800 such attacks at the high point, between January 1969 and April 1970. The Department of Defense acknowledges 503,926 incidents of desertion between 1966 and 1973.[101] Deserters in foreign countries became politically active there. In 1975 the American Civil Liberties Union reported that 750,000 Americans were in need of amnesty because they had gone into exile or otherwise avoided the war.[102]

The most profound rebellion occurred within the military. According to the *Armed Forces Journal* in 1971,

> the morale, discipline and battle-worthiness of the U.S. Armed Forces are, with a few salient exceptions, lower and worse than at anytime in this century and possibly in the history of the United States. By every conceivable indicator, our army that now remains in Vietnam is in a state approaching collapse, with individual units avoiding or having refused combat, murdering their officers and non-commissioned officers, drug-ridden, and dispirited where not near mutinous.

Among the evidence: 109 "fragging" incidents in 1970, soldier slang for the murder of officers and NCOs; some 144 underground newspapers published on or aimed at US military bases; at least 14 GI antiwar organizations; a semi-underground network of lawyers "which tries to coordinate seditious antimilitary activities throughout the country"; "a community of turbulent priests and clergymen," which visits "military posts, infiltrates brigs and stockades in the guise of spiritual counseling," works to recruit military chaplains, and consecrates draft-dodging; and at least eleven off-base antiwar coffee houses with rock music, antiwar literature, and how-to-do-it tips on desertion, the best-known being The Shelter Half (Ft Lewis, Wash.), Home Front (Ft Carson, Colo.), and Oleo Strut (Ft Hood, Tex.). The Movement for a Democratic Military specialized in theft of weapons from military bases in California.[103] In Vietnam, wrote one military paper, "the Lifers, the Brass, are the true Enemy, not the enemy." "Word of the deaths of officers will bring cheers at troop movies or in bivouacs of certain units."

In this atmosphere, the New Left – the left wing of the antiwar movement – sought to expose the relations between American racism and the war. Once again, whites were confronted with a darker, weaker, poorer people.[104] "They were dinks, you know, subhuman." "They all hold fucking hands. I hated that."[105] Even the racial epithet the Americans used for the Vietnamese – "gook"

– had been invented during the American occupation of Haiti. Slavery and imperialism were two moments in the development of capitalism. Taken along with the regular confrontations between black youths and police, the growth of black power, the understanding of the war in Vietnam as a "war of national liberation," and the fact that US spending for Vietnam made "the war on poverty" unaffordable, antiwar sentiment drove the civil rights movement to the left.

The emergence of the issue of armed self-defense in the black community, as shown by the Black Panther Party and the Revolutionary League of Black Workers, exemplified this. Robert F. Williams, who advocated black self-defense as against King's nonviolence in 1960, and fled the country the following year to avoid the FBI, became an international figure in the antiwar context. As an eleven-year-old in Monroe, North Carolina, Williams had witnessed the beating and dragging of a black woman by a white policeman.[106] According to his biographer, "Williams revisited the bitter memory on platforms that he shared with Fidel Castro, Ho Chi Minh, and Mao Zedong. He told it over Radio Free Dixie, his regular program on Radio Havana from 1962 to 1965, and retold it from Hanoi in broadcasts directed to African-American soldiers in Vietnam. It echoed from transistor radios in Watts in 1965 and from gigantic speakers in Tiananmen Square in 1966." His autobiography, "While God Lay Sleeping," which he completed just before his death in1996, also opens with the story. "I don't consider myself American; I am a Black Muslim man of African heritage," said Williams, echoing Frederick Douglass and Malcolm X.[107]

The antiwar struggle fueled the New Left's interest in the vast body of critical social thought described by C. Wright Mills as "to the left of [John] Dewey." In part this meant Marxism, because the war only seemed explicable once the centrality of imperialism – "the last stage of capitalism" – had been granted. But it also meant Freudo-Marxism, Frankfurt School critical theory, Guy Debord's *Society of the Spectacle*, Situationism – all expressions of the New Left's desire to place subjectivity, albeit thwarted subjectivity, at the center of its conception of capitalism. Marcuse's *Reason and Revolution*, which advanced a view of history as a project of self-realization, had been written in 1941 but now found its audience. Beginning in 1960 *New Left Review* began translating and publishing the long-ignored works of dissident or Hegelian Marxists like Karl Korsch, Lucio Colletti, Jean-Paul Sartre, Georg Lukacs, Max Horkheimer, Theodor Adorno, and Antonio Gramsci, works that emphasized the struggle for position in civil society rather than the state. A global theory of revolution also began to emerge in the works of Régis Debray, based on the Cuban and other Latin American experiences, and Immanuel Wallerstein, who formulated a theory of the capitalist world-system. In all of these works, New Leftists were searching for that structure of unreason that lay behind an otherwise inexplicable war, as well as behind a superficially rational technocapitalist facade.

For many Americans, the turning point – the moment when the war's irrationality became palpable – occurred on March 16, 1968 when a company of American infantrymen landed in the village of My Lai by helicopter.

> Many were firing as they spread out, killing both people and animals. There was no sign of the rumored Vietcong battalion and no shot was fired at Charlie Company all day, but they carried on. They burnt down every house. They raped women and girls and then killed them. They disemboweled some villagers or cut off their hands or scalps. There were gang rapes and killings by shooting or with bayonets. There were mass executions. Dozens of people at a time, including old men, women, and children, were machine-gunned in a ditch. In four hours, nearly 500 villagers were killed.[108]

The massacre, the *New York Times* noted, "struck a blow against one of our fondest illusions, the American fighting man as G.I. Joe ... slogging through Europe with a wisecrack on his lips, a wink in his eye, and a chocolate bar in his hand for the orphaned Paisano kids."[109] The *Nation* observed that the "pseudo-moral discussion" that followed the My Lai revelations "would be a good thing if it resulted in a lasting change of heart, but it is as ephemeral as the frontier evangelism from which it is derived."[110]

Historians describe the United States as a divided nation in the late sixties, but this is misleading. There was intense loyalty to slain Americans, and to the nation in general, but support for the war, as opposed to the troops, was a distinctly minority view. In particular, all polls demonstrate that manual workers were consistently more opposed to the war, and more in favor of withdrawal, than the college educated, who did not have to fight.[111]

Nevertheless, after My Lai the nation's outlook truly darkened. Westerns and war movies no longer were shown. In some cases, families were torn apart. He loved America, Philip Roth wrote of his hero in *American Pastoral*, "loved being an *American*. But . . . he hadn't dared begin to explain to [his Weatherman daughter] why he did, for fear of unleashing the demon, insult."[112] An indication of the darkening mood lay in music: "There's something happening here./ What it is ain't exactly clear./ There's a man with a gun over there,/ Telling me I got to beware./ I think it's time we stopped, children, what's that sound?/ Everybody look what's going down." The cult of failure spread. Dustin Hoffman in *The Graduate* listened to the Paul Simon song: "Where have you gone, Joe DiMaggio?/ A nation turns its lonely eyes to you." And of course Dylan: "He said his name was Columbus/ And I just said good luck."

By 1968 the continued escalation of the war, My Lai, the ghetto uprisings, the demonstrations and sit-ins in the universities, all meant that the United States was in a profound crisis of authority – what Jürgen Habermas was soon to call a "legitimation crisis" – comparable in depth, if not long-term impact, to those Lincoln and Roosevelt faced when they took office. What has only become clear with hindsight is that the crisis of authority corresponded to a structural crisis. Two possible paths lay ahead. The first maintained a militarist posture and military spending as the basis for an increasingly dysfunctional, finance and debt-driven neoliberal economy. The second would divert military spending toward domestic needs, beginning with the ghettos, and would shift out of the Cold War mode toward an international order based on equality between peoples. Faced with similar turning points, both of Lyndon Johnson's two great predecessors, Lincoln and Roosevelt, had moved toward refoundings, using the ideal of equality as their lodestar. Tragically, Lyndon Johnson did not follow in their footsteps.

Since the Tet offensive in January 1968 Johnson's administration had lost nearly every base of its support except for the older *nomenklatura* of party politicians and labor officials. "The major threat we face is from the doves," Johnson explained. "I felt I was being forced over the edge by rioting blacks, demonstrating students, marching welfare mothers, squawking professors, and hysterical reporters."[113] "Just like FDR and Hitler, just like Wilson and the Kaiser," he insisted, "it's just perverted history to claim that [the war in Vietnam is a] civil war, just pure bad history manufactured by the Harvards and the [John Kenneth] Galbraiths."[114] Those pushing for negotiations with the North Vietnamese, he added, were "fuzzy folks . . . happy [go] lucky fellows that smoke a little marijuana."[115] Nor was Johnson the only person in the White House so deluded in his perceptions. When Robert Lowell refused to participate in a White House Festival of the Arts and when Eartha Kitt protested the war at an administration event, Johnson's assistant Jack Valenti denounced the "tawdry lengths that some people would go to in impoliteness and incivility." When Richard Helms, head of CIA, told the administration there was no evidence that Communists were manipulating the demonstrators, Dean Rusk refused to believe him.[116]

Given Johnson's isolation, Democrats began to look for an alternative candidate for the 1968 election. Allard Lowenstein, who was seeking to convince leftists that they could "work within the system," persuaded Senator Eugene McCarthy to run. McCarthy got 42.4 percent of the vote in the New Hampshire primary. As the economy began to tank, the so-called "wise men," including Dean Acheson, led by the senior Democratic advisor, Clark Clifford, told Johnson "that major elements of the national constituency – the business community, the press, the churches, professional groups, college presidents, students, and most of all the intellectual community – have turned against this war." "What the President needs is not a war speech but a peace speech," Clifford added.[117] Walter Lippmann warned that Johnson's re-election "will not arrest but will force the disintegration of the [Democratic] party."[118] In March 1968, Johnson announced that he would neither seek nor accept reelection. On April 4, Martin Luther King was assassinated. On June 5, Robert Kennedy was slain, just after winning the California Presidential primary. April brought the uprising in Prague, and May the general strike in Paris. In Mexico City left-wing students were massacred at the university. Soon after in Chile, Paraguay, Brazil, Argentina, and Uruguay, New Left activists were "disappeared," in some cases thrown alive from military airplanes.

In June, Richard Nixon won the Republican nomination. In August, meeting in Chicago, the Democrats nominated Hubert Humphrey, the prowar candidate of the party bosses and labor officials, even as the party was falling apart both inside and outside the convention hall. Walt Rostow, the White House's "expert" on the demonstrators, denounced the "put-up job between the TV people and the demonstrators. It was all mounted . . . just the way the Buddhist thing was mounted in Hue . . . They made sure the cameras were there when these guys set fire to themselves."[119] After the convention, there was a widespread "sense that American society was degenerating into an uncontrolled disorder which authority could not halt."[120] Lippmann warned gravely that it had become necessary to repress "irreconcilable revolutionary dissent." The country, he wrote, "has entered a period of revolutionary change of which no one can foresee the end or the consequences. For we are living in a time when the central institutions of the traditional life of man are increasingly unable to command his allegiance or his obedience."[121]

The election of Nixon in November ended the sense of immediate crisis, but without turning the country in a direction that could resolve the crisis on the basis of America's core egalitarian values. On the contrary, Nixon's chief ally, Henry Kissinger, seemed to many to despise those values. Even after Nixon's landslide re-election in 1972, his Presidency lacked legitimacy, as was shown by the Watergate events the following year. Some hold that the election of Reagan in 1980 resolved the tear in the American fabric that the war had opened, but this view cannot be sustained by historical analysis. A new, neoliberal order did follow the sixties, but based on sharpening, not resolving, the divide between rich and poor, it has arguably never become hegemonic. In any event, "the decisive realignment election that political observers anticipated all through the [post-sixties] period, waiting for the Republican party to sweep aside its rivals as the Democratic party had so dramatically done in 1932, failed to take place."[122] Instead, in the words of John Lewis, a founder of SNCC and currently a Congressman,

> Something died in America in 1968. It was that sense of hope, that sense of optimism, a sense of what could be. The sense of possibility died in all of us. I'm not so sure as a nation, as a people, those of us who came through that period have been able to get over that, really. It was the worst of times to see two young leaders cut down like they were cut down . . .[123]

Even Newt Gingrich has written, "in a real sense we have not regained [our bearings] . . . If you go back to '67, you'd find a kind of generalized broad optimism which disappeared sometime during the crucible of '68 and from which we have not to this day fully recovered."[124]

The scholarly literature assumes that 1968 also saw the end of the New Left. Among the prevailing explanations one reads that the New Left failed because it did not support the Democrats in the election of 1968 and because its participants turned (a) to Marxism or (b) violence or (c) against traditional American values and spat on returning soldiers (Todd Gitlin); because it was a generational uprising, a student movement, an expression of the baby boomers, which naturally ended as people reached thirty (many popular accounts, Edgar Morin); because it turned its back on women's liberation, leaving women no recourse but to form their own all-female organizations, thus depriving New Left men of sexual services (Alice Echols, Ruth Rosen, many Hollywood movies such as *Forrest Gump*); because it was really a cultural revolution, not political at all, and in that sense was a big success as shown by the huge wave of narcissism and desire that it unleashed (Daniel Cohn-Bendit, Judith Butler); because it was actually moral rather than political, and so transformed our habits and lifestyle, though not our laws (Richard Rorty); because it was a shock troop subtly introducing a new phase in the history of capitalism, namely post-Fordist network capitalism, either through its critique of bureaucracy (Richard Sennett), the family wage (Nancy Fraser), or through the cooptation of its "artistic" critique (Luc Boltanski, Ève Chiapello, Thomas Frank), and thus its fate demonstrated "the ruse of capitalism" or "the cunning of history" (Régis Debray); and finally because "the New Left was nothing at all, only Prague 68 was important because it led to the end of Communism" (Wolf Lepenies).

Was an alternative possible? Could a refounding have occurred? Was there a possibility of uniting the working class, which was sacrificing its sons, with the passionate, irreconcilable hatred of the war that animated the antiwar movement, hatred comparable to that of the abolitionists toward slavery? In both previous cases, those of slavery and of the Great Depression, the country had been faced with seemingly irreconcilable internal divisions. Yet, in both cases it found a way through based on the convergence of liberals (or republicans) and leftists on the principles of equality and social justice. Why did the crisis of Vietnam turn out to be different? The historian's task, as Walter Benjamin argued, is to fan the spark of hope in the past, to find those moments which indicate that history could have gone differently, to refuse the trope of inevitability on which triumphalist narratives rely.[125] In the 1960s, the spark lay in the working class.

Before 1968 the New Left was unable to offer a credible alternative to the administration because as a student movement it was largely cut off from the material processes – economic necessity, labor, the family – that had given rise to the crisis in the first place. After 1968, however, many sought to ground the New Left in the new, technologically and scientifically transformed working class that emerged in the sixties. In this project, two efforts were especially important. First, the cultural revolution – the prefigurative politics, the anti-authoritarianism, the psychology of disidentification and expanded solidarity – had to be reinterpreted in terms of the transformation of capitalism, especially the transition from a form of family life directly grounded in the economy to new forms of personal emancipation. In this regard, as we shall see, women's liberation, its place in the New Left, and in later struggles over abortion, would prove crucial. Second, it was necessary to understand the changing character of the working class, its diversity, its decentralized, even centripetal character, and its global dimensions.

In the 1968 conjuncture, the politics of organized labor, made strongly anti-Communist in the McCarthy period, was fateful. Labor leaders opposed the student risings, supported the war in Vietnam, and rejected busing, affirmative action, and housing integration. Figures like Gus Tyler of the International Ladies Garment Workers Union complained in 1968 that the "new politics" represented by Al Lowenstein, Eugene McCarthy and Robert Kennedy was changing the whole point of the liberal tradition, "away from economics to ethics and aesthetics, to morality and culture," thus abandoning workers "to the Republican wolves."[126] Figures like Lowenstein responded that the demography of the country was shifting to the young, and that a new politics could not be based on economics alone. In this regard the war, and the violence associated with the war, was crucial.

Working-class sentiments were not prowar, but many workers

and their families hated the antiwar movement as a symbol of elitism and as a challenge to their patriotism. Perhaps even more important, as Alan Brinkley has argued, "the violence that was unleashed [especially after King's slaying] came to be seen by many people as the vision of America's future, and gave salience to law and order as an issue."[127] A fireman who lost his son Ralph in Vietnam, and who was interviewed by Robert Coles, exemplified a widespread sentiment:

> I'm bitter. You bet your goddam dollar I'm bitter. It's people like us who give up our sons for the country. . . . Let's face it: if you have a lot of money, or if you have the right connections, you don't end up on a firing line in the jungle over there, not unless you want to. Ralph had no choice. He didn't want to die. He wanted to live. They just took him – to 'defend democracy,' that's what they keep on saying. Hell, I wonder.

Why didn't this man see the antiwar movement as trying to save the life of his son? A few years later a young black man warned then Presidential candidate George McGovern, "This election is going to break your heart. People aren't as decent as you think they are. They don't like black people; they're resentful of the kids, and they want to forget about the poor. They don't care about peace and human rights and the Constitution. Every guy is just trying to make it for himself."[128] Was this man expressing an eternal truth about American politics or, as I believe, was he dispensing the new, neoliberal wisdom that would emerge in the 1970s?

Two figures seemed at the time to understand the possibility of a broad left-liberal response to the crisis, a response that was simultaneously antiwar and pro-working class. These were Martin Luther King and Robert F. Kennedy, both assassinated in 1968. Before he died, King had reinvigorated his Popular Front roots, increasingly focusing on economic issues, and arguing that the return to order had to be based on social justice. Commenting on the urban uprisings, he said, "I could never again raise my voice against the violence of the oppressed in the ghettos, without having first spoken clearly to the greatest purveyor of violence in the world today – my own government."[129] Kennedy too was genuinely transformed by the events of the sixties. Touring Spanish

Harlem, he explained his decision to run for office to the boxer José Torres: "I found out something I never knew. I found out that my world was not the real world." Entering the Democratic primaries after Gene McCarthy had demonstrated the strength of the antiwar sentiment, and boasting strong Catholic law-and-order credentials, Kennedy told David Frost,

> I think there has to be a new kind of coalition to keep the Democratic Party going, and to keep the country together. We have to write off the unions and the South now. And to replace them with Negroes, blue-collar whites, and the kids. We have to convince the Negroes and the poor whites that they have common interests. If we can reconcile those hostile groups, and then add the kids, you can really turn this country around.[130]

The polls and voting records show that this was not unreasonable. Until the election of Reagan in 1980, the industrial working class vacillated between some mix of old and New Leftism, on the one hand, and Nixon's "Silent Majority" on the other. A crucial factor was the ongoing transformation of the US economy, including its industrial sector. With the emergence of a transnational division of labor, the working class was increasingly composed of young, cheap, immigrant and female labor, often responsive to New Left appeals. The year 1970 witnessed the second largest strike wave in American history (after that of 1946) as 2.4 million workers joined strikes, wildcats, slowdowns and other labor conflicts. *Newsweek* described the 1970 Lordstown strike, as follows: "With all the shoulder-length hair, beards, Afros and mod clothing along the line" it looks like an "industrial Woodstock." The case of Dewey Burton, a white Detroit autoworker born in 1946, and regularly interviewed by the *New York Times*, demonstrates the lost possibilities. In 1970, Burton, a New Deal Democrat with a strong sense of entitlement, had long sideburns, slicked-back hair and mod striped pants, but was livid over his son being bussed away from his neighborhood school. By 1980 he had become a Reagan Democrat, his sense of entitlement gone, largely because his job had become so insecure that he was grateful to his employer for whatever he could get.[131] It took much of the seventies to fully destroy the hope for a broad, multidimensional left-liberal solution to the crisis posed by the new economy, the hope in other words for a third refounding. The politics of the family, to which we now turn, was critical in shaping the ultimate outcome.

The New Left, as we have seen, was intervening in a series of upheavals that it had not created: first civil rights, and then the antiwar movement. In the late sixties it responded to the third great upheaval of the epoch: feminism. Like civil rights, and like the decline in American global supremacy, the dismantling of the family wage and the large-scale entry of women into the workforce seems in retrospect to have been inevitable. However, the meaning of this change was ambiguous. On the one hand, feminism could strengthen the tendency toward an individualistic, meritocratic society, which valorized "empowerment" and "achievement" in the context of an increasingly unequal society. Or feminism could point toward a more deeply egalitarian society, one in which the organization of work was not based on status hierarchies. The latter possibility, which required connecting feminism with civil rights and the antiwar movement, would have sought to destroy invidious racial and gender hierarchies, both at home and abroad. That was the possibility articulated within the New Left.

As with civil rights and the antiwar movement, the New Left did not invent the issue of women's rights. On the contrary, "liberal feminism," as it was later called to distinguish it from radical feminism and socialist feminism, was a powerful force throughout the sixties, focused on expanded possibilities for women, especially working-class women, in employment and public life. As a result of the structural transformation of American capitalism, large-scale changes in the gender order were underway. "Between 1950 and 1998 the proportion of women working outside the home in America rose from 33.9 to 59.8 percent. . . . The number of married women with young children at work rose from 12 percent in 1950 to 40 percent in 1990."[132] The increase reflected the incipient decline of heavy industry, the rise of services, finance and marketing, and the expansion of a consumer economy. While women had worked outside the home before, they had mostly done so as a response to national emergencies, especially wars. The changes of the sixties, however, were structural: they entailed the end of the family wage and the creation of the two-earner family.

The pre-New Left liberal feminism of the 1960s was enormously effective. The contraceptive pill, which had become available in 1957, helped spark women's liberation. Betty Friedan's *The Feminine Mystique* was published in 1963. The Civil Rights Act of 1964, which forbade discrimination on the basis of race, also forbade discrimination on the basis of sex, as an accidental result of a ploy by opponents of the bill. The National Organization for Women was founded in 1966. The National Association for Repeal of Abortion Laws was founded in 1967. Between 1965 and 1969 the entire apparatus of protective legislation aimed at women was dismantled. In 1972 Congress enacted Title IX of the Educational Amendments Act, which banned discrimination in any education program receiving federal aid, leading to a revolution in women's sports. 1973 saw *Roe v Wade*, legalizing abortion on the basis of the "right to privacy," a right established by the courts which were outlawing anticontraception legislation. Second wave feminism, then, was well launched in the sixties, its ideology largely drawing on the New Deal and Popular Front tradition, on the rights revolution, as well as on the legacy of American feminism, among the strongest feminist traditions in the world.

Yet the feminism of the sixties was feminism without a left. Just as the New Left changed the meaning of civil rights and of the antiwar movement, so it changed the meaning of feminism. While the structural, institutional and legal revolution associated with feminism was well underway in the sixties, it was not until its encounter with the New Left that "equal rights for women" became "women's liberation" and "radical feminism." Not surprisingly, women's experience in the mixed left afforded a deeper insight into patriarchal structures and psychology than was available in the more practical, less process-oriented or participatory organizations of mainstream feminism.

The early SNCC and SDS memos on women's liberation demonstrate the process by which the regulatory ideal of participatory democracy was turned inward, against hierarchy in the radical movement itself. One of the earliest SNCC memos, that of Mary King and Casey Hayden, asked, "Who sweeps the office floor?" and "Who takes the minutes?" "The average white person," Hayden and King added, "finds it difficult to understand why the Negro resents being called 'boy' ... because the average white person doesn't realize that he assumes he is superior. So too the average SNCC worker finds it difficult to discuss the woman problem because of the assumptions of male superiority."[133] In 1967 women in SDS passed the following resolution:

> As we analyze the position of women in capitalist society and especially in the United States we find that women are in a colonial relationship to men and we recognize ourselves as part of the Third World. Women, because of their colonial relationship to men, have to fight for their own independence. . . . Only the independent woman can be truly effective in the larger revolutionary struggle.

These and similar statements reflect the way in which women's liberation moved beyond mainstream feminism.

Just as the antiwar movement had built on the civil rights movement, so early proponents of women's liberation built on the antiwar movement. They saw women's subordination as another in the series of wrongs that men and women of the New Left would address together. The 1967 SDS resolution exclaimed, "the struggle for liberation of women must be part of the larger fight for human freedom. We recognize the difficulty our brothers will have in dealing with male chauvinism and we will assume our full responsibility in helping to resolve the contradictions. Freedom now! We love you!"[134] A 1968 memo by Naomi Jaffe and Bernardine Dohrn, both of whom later became Weathermen, stated,

> We realize that women are organized into the Movement by men and continue to relate to it through men . . . the difficulty women have in taking initiative and in acting and speaking in a political context is the consequence of internalizing the view that men define reality and women are defined in terms of men. We are coming together not in a defensive posture to rage at our exploited status vis-à-vis men, but rather in the process of developing our own autonomy.[135]

Here, too, the implication was that the same struggles for self-definition that had inspired men and women in Mississippi, and that had turned Vietnamese peasants into revolutionaries, also underlay women's struggles in the American heartland.

The early women's liberation writings were fragmentary and exploratory, symbolized by the well-worn, mimeographed articles that for several years were the movement's basic texts.

Notes from the First Year began publication in 1968. In 1970 two powerful works appeared, Kate Millett's *Sexual Politics* and Shulamith Firestone's *The Dialectic of Sex*. Both of them took the psychoanalytic worldview, which was founded on sexuality, and replaced sexuality with power. According to Millett, coitus "appears a biological and physical activity" but in fact it is "a charged microcosm" of "power-structured relationships ... whereby one group of persons is controlled by another." Therefore, politics needed to be extended from the spheres of the state, and the economy, to include power relations of "personal contact and interaction between members of well-defined and coherent groups." Firestone, in turn, sought "the ultimate cause and the great moving power of all historic events" in the "biological family," which has given rise to a "power psychology," a "psychological pattern of dominance-submission." What Freud called penis envy was in fact power envy. Firestone also distinguished radical feminists, who attacked the "sexual class system," from "conservative feminists," "politicos," and "Ladies Auxiliaries of the Left."

Distinct though they were, women's liberation and liberal feminism converged with explosive immediacy around 1968–9. Intense feelings of solidarity between women produced the convergence. The year 1968 witnessed the iconic protest against the Miss America ceremony at Atlantic City, when women burnt high-heeled shoes, girdles, bras, and curlers. The next year, on the fiftieth anniversary of the Suffrage Amendment, 50,000 women strode down Fifth Avenue. Influential female journalists like Susan Brownmiller, Gloria Steinem, Nora Ephron, and Ellen Goodman brought the women's issue into the mass media. In 1970 forty-six women at *Newsweek* filed a sex discrimination suit against their employer; two days later, their colleagues at *Ladies Home Journal* staged a sit-in, soon followed by the women at Time Inc. "It was as if the standard of rebellion had been raised in the corridors of the emperor's seraglio," wrote Geoffrey Hodgson.[136]

The discovery of women's liberation was accompanied by tremendous feelings of joy, the lifting of a repression. Kathy Amatniek, one of the inventors of "consciousness-raising," wrote that "when those meetings began ... Suddenly everyone had a story about the negative response of the man she lived with." For Nancy Hawley, one of the originators of *Our Bodies, Ourselves*,

"The flood broke loose gradually and then more swiftly. We talked about our families, our mothers, our fathers, our siblings; we talked about our men; we talked about school; we talked about 'the movement' (which meant New Left men). For hours we talked and unburdened our souls and left feeling high." Carol Hanish, who popularized the phrase "the personal is political," wrote, "the last eight months have been a personal revolution."[137] Joanne Cook, a feminist economist, recalled that "not one woman apologized for complaints about her lot . . . Every woman was a sister."[138] The euphoria of sisterhood also brought intense expectations of loyalty and unity, which found expression in pressures to leave heterosexual relationships, and enter lesbian ones.

Even though women's liberation took on a mainstream character almost immediately, its deepest insights were part of the New Left's attempt to extend the ideal of equality into everyday life. Women and men, women's liberationists argued, are made into sexes as we know them by the social requirements of heterosexuality, which institutionalizes male dominance and female sexual submission. Sexuality is the lynchpin of gender inequality, the analogue to labor in the Marxist worldview.[139] Sex is "something men do to women." "Domination, penile penetration, possession, constitute the male definition of sex."[140] "A woman is a being who identifies and is identified as one whose sexuality exists for someone else, who is socially male."[141] There is at least a touch of rape in all heterosexuality; even when they appear voluntary, sexual relations between men and women are eroticized forms of dominance and submission. "So many distinctive features of women's status as second class – the restriction and constraint and contortion, the servility and the display, the self-mutilation and requisite presentation of self as a beautiful thing, the enforced passivity, the humiliation – are made into the content of sex for women. Being a thing for sexual use is fundamental to it."[142] Not all women agreed with these formulations, but none failed to be affected by them.

From a very early period, men were considered irrelevant to the powerful ties that formed among women. Instead, the valorization of the "woman-identified woman" gave rise to what was soon to be called identity politics. Identity politics differed fundamentally from the "shattering of social roles" that had characterized the New Left. Cathy Cade, a lesbian documentary photographer, explained that "in the black movement I had been fighting [to end] someone else's oppression and now there was a way that I could fight for my own freedom." For Mimi Feingold, "women couldn't burn draft cards and couldn't go to jail so all they could do was to relate through their men and that seemed to me the most really demeaning kind of thing." Another feminist collective proclaimed that "the most profound and potentially the most radical politics come out of our own identity, as opposed to working to end somebody else's oppression."[143] The importance of what women's liberation called the woman-identified woman found theoretical expression in Nancy Chodorow's 1978 *The Reproduction of Mothering* and historian Carol Smith-Rosenberg's 1975 "Female World of Love and Ritual." Adrienne Rich summarized: "women are talking to each other, recovering an oral culture, telling our life-stories, reading aloud to one another the books that have moved and healed us, analyzing the language that has lied about us, reading our own words aloud and to each other."

A similarly rapid evolution occurred within Gay Liberation, generally dated from the Stonewall uprising, June 27, 1969. Earlier, Gay Liberation had been part of the antiwar movement, sporting such slogans as "No Vietnamese ever called me queer" and insisting, "We will not help to perpetuate a society that oppresses us and discriminates against us, nor will we fight in its army." In 1969 an activist explained: alienation from one's body is "the first imperialism. For this reason we gay (powerless) males must of necessity of our condition be antiwar and anti-imperialist. We are already a conquered country."[144] In 1970 the Gay Liberation Front was formed, describing itself as "a nation-wide coalition of revolutionary homosexual organizations creating a radical counter culture ... Politically it's part of the radical 'Movement' working to suppress and eliminate discrimination and oppression"[145] By the early to mid-seventies, however, homosexuals began to think of themselves less as members of a radical movement than as persons with a distinct way of life, persons who belonged to a historically specific community. Homosexuality, then, became an identity, something that was based on membership in a community, and to which radical politics was essentially irrelevant.[146]

With the development of identity politics, the issue of "leaving the left" arose within women's liberation. We can get a sense of what "leaving the left" meant by examining the relations of Barbara

Deming and David McReynolds, both lifelong pacifist activists, close friends in the civil rights and antiwar movements, and both gay. When Deming became a feminist separatist, McReynolds told her he refused to "read a book written by someone who won't attend planning meetings with men, someone who insists on separate demonstrations, separate book stores, separate bars." He also wanted her to know that his support for her separatist feminism was not unconditional. "When women tell me they know all about men or that men are such and such, I know they speak part of the truth," he explained, but only part. For some time now she'd talked of "waiting, of silence, of hoping men would change and see patriarchy as the enemy," yet in his view "the attack on the patriarchy is possible only because it is, in a sense, already over." He remained puzzled about the degree to which the women's movement was concerned about political issues other than feminism. Barbara's pain, McReynolds tried to convince her, was "a human condition, not a female one" and he believed she was edging away "from the overarching humanity, which is at the core of nonviolence." "We need one another," he wrote, "our common humanity being more urgent in this short life than our blackness, whiteness, or elseness. That is a truth you once knew and I sense you have lost or are losing it somewhere along the way."

But Deming felt that "our lives, women's lives, are not real to you (and to men generally) – except in so far as they support the lives of men." Those who called themselves "anti-imperialists," she added, needed to recognize "that women are treated as a colonized people – here and everywhere." There was only one man on the left, David Dellinger, she claimed, who had read the extraordinary books that feminists had written over the last few years. "The bond is still there," she added in a note to herself, but she wasn't sure that men and women could "any longer struggle side by side . . . It is going to take non-cooperation with [men] to make them change." To the end Deming insisted that feminists saw the connections "between the liberation of women as women and the elimination of capitalism, racism, and imperialism," and she did agree with her friend, Weatherman Susan Saxe, that "the split between the left and feminists [is] a tragedy."[147]

Some white women and most black women rejected the idea of a separate women's movement. Barbara Epstein, a radical historian and feminist, wrote, "There is an emotional reason why I feel uncomfortable calling myself a socialist-feminist," a term which implied two separate movements, one aimed at socialism, the other at feminism.

> I was very much involved in the peace movement when I was in high school. I joined the Communist Party when I was in my first year in college, and so the left really became my history, my identification, my family. I experienced the women's movement as telling me that I was no longer allowed to belong to the left. I really felt the women's movement tore apart the home that I had made for myself.[148]

Furthermore, "the issue that was being raised was why didn't women get listened to in meetings. Women were saying we are the wives and girlfriends; we do the shit-work and we don't play a leadership role. I didn't fit into those categories. I really was taken seriously and was not regarded as an appendage to some man." This echoed an earlier remark of black SNCC worker Ruby Doris Smith Robinson that the charge that women's role was limited to office work "didn't make sense to me because at the time I had my own project in Bolivar County, Mississippi."[149]

Other women also felt uncomfortable by the gap opening between feminists and the left. Gloria Emerson, covering the war in Vietnam, wrote,

> There were people who were exasperated and puzzled by my indifference to the women's liberation movement, which I had first known and admired in England when I lived there. I knew the immense value of the movement but I could not bear the posters SAVE OUR SISTERS IN DANANG or the women who would not join the antiwar movement because they felt it did not sufficiently stress rape as a crime, although, of course, it did . . . Perhaps the interest in the women's movement, the early excitement over its huge importance, ended that night in Saigon in 1971 when Germaine Greer was there on a brief visit . . . What really provoked her, she said, was seeing a group of Vietnamese women filling sandbags near Long Binh, the biggest US Army base in Vietnam, the ugliest of places. What she resented was a sign in English, near the Vietnamese women, that said MEN AT WORK.

"I had always known how women were leashed, confined, made so small, and uncertain," Emerson reflected. "But in Vietnam, among the most helpless and humiliated were the soldiers themselves."[150]

This was also the period in which the New Left was changing from an inchoate mass of spontaneous upheavals into an organized social movement. Marxian theory was evolving, some of it responding creatively to the feminist critique of gender hierarchy. Here I can speak from personal experience. My book *Capitalism, the Family and Personal Life* began as a review of Firestone's *Dialectic of Sex* and was published in 1972 in the neo-Marxist journal *Socialist Revolution*. In it I argued that what Marx called the social relations of production – "the total ensemble of social relations entered into in the social production of existence" – necessarily included the family, and that mass consumption and the technological-scientific revolution had made a new, "post-economic" consciousness possible. The rise of industrial capitalism, I explained, for the first time, created the modern division between the public and the private.[151]

Meanwhile, the waning of the "Golden Age of Capitalism" also directed attention to socialist ideas. Beginning around 1968, signs of a crisis of capital accumulation (i.e., profitability) appeared everywhere. Nixon's response was a huge wave of regulatory reform, including wage and price controls, income maintenance, tax reform, environmental controls, and consumer protection.[152] Radical unions flourished, organizing hospital workers, hotel workers, waitresses, and farmworkers. Third world cultural radicalism flourished in such forms as the Young Lords, Third World Newsreel, and the LA Rebellion. Efforts were made to begin leftist political parties, for example by Arthur Kinoy and James Weinstein.

The strongest example of the maturation of the New Left was Michael Harrington's Democratic Socialist Organizing Committee (DSOC), founded in 1973 and later merged with the New American Movement (NAM). According to Harrington, "The Democratic Socialists envision a humane social order based on popular control of resources and production, economic planning ... and racial equality. I share an immediate program with liberals in this country because the best liberalism leads toward socialism." "I want to be on the left wing of the possible," he added. Like NAM, DSOC was explicitly feminist; Gloria Steinem was a founding member. Working in alliance with major labor unions, DSOC became a powerful presence within the Democratic

Party. The goal, Harrington argued, was to join the New Left of the 1960s with the old left and the labor movement in a "united political movement of the liberal-left" that would operate within the Democratic Party not to rally it once more as the "party of Roosevelt," but to "look beyond the New Deal, the Fair Deal, the New Frontier and the Great Society."[153]

In spite of such efforts, the sense of a burgeoning, diverse radical movement was gone by the mid-seventies. For many, there was a wrenching emotional aftermath. Survivors held on to the ephemera accumulated over the years, as if it were vital to conserve tracts, posters, journals, brochures, bulletins, even scraps of paper.[154] Luisa Passerini, who interviewed survivors of both the Popular Front and the New Left in Italy, wrote, "My interviews with the elderly about their memories of Fascism had absorbed and moved me, but they weren't so weighty, so unresolved, so enigmatic" as those of the 1968 generation.[155] Later students asked, "Why did there seem to be so little guidance available to those who were only then coming to a critical outlook on their society? Why were the connections to the past severed so cleanly?"[156] A new generation of singers emerged to ask "Remember when everyone was doing the ban-the bomb songs?" adding "the minute you preach, you're interfering with somebody else's life."[157] Radical Chic, explained Thomas Wolfe, writing about a Panther-support party, "is only radical in style; in its heart it is part of Society and its traditions."[158]

The war in Vietnam passed into the realm of the apolitical. Barbara Tuchman called it a "march of folly." Michael Herr underwent psychoanalysis to produce his feverish, free-associational work *Dispatches*, which offers no politics, no morality, "no clear outline of history."[159] Tim O'Brien wrote, "They did not know even the simple things: a sense of victory, or satisfaction, or necessary sacrifice. . . . They did not have targets. They did not have a cause. They did not know if it was a war of ideology or economics or hegemony or spite."[160] According to Oliver Stone's *Platoon*, "we did not fight the enemy, we fought ourselves." When the war finally ended on May 11, 1975, 60,000 people came to Central Park to hear Joan Baez, Pete Seeger, Phil Ochs, and Odetta sing, but there was a sense of anticlimax: "People sat on the hard ground in Sheep Meadow, a large area in Central Park where there are deep, bald patches in the grass."[161]

Order returned slowly. What Tom Wicker called Nixon's "repressed, introverted, driven" personality, his identification with losers, his resentment of privilege, facilitated the transformation of the Republicans into the party of protest and discontent.[162] The resulting alliance of wealth and ressentiment produced "a French Revolution in reverse – one in which the sans-culottes pour down the streets demanding more power for the aristocracy."[163] All the way down to the Tea Party, the strength of the Republicans lay in their ability to capture and transform the New Left's anti-elitism.

Even as leftist energies waned, "the Sixties" came to dominate American politics just as the Civil War and the New Deal had dominated the political landscapes that followed them. Indeed, the effects of the New Left on American society and culture have been almost incalculable. An entirely new consciousness of both race and gender has transformed language, lifestyle and institutions. There is a persistent skepticism toward American intervention abroad. Academic life has been transformed, not only by the entry of minorities and women, but also by the creation of whole new subfields and by the transformation of canonical knowledge. The press owes whatever willingness it has to challenge authority to the New Left. A host of new political issues including abortion, gay marriage and ecology occupy center stage. A moral revolution in the treatment of prisoners, the mentally ill, patients, and immigrants occurred. The churches, perhaps especially the Catholic Church, developed liberation theologies. The election of a black President in 2008, whatever his politics, testifies to the impact of the civil rights movement. We are only at the beginning of understanding the full implications of the attack on patriarchy and on "compulsory heterosexuality," and of the questions of "identity" that opened up in the early seventies.

Yet the New Left is widely considered a failure today, and this must be directly addressed. Two different senses of "failure" need to be distinguished. In one sense the left will always "fail," because it stands for sometimes utopian ideals that cannot and will not be realized in the immediate present. This "failure" is actually a form of success, because it means that the left is guided by the long-term project of deepening equality, in a society understandably preoccupied with immediate gain and loss. In another sense, however, the left may fail by committing remediable errors, errors that need to be corrected if future lefts are to flourish. It is my view that the end of a mixed left in the early to mid-seventies was one such remediable failure. Beginning in the early seventies, unprecedented resources went into building the neoliberal order but the New Left could never have been destroyed from the outside. To the extent that the New Left's achievements have been forgotten, the "forgetting" was generated by "third way" theorists, advocates of the "cultural turn," Kantians, Freudians, Foucauldians, sexual emancipators, historical revisionists, subaltern postcolonialists, "progressive" social scientists and, especially, by second wave feminists, in other words by the left itself. Nevertheless, rather than speaking in terms of success or failure, it is preferable to ask today what legacy the New Left left behind. A concluding chapter addresses this question.

In the sixties, then, the country faced, for the third time in its history, simultaneous crises in its structure and its identity. In this case, however, the two crises had different resolutions, at least in the short run. The structural crisis, the transition from state-guided industry and global hegemony to neoliberal financialization and nonhegemonic militarization, proceeded relatively smoothly for a while. But the country did not deepen its core commitment to equality. On the contrary, it rejected its egalitarian traditions, suppressed much of the memory of the three lefts that had been so closely tied to those traditions, and embraced a culture of meritocracy, class division, and inequality that was fundamentally alien to its history. The result was not refounding but long-term decline. As of this writing, the structural crisis and the identity crisis seem to be converging once again. What is called the economic crisis that began in 2007 cannot be solved without a renewed left/liberal politics centered on social justice and equality. That brings us to our final subject: the prospects for the left today.

Conclusion

The American Left Today

When American history is understood as it should be, as a series of deep, successive structural crises – slavery, industry, and global finance – and not as a linear unfolding, we can see that the left has been central to its history. America needed a left during the crisis over slavery in order to give abolition the meaning of racial equality. It needed a left during the crisis over industrialization in order to give the welfare state the meaning of social equality. And it needs a left in today's crisis over neoliberalization in order to give America's great technological advances and reorientation to a globalizing world the meaning of equality.

In thinking about the tasks facing the left today it is easy to become discouraged, but this would be a mistake. History encourages the long view. Each of America's three great crises has been a secular crisis, stretching over decades, not years. Everyone in the United States today knows that the country has been in a major economic crisis since 2007, and no one knows how and when it will end. What many do not realize, however, is that today's crisis is the latest expression of the long-term political, social and cultural crisis that began in the 1960s. Marginalized, confused and intimidated as the left is today, it has to be patient and reflective, because the country is again at a turning point. Far from awaiting "recovery," the US needs to reanimate its core identity in the face of a major structural transformation. Only a left can precipitate the kind of discussion that America needs today.

Let us begin to think about today's crisis and the potential role of the left in it by recapping the argument of this book. In the past, the left has emerged when the country was at a moment of crisis. As we saw, such crises were never simply economic crises, but rather turning points, correlated with epochal shifts in the structure of capitalism. Each of our three moments of crisis – slavery, industrialization, and neoliberalism – had two dimensions: a system dimension, whose resolution demanded a structural transformation, and an identity dimension, whose resolution demanded that the structural shift be given a meaning that deepens the country's core identity. In each crisis, the left has been indispensable to the country's struggle to deepen its understanding of what it means to be an American. In each case, the left's contribution lay in its expansive defense of America's core value, namely, equality. For each left, equality correlated with democracy, understood not in terms of voting, or blogging, but in terms of a common culture, of geographic, intellectual or psychical spaces where fellow citizens meet each other as equals. The left preserves this egalitarian democratic ideal through ordinary times, and safeguards it through emergencies. In crises, however, the left extends and deepens the ideal of equality in light of a new constellation of historical challenges.

The question, then, is whether we now face such a crisis moment. Does the United States today face a system crisis arising from a tectonic shift in the structure of capitalism, one that can be likened to the slavery crisis and to the industrialization crisis? Do we stand at a turning point where the nation's identity and core values are again put into question? In my view, the answer is yes on both counts. To explain why, I shall sketch the contours of the present situation, identifying three great interconnected structural shifts that began in the 1960s: neoliberal financialization, a shift in the geography of production, and a transformation in the "natural" order as expressed both in gender and in ecology. These, I will argue, constitute the objective vectors that have led us to a turning point, one whose successful resolution requires a renewed and deepened commitment to equality, hence a left.

Recall that the New Deal order that began to unravel in the 1960s was based on a strong state, robust controls over financial speculation, and American supremacy over the global trading system. The Bretton Woods Agreement (1944) made the dollar, whose value was fixed in gold, the international trading currency. As long as American industry reigned supreme, dollars were needed to buy American goods and were not redeemed in gold. Beginning in 1968, however, the Vietnam War induced inflation and a balance of payments crisis, while the revival of Western Europe and Japan threatened American markets. As a result, several nations, starting with France, began to demand gold for their dollars. In 1971 Nixon took the United States off the gold standard, leading to the creation of a vast new international currency and capital market largely run by US banks, insurance companies, and investors. Henceforth, investment houses, not national governments, would set exchange rates. In 1974 all controls on capital flows abroad were lifted. Soon after, financial flows outstripped global trade and productive output. In the 1980s President Reagan combined tax cuts with increased military spending, making the US a debtor nation for the first time since World War One. Leveraged buyouts increased the burgeoning debt. As the share of the national income going to wages declined, households tried to maintain their living standards by increasing their debt as well. The reliance on debt built the new "risk management" industries. The Black–Scholes equation enabling the calculation of derivative prices, which in turn enabled the recent speculative bubbles in technology and housing, was invented in 1973.

With the rise of financialization, the United States did what Great Britain did a century earlier. It relinquished its industrial primacy and encouraged its capitalists to invest abroad. In the words of Thomas McCormick, the US accepted its transformation into "a rentier nation, living off the income of its rents – that is to say, its direct and indirect overseas investments."[1] When Gilbert Williamson, president of the NCR Corporation, a technology corporation later acquired by AT&T, was asked about United States competitiveness in 1989 he replied, "I don't think about it at all. We at NCR think of ourselves as a globally competitive company that happens to be headquartered in the United States."

The result was a structural shift in the geography of production. On the one hand, the deregulation of aviation, trucking, railroads, and telecommunications, along with the advent of containerization and computerized inventory control, intensified what David Harvey has called space–time compression. Manufacturing relocated to low-wage countries, leading to "deindustrialization," the "rustbelt," and "downsizing," all terms invented in the 1970s. Labor unions were blamed for the great inflation of the period and, with the threat of capital migrating, began to accept weaker and weaker contracts, soon going into decline. Michael Harrington's 1974 article "A Collective Sadness" reflected on the lost sense of the meaning of work, while other authors evoked the new age of "limits," "diminished expectations," and "austerity." Rising poverty, declining real wages, and drug epidemics in rural America drove many workers despairingly to the right. Thomas Frank neatly captured the paradox of "small farmers proudly voting themselves off the land ... devoted family men carefully seeing to it that their children will never be able to afford college or proper health care ... working class guys in Midwestern cities cheering as they deliver up a landslide for a candidate whose policies will end their way of life."[2]

On the other hand, the opening of new markets for investment elsewhere in the world, especially after the fall of Communism in 1989, sparked a new wave of productive activity. As manufacturing shifted to India, China, Korea, Taiwan, Brazil, Mexico, and Eastern Europe, 1–2 billion people were brought into the middle class. The same dynamic, however, ensured that 3–4 billion other people were involuntarily excluded from the global economy, while another 2 billion scraped by on its margins, subsisting through the "informal" economy. Often associated with the developing world, a chunk of the latter lived in fact in the United States, which increasingly turned into a two-tier society, one tier able to benefit from the expansion of global finance and trade, the other tied to the declining industrial economy, to low-paid service work, and increasingly to casual or irregular labor. The result was a continuing series of productivity crises, competitiveness crises, financial crises, and global imbalances, punctuated by manic moments in which the country insisted it had "licked the Vietnam syndrome" and returned to being "number one."

These developments were deeply entwined with the transformation of the gender order and the uprooting of the ecological order in which, especially outside the West, the peasant and rural family had been rooted. In the developed countries, an enormous wave of commoditization marketized household functions: witness the rise of fast food, and for-profit nursing homes and child care, all premised on low-wage labor, much of it performed by women and immigrants. Meanwhile, the size of the workforce doubled as women entered paid labor, definitively suppressing the family wage ideal. In China, Malaysia, Indonesia, South America, and in Mexican maquiladoras, women manned global assembly lines in such export-oriented industries as electronics, toys, shoes, and textiles. Conservative obstacles to marketization, such as the "natural economy" and communal life forms, swiftly collapsed, while nepotism and the "old boys' network" weakened. At the same time, the ecological conditions for sustaining life were undermined, no one knows to what extent. Biodiversity declined; species vanished; the planet warmed; pollution surged; bodies of water died; energy and water become increasingly scarce; demographic crises mounted; diseases rampaged across the world.

These three changes – financialization, a shifting geography of production, and the uprooting of nature and tradition – all well underway in the seventies, converged to create the neoliberal social order. Like the market society in which slavery flourished, and like the industrial society in which the working class emerged, the neoliberal order cannot be understood in economic terms alone. It is above all a moral order with a fatal flaw. Both the order and its flaw can be seen when we consider the decline of the New Left. In a word, neoliberalism incorporated the new libertarian and egalitarian values of the sixties, but turned them into rationales for an unequal social order.

The key move was to separate the cultural revolution of the sixties from the political transformation espoused by the left. Sixties' culture – the so-called "counterculture" – had fostered antinomianism, the worship of youth, and do-your-own thing individualism. In the course of the neoliberal transformation, these qualities became detached from the anticapitalist ethos of the New Left. Depoliticized, they served to animate the "spirit" of a new mode of capitalism, one based on hedonism, consumerism, and "empowerment."[3] Likewise, neoliberalism adapted the rights revolution to its own purposes. Uprooted from ideas of collective struggle, rights were reinterpreted in terms of "diversity," meritocracy, and market opportunity. As "choice" became the neoliberal mantra, the country's commitment to equality was suppressed. That suppression is the fatal flaw of the neoliberal order. To understand this more deeply, let us consider the fate of the three great social movements of the 1960s – civil rights, antiwar, and feminism.

Recall once more the democratic spirit of the early sixties. At that time, civil rights did not mean simply the end of segregation, nor did it apply only to blacks. Pressed by its radical currents, the civil rights movement encompassed social and economic equality, and was aimed at all poor, excluded and denigrated Americans – witness the Kennedy administration's interest in Michael Harrington's *The Other America*, the great 1963 Civil Rights March "for Jobs and Freedom," and the war on poverty. These were the years in which Medicare was created and Social Security extended, both conceived as "entitlement" programs, hence as *rights*, rooted in the social compact, not as economic proffers that could be adjusted or taken away as the budget-of-the-day required.

In the neoliberal order, however, civil rights was reinflected to signify meritocracy instead of equality. As if to illustrate the famous slogan of China's neoliberal expansion, "a few get rich first," some blacks rose dramatically in the professions and business, while others were driven into prisons, the drug trade, and urban violence. As the "victim rights" movement became the largest social movement in America, the death penalty was restored, and over 10 percent of all young black men were incarcerated at any given time. The fact is that the civil rights revolution was ambiguous in its implications. Only a left could give civil rights the full meaning of equality. Absent a left, that meaning receded and the alternative, market-centered, meritocratic meaning triumphed.

A similar fate befell the antiwar movement. In its heyday, the movement's left wing had not cast the war as a "mistake." Nor had it claimed that the US should negotiate rather than resort to force; still less that the US should not intervene abroad. What the New Left wanted, rather, was a peace-oriented global order in which peoples could interact on the basis of equality; hence the call to "end US imperialism" and disband the US-dominated Cold War alliance. Moreover, peace abroad had been connected to justice at home. In 1972 Senator George McGovern had run for President on the Democratic ticket proposing not only an immediate end to the Vietnam War, but an "alternative military budget" with deep cuts in military spending, the savings going toward efforts to end poverty and guarantee decent paying jobs.[4]

Later in the seventies, however, the legacy of the antiwar movement shifted from global justice and equality to universal human rights. As the Russian dissident and human rights activist Andrei Sakharov explained, "What we need is a systematic defense of human rights and ideals, and not a political struggle, which would inevitably incite people to violence, sectarianism, and frenzy."[5] American support for human rights, wrote Ronald Steel, was an effort to reestablish "the country's moral and missionary credentials . . . 'after groveling in the moral muck so long.'"[6] What followed was a raft of new military interventions justified in the name of human rights – witness Nicaragua, Panama, Grenada, Yugoslavia, Lebanon, Iraq, and Afghanistan. Often, to be sure, these exercises in "military humanism" were viewed cynically, especially abroad. But they demonstrate that human rights, like civil rights, are ambiguous. They can justify American domination or they can contribute to the project of social justice on a global scale. Only a left can pave the way to the second alternative.

Similarly, feminism has triumphed in the form of meritocracy, not equality. College-educated female bank-tellers became branch managers and clerical workers in publishing companies became editors, just as unions were being destroyed, benefits were being cut back, and the mass of women both in the United States and internationally were confined to low-paying jobs. Microsoft recruited college-educated women while Wal-Mart built its fortunes in the "the aisles and break rooms of Southern discount stores, in small group Bible study and vast Sunday-morning worship services."[7] Certainly, feminists were conscious of the disparity and worked to build solidarity among women of different classes, races and nationalities, but female solidarity is not the same as social equality. With the New Left's decline, the left wing of feminism – socialist feminism – was increasingly marginalized. As a result, feminists never forged connections between the struggle for gender equality and struggles against forms of exploitation and domination not based on gender. On the contrary, with its left marginalized, a hegemonic feminism was invoked to legitimate the spread of US corporations and US armies throughout the world.[8]

What gave neoliberals the opportunity to recuperate the movements of the sixties was the emergence of a two-tier society. The shift from equality to meritocracy was prefigured as New Left communes and political organizations broke up in the early seventies and some members became tenured professors and bought homes, while others took part-time positions, moved through a series of dead-end jobs, and lived like graduate students well into mid-life. Many of the radical students who filled the New Left ranks in the sixties morphed into privileged, educated elites who benefit from the global economy, turning their backs on the egalitarian vision that had arisen with the new, mass universities. Unlike the classical middle classes, who justified their privileges by their role in the accumulation process, the new elites justified their privileges by the claim of being smarter, better educated, a more valuable form of "human capital," or by their control over credentials and licensing.[9] More important than property, they passed on to their children social and cultural capital, including access to the best schools (increasingly private), but also "taste," as in knowledge of food, wine, travel, fashion, and clothes. The new elites were also cosmopolitan and global; they had more in common with elites in other countries than with their fellow nationals.

As with previous transformations in the mode of production – those of the 1850s and the 1930s – intellectuals played a crucial role in the construction of the new order. In the era of neoliberalism, however, many abandoned their skepticism toward business, their sympathy for the poor, and their antipositivistic slant. It had been axiomatic in the 1960s that a society needed history, literature and social thought in order to figure out what its core values were, and what direction it aspired to move in. It seemed obvious then that genuine insight could only come from critical reflection grounded in one's own historical situation, and not from inquiry that purported to adopt "the view from nowhere." The seventies, however, witnessed the beginnings of the triumph of neoclassical economics, the rational choice revolution in political science and sociology, the reduction of psychoanalysis to neurobiology, and the postmodern attack on subjectivity. Rational choice theory remapped "the world of politics and legislative action as a field of individual preference-satisfying behavior." Game theorists demonstrated "the tragedy of the commons," in other words that collective solutions invariably produced "free riders," "short-term outlooks," "fundamental and inescapable arbitrariness," "suboptimal results." "Under the weight of these analyses the idea of governance as an expression of the public good all but evaporated."[10]

The neoliberal state that began to take shape during the Carter Presidency (1976–80) was economistic. All market societies require strong political centers in order to counter the centrifugal, particularizing and dispersive tendencies built into markets, but because of its volatile character, the finance-driven economy unleashed in the 1970s needs more guidance, more politics, more leadership than the industrial economy that preceded it. Yet since the 1970s American society has lost the political language it needs to even comprehend its situation. The heart of the neoliberal crisis is political, not economic. Witness the current state of our party system. Parties, in America, particularly in times of crisis, have never been vote-getting machines. Rather they have incubated public debates that give meaning to the transformation of capitalism. Today, for the first time in American history, we have a secular transformation of capitalism – neoliberalism, globalization, the two-earner family – that is being led from the right. What is most striking is how completely the Democratic Party has abandoned all traces of its New Deal heritage, in favor of the language of taxes, budgets and deficits, of "evidence-based" "scientific measurement," "efficiency," and "waste." In 1981, when Senator Paul Tsongas called for liberals to become more conservative on economic issues and more radical on cultural issues, like feminism and gay rights, he was applauded for "cutting through" a "sterile" left/right distinction.[11] By the time of the Clinton Presidency, when Thomas Frank moved to Washington DC, he noted an "aversion, bordering on hatred, for the left, especially among Democrats. People who dominate discussions in Democratic circles despise the left."[12]

Neoliberalism, then, has created a cold rationalistic world, divided between highly educated and pampered elites and vast, vulnerable, struggling underclasses, a deracinated world in which individuals rely on technology and cost-benefit analyses, a mean world in which the dominant classes tolerate injustice in the name of economic necessity or other forms of pseudo-science. Many of these characteristics were evoked in Kazuo Ishiguro's 2005 novella *Never Let Me Go*. The premise of the novel is that "medical breakthroughs" beginning in 1956 led to the mass production of genetically engineered clones who are brought up to become organ donors, which, of course, means they die young. The novel focuses on two girls and a boy, around ten years old, who are at the ultraprivileged school for clones, Hailsham, a sort of junior Harvard. The entire system is maintained by cultivating a sense of specialness in the children: their school is special, they produce art which is exhibited in a "gallery," they receive "tokens" for exemplary performances which they trade for what they fail to recognize as the "normals'" castoffs, and when they reach their short adulthood they are beset by false rumors that "deferrals" are possible for those who can prove (especially through their art) that they are "truly in love." Later they learn that Hailsham was a failed experiment by loser do-gooders seeking to demonstrate that clones had souls.

Neoliberalism has brought about a world that has much in common with the one described by Ishiguro. Highly privileged educated global elites benefit vastly from the new opportunities of travel and high-end consumption made possible for those who can create "value" in a fast-changing, highly competitive "flat-world" search for capital. Meanwhile a vast, mostly colored global underclass does in fact sell body parts, often in order to migrate illegally to the world of "normals" where work might be found. Babies, sexual services, drugs, housekeeping, child care, gardens, flowers and much else serve as the "tokens" – that is, commodities – through which the underclass can purchase the cast-off rejects of the "normals." Working through the individuation and personal life characteristic of consumer society, rather than through the mass coercive techniques characteristic of mass production, narcissism supplies the oil that makes the gears of globalized, rational-choice capitalism mesh. This is the world out of which a new left has to take shape.

Slavery put the whole project of America into question long before the slavery crisis sharpened in the late 1850s. The rise of the "trusts" and the exploitation of labor endangered America's republican character for a century before the New Deal addressed the problem. Similarly, the neoliberal order has been undermining American democracy for decades. In recent years, our awareness of the crisis-like character of American society has heightened, perhaps beginning with the impeachment of Clinton in 1998 and the stolen election of 2000. The truly irrational character of the US response to the attacks of September 11, 2001 should have served as a wake-up call: two fruitless and destructive wars, and a complete failure to address large-scale international problems of poverty, climate, resource management and global justice. Since 2007 the naked subordination of the government to finance has been unmistakable. Can a new left intervene in the present crisis in such a way as to help redefine American identity once again, and thereby make a resolution of the crisis possible?

The key to answering this question lies in understanding that the New Left was never fully absorbed by the rise of neoliberalism. Like earlier lefts, it left behind a remainder, a "promissory note" for "future use." As with previous lefts, that remainder was an expanded sense of equality. Only when we return to the core egalitarianism that the left stands for can we reclaim the mantle of freedom – not the shallow freedom of choice upheld by neoliberalism but a critical conception of freedom rooted in equality. For the New Left, it was axiomatic that one could not be free so long as blacks were subjected to racism in Mississippi, so long as peasants were being napalmed in Vietnam, or so long as women were dying from illegal abortions or from other forms of violence at the hands of men. With that as our heritage, the left today must reject liberals who counterpose equality to freedom and must insist on a deeper conception of freedom than that provided by the market. We have our own Mississippi in Katrina; we have our own Vietnam in Palestine; we have our own lynching in the murder of the young gay man Matthew Shepherd.

That the tradition of the left never died in America was apparent during the 2008 Democratic primary. Hope is invariably the basis for the left, and "hope" was the slogan of Barack Obama's campaign. When people tell me today that they were not stirred by that campaign, I don't believe them. Only someone without a heart could have failed to be moved by a call not for a change in policy but for a change in mindset. Had Obama moved in the direction his campaign implied, we would today be witnessing the characteristic conflict between liberalism and the left that marks the great eras of reform. Instead he chose to occupy a vacuous "bipartisan" "center," which inevitably let the right and its corporate allies hold the country hostage, greatly deepening the crisis we are in. It will not be easy to turn our backs on the country's first black President but it is necessary if we are to make any progress at all.[13]

Occupy Wall Street represents a stark contrast to the missed opportunities of the Obama Presidency. The protests on behalf of the 99%, which began on September 17, 2011, bear out one central claim of this book: the irrepressible character of the American commitment to equality, and speak to a second: the impossibility of a successful resolution of the current crisis without a robust, independent left. Given the fact that Occupy Wall Street has already transformed the discourse of American politics, nothing could be more harmful than for the movement to be reabsorbed into the neo-liberal, corporate dominated Democratic Party. Instead, its goal should be to recreate a permanent radical presence in American life.

For that to happen, "progressives," "liberals," feminists, ecology activists, gay liberationists, pacifists, anti-war activists as well as Occupy Wall Street militants, have to reaffirm their common identity as a left. The consolidation and clarification of identity is central to every founding. It is what the abolitionists did when they got started, what the socialists did when they got started, and what the New Left did when it got started. Like our predecessors, today's activists need to know themselves as a left, as part of an indispensable tradition. To be sure, no one can know exactly what programs today's left should espouse, nor what balance it should strike between government and markets, efficiency and distributive justice, the focus on status and on class, global, national and local frameworks and the like. But that does not mean that we do not know the difference between a left, committed to the nation's core egalitarian values, and technocratic, pragmatic "problem-solving" committed to corporate power. Almost every voice in America today is in thrall to the rich, the banks, the military, the technology companies, to celebrity culture, and to the academic elites. Only a left could develop the commitment and capacity to go deeper and to think independently on the basis of the country's core values. To be sure, our history as a left has been fraught, just as the country's history has been fraught. We lost our way in the 1970s, just as our predecessors did in 1867, 1896, and the 1950s. But what was lost in those moments was not lost forever. On the contrary, the history of the American left constitutes a living legacy, one that now includes Occupy Wall Street. It remains for us to reclaim and extend that legacy. The times demand nothing less.

Notes

Introduction

1 Robert Hertz, *Death and the Right Hand* (Glencoe: Free Press, 1960).
2 Christopher Hill, *The World Turned Upside Down* (New York: Viking, 1972), 15.
3 Steven Lukes, "The Grand Dichotomy of the Twentieth Century," in Terence Ball and Richard Bellamy, eds, *The Cambridge History of Twentieth Century Political Thought* (London: Cambridge University Press, 2003), 606.
4 J. A. Laponce, *Left and Right: The Topography of Political Perception* (Toronto: University of Toronto Press, 1981), 27.
5 Lukes, "Grand Dichotomy," 611. See also Norbert Bobbio, *Left and Right: The Significance of a Political Distinction* (Chicago: University of Chicago Press, 1996).
6 Lukes, "Grand Dichotomy," 604.
7 David Brion Davis, *Inhuman Bondage: The Rise and Fall of Slavery in the New World* (Oxford: Oxford University Press, 2008), 248.
8 Daniel T. Rodgers, *Age of Fracture* (Cambridge: Belknap Press of Harvard University Press, 2011).
9 Doug Rossinow, *The Politics of Authenticity* (New York: Columbia University Press, 2002), 3.
10 John Macmillan and Paul Buhle, *The New Left Revisited* (Philadelphia: Temple University Press, 2002), distinguishes the New Left and the movement. In my experience the "New Left"

was the journalistic term, whereas participants referred to "the movement."

1 Abolitionism and Racial Equality

1 David Armitage, *The Declaration of Independence: A Global History* (Cambridge: Harvard University Press, 2007), 68; R. R. Palmer, *Age of Democratic Revolution: A Political History of Europe and America, 1760–1800* (Princeton: Princeton University Press, 1969).
2 Eric Foner, "American Freedom in a Global Age," *American Historical Review* 106 (Feb. 2001), 9.
3 Richard Rorty, *Achieving Our Country: Leftist Thought in Twentieth-Century America* (Cambridge: Harvard University Press, 1998), 11.
4 John L. Thomas, *The Liberator: William Lloyd Garrison* (New York: Little Brown, 1963).
5 Michael Walzer, *The Revolution of the Saints* (Cambridge: Harvard University Press, 1965), 3–4.
6 Hannah Arendt, *On Revolution* (New York: Penguin Classics, 2006), 110.
7 David Brion Davis, "Free at Last: The Enduring Legacy of the South's Civil War Victory," *New York Times*, Aug. 26, 2001.
8 Charles Sellers, *The Market Revolution: Jacksonian America, 1815–1846* (New York: Oxford University Press, 1994). For a nuanced critique see Richard Bushman, "Markets and Composite Farms in Early America," *William and Mary Quarterly* 55:3 (July 1998), 351–74.
9 The Portuguese word *feitoria*, the African site for gathering slaves, is derived from the same root as the English "factory."
10 Quoted in Robin Blackburn, *The Making of New World Slavery: From the Baroque to the Modern, 1492–1800* (New York: Verso, 1997), 11, 6, 260; Robin Blackburn, *The Overthrow of Colonial Slavery: 1776–1848* (New York: Verso, 2011), 6.
11 Eric Hobsbawm, *The Age of Revolution: 1789–1848* (New York: Vintage, 1996), 34. The actual economic contribution of slavery to industrialization has been the subject of many disputes.
12 Sellers, *The Market Revolution*, 398.
13 This paragraph follows Davis, "Free at Last."
14 Eric Foner, *Free Soil, Free Labor, Free Men: The Ideology of the Republican Party before the Civil War* (New York: Oxford University Press, 1995).

15 Michael Paul Rogin, *Fathers and Children: Andrew Jackson and the Subjugation of the American Indian* (Piscataway: Transaction, 1991), 167.

16 Thomas Brown, "From Old Hickory to Sly Fox: The Routinization of Charisma in the Early Democratic Party," *Journal of the Early Republic* 11:3 (Autumn 1991), 342.

17 Rogin, *Fathers and Children*, 167.

18 Sellers, *The Market Revolution*, 165.

19 David Morris Potter, *The Impending Crisis, 1848–1861* (New York: HarperCollins, 1976), 226.

20 Sellers, *The Market Revolution*, 290, 294.

21 Ibid., 242–3.

22 Typically, a hurt mother in a Lydia Huntley Sigourney story laments the attitude of her son: "He despised my woman's voice, my motherly love." Ann Douglas, *The Feminization of American Culture* (New York: Macmillan, 1977), 47.

23 Howard Temperley, "Capitalism, Slavery and Ideology," *Past and Present* 75 (May 1977), 105.

24 John Millar quoted in Blackburn, *The Overthrow of Colonial Slavery*, 52; David Brion Davis, *The Problem of Slavery in Western Culture* (New York: Oxford University Press, 1988), 298–9.

25 Robin Blackburn, "Haiti's Slavery in the Age of Democratic Revolution," *William and Mary Quarterly* 63:4 (Oct. 2006), 633–44.

26 Davis, *Inhuman Bondage*, 165.

27 See Eugene Genovese, *From Rebellion to Revolution: Afro-American Slave Revolts in the Making of the Modern World* (Baton Rouge: Louisiana State University Press, 1979), for this point.

28 Lester D. Langley, *The Americas in the Age of Revolution, 1750–1850* (New Haven: Yale University Press, 1998), 137; Genovese, *From Rebellion to Revolution*, 87.

29 Blackburn, *The Overthrow of Colonial Slavery*, 360.

30 I am here following Davis, "Free at Last."

31 David Brion Davis, *The Problem of Slavery in the Age of Revolution, 1770–1823* (New York: Oxford University Press, 1999), 251.

32 David Brion Davis, *Inhuman Bondage: The Rise and Fall of Slavery in the New World* (New York: Oxford University Press, 2006), 248.

33 Blackburn, *The Overthrow of Colonial Slavery*, 143.

34 Barrington Moore, Jr, *The Social Origins of Dictatorship and Democracy: Lord and Peasant in the Making of the Modern World* (Boston: Beacon, 1993).

35 Davis, *Inhuman Bondage*, 285.

36 Blackburn, *The Overthrow of Colonial Slavery*, 440.

37 Lawrence Jacob Friedman, *Gregarious Saints: Self and Community in American Abolitionism, 1830–1870* (Cambridge: Cambridge University Press, 1982), 162.

38 Eric Foner, *The Fiery Trial: Abraham Lincoln and American Slavery* (New York: Norton, 2010), 19. This book appeared too late for me to fully use.

39 Sean Wilentz, *The Rise of American Democracy: Jefferson to Lincoln* (New York: Norton, 2006), 406.

40 Quoted in Davis, *Inhuman Bondage*, 154.

41 Quoted in Wilentz, *The Rise of American Democracy*, 406.

42 Grimké in Kathryn Kish Sklar, *Women's Rights Emerges within the Antislavery Movement, 1830–1870: A Brief History with Documents* (Boston: Bedford/St Martins, 2000), 222.

43 There is also the example of Ernestine Rose, a Jewish freethinker and Owenite from Poland. According to Ellen DuBois, "Rose's republican emphasis on the Declaration of Independence as a foundational text, her early attention to the centrality of enfranchisement, her emphasis on what we would call the social construction rather than the sin of inequality, her focus on legal reform rather than moral transformation, and her insistence that marriage was a personal rather than a sacred relationship" were not restricted to the single non-Christian. DuBois in Sklar, *Women's Rights Emerges*, 285, 286–7.

44 Sellers, *The Market Revolution*, 157.

45 Avihu Zakai, *Jonathan Edwards's Philosophy of History: The Reenchantment of the World in the Age of Enlightenment* (Princeton: Princeton University Press, 2003), 3. Hulme notwithstanding, there are reasons not to circumscribe abolitionism within a narrowly religious frame. To begin with, it is often hard to determine how much of American millennialism was nationalist and how much involved religion per se. As Perry Miller wrote, "the steady burning of the revival, sometimes smoldering, now blazing into flame, never quite extinguished until the Civil War, was a central mode of the culture's search for national identity." Perry Miller, *The Life of the Mind in America: From the Revolution to the Civil War* (Boston: Mariner, 1970), 6.

46 Wilentz, *The Rise of American Democracy*, 402.

47 John Stauffer, *The Black Hearts of Men* (Cambridge: Harvard University Press, 2002), 1.

48 Quoted in Jane H. Pease and William H. Pease, *They Who Would Be Free: Blacks Search for Freedom 1830–1861* (Champaign: University of Illinois Press, 1990), 15.

49 Friedman, *Gregarious Saints*, 165.

50 Ibid., 176.
51 Davis, *Inhuman Bondage*, 160.
52 Foner, *The Fiery Trial*, 21.
53 Friedman, *Gregarious Saints*, 176–7.
54 Ibid., 63–4, 21–35.
55 Linda Kerber, "The Abolitionist Perception of the Indian," *Journal of American History* 62:2 (Sept. 1975), 271–95.
56 Friedman, *Gregarious Saints*, 137.
57 Richard S. Newman, *The Transformation of American Abolitionism: Fighting Slavery in the Early Republic* (Chapel Hill: University of North Carolina Press, 2002).
58 Lewis Perry, *Radical Abolitionism: Anarchy and The Government of God in Antislavery Thought* (Knoxville: University of Tennessee Press, 1995), 230; Blanche Hersch, *The Slavery of Sex* (Champaign: University of Illinois Press, 1978), 7.
59 Friedman, *Gregarious Saints*, 141.
60 Hersch, *The Slavery of Sex*, 234.
61 Friedman, *Gregarious Saints*, 131.
62 Grimké in Sklar, *Women's Rights*, 227.
63 Ibid., 230–1.
64 Eric Foner, *Politics and Ideology in the Age of the Civil War* (New York: Oxford University Press, 1981), 40.
65 Walters, *The Antislavery Appeal: American Abolitionism after 1830* (New York: Norton, 1984), 19.
66 Quoted in Aileen Kraditor, *Means and Ends in American Abolitionism: Garrison and His Critics on Strategy and Tactics, 1834–1850* (Lanham: Ivan R. Dee, 1989), 23.
67 James Oakes, *The Radical and the Republican: Frederick Douglass, Abraham Lincoln, and the Triumph of Antislavery Politics* (New York: Norton, 2007), 13.
68 Dwight Dumond, *Antislavery Origins of the Civil War in the United States* (Ann Arbor: University of Michigan Press, 1959), 56.
69 Kraditor, *Means and Ends*, 6.
70 Wilentz, *The Rise of American Democracy*, 403–4.
71 Foner, *Politics and Ideology*, 41.
72 James McPherson, *Battle Cry of Freedom: The Civil War Era* (New York: Oxford University Press, 1988), 41.
73 Foner, *Politics and Ideology*, 36.
74 Potter, *The Impending Crisis*, 250. Indeed, "the Republican party received a permanent endowment of nativist support which probably elected Lincoln in 1860 and strengthened the party in every election for more than a century to come," quoted in Aristide R. Zolberg, *A Nation by Design: Immigration Policy in the Fashioning*

of America (Cambridge: Harvard University Press, 2006), 165;
Potter, *The Impending Crisis*, 259: "No event in the history of the
Republican Party was more crucial or more fortunate" than its
"sub rosa union" with nativism, that is with the rural, Protestant,
Puritan-oriented population of the North.

75 Quoted in Merle Curti, "The Impact of the Revolutions of 1848 on
American Thought," *Proceedings of the American Philosophical
Society* 93:3 (June 1949), 210.

76 Quoted in Michael Kazin, *American Dreamers: How the Left
Changed a Nation* (New York: Knopf, 2011), 10.

77 Sellers, *The Market Revolution*, 237–8.

78 Quoted in Foner, *The Fiery Trial*, 173.

79 Daniel Walker Howe, *The Political Culture of the American Whigs*
(Chicago: University of Chicago Press, 1979), 21.

80 Oakes, *The Radical and the Republican*, 13.

81 Kraditor, *Means and Ends*, 29. The American Anti-Slavery Society
stated in 1833, "after the sternest immediatism of doctrine, the
practical reformation will be sufficiently gradual."

82 Kraditor, *Means and Ends*, 27.

83 Quoted in ibid.

84 Quoted in McPherson, *Battle Cry of Freedom*, 118, 122, 126.

85 David Donald quoted in Richard Carwardine, *Lincoln: A Life of
Purpose and Power* (New York: Knopf, 2006), 69.

86 Quoted in McPherson, *Battle Cry of Freedom*, 181–2.

87 Oakes, *The Radical and the Republican*, 71–2.

88 Ibid., 23.

89 Quoted in ibid., 46.

90 Carwardine, *Lincoln*, 26.

91 Oakes, *The Radical and the Republican*, 88.

92 Ibid., 83–4. The phrase beginning "This, and only this" comes from
Lincoln. The rest is Oakes's summary.

93 Quoted in McPherson, *Battle Cry of Freedom*, 186.

94 Quoted in ibid., 494–5.

95 Quoted in ibid., 495–6.

96 Quoted in Geoffrey C. Ward, "Death's Army," *New York Times*,
Jan. 27, 2008.

97 Oakes, *The Radical and the Republican*, 122.

98 Davis in Sklar, *Women's Rights*, 16.

99 Pauline Maier, *American Scripture: Making the Declaration of
Independence* (New York: Knopf, 1997), 136; Garry Wills, *Lincoln
at Gettysburg: The Words that Remade America* (New York: Simon
& Schuster, 1993).

100 Quoted in McPherson, *Battle Cry of Freedom*, 497.

101 James McPherson, *For Cause and Comrades: Why Men Fought in the Civil War* (New York: Oxford University Press, 1997).

102 Foner, *The Fiery Trial*, 323.

103 Quoted in McPherson, *Battle Cry of Freedom*, 497.

104 George Fredrickson, *White Supremacy: A Comparative Study in American and South African History* (New York: Oxford University Press, 1982), 182.

105 Steven Hahn, "Class and State in Post-emancipation Societies: Southern Planters in Comparative Perspective," *American Historical Review* 95:1 (Feb. 1990), 84.

106 Moore, *Social Origins*, 131–2, 138.

107 Davis, "Free at Last," 1.

108 Eric Foner, "Abolitionism and the Labor Movement," in Foner, *Politics and Ideology*, 67.

109 Quoted in ibid., 62–3.

110 Robin Blackburn, "Fin de Siècle: Socialism after the Crash," *New Left Review* I/185 (Jan.–Feb. 1991), 153.

2 The Popular Front and Social Equality

1 Michael Denning, *The Cultural Front: The Laboring of American Culture in the Twentieth Century* (New York: Verso, 1998), 67, 75.

2 Richard Pells, *Radical Visions and American Dreams: Culture and Social Thought in the Depression Years* (New York: Harper & Row, 1973), xvii–xviii.

3 Christopher Lasch, *The Agony of the American Left* (New York: Vintage, 1969), 3.

4 John Locke, *Two Treatises of Government and a Letter Concerning Toleration*, ed. Ian Shapiro (New Haven: Yale University Press, 2003), §§25.

5 Eric Foner, *A Short History of Reconstruction: 1863–1877* (New York: Harper & Row, 1990), 383.

6 Gary Gerstle, *American Crucible: Race and Nation in the Twentieth Century* (Princeton: Princeton University Press, 2001), 166.

7 So powerful was this recognition that an Italian stowaway was discovered who knew only one word of English, "McKinley."

8 Pells, *Radical Visions and American Dreams*, 5.

9 James Weinstein, *Ambiguous Legacy: The Left in American Politics* (New York: New Viewpoints, 1975), 4.

10 Christopher Lasch, *The Agony of the American Left* (New York: Vintage, 1969), 35.

11 Christopher Lasch, *The True and Only Heaven: Progress and Its Critics* (New York: Norton, 1991), 337–8.
12 Denning, *The Cultural Front*, 3.
13 Zeev Sternhell with Mario Sznajder and Maia Asheri, *The Birth of Fascist Ideology: From Cultural Rebellion to Political Revolution*, trans. David Maisel (Princeton: Princeton University Press, 1994), 31.
14 Randolph Silliman Bourne, *War and the Intellectuals: Collected Essays: 1915–1919*, ed. Carl Resek (New York: Harper & Row, 1964), 2; Richard P. Adelstein, "'Islands of Conscious Power': Louis D. Brandeis and the Modern Corporation," *Business History Review* 63:3 (Autumn 1989), 167.
15 David W. Noble, *The Paradox of Progressive Thought* (Minneapolis: University of Minnesota Press, 1958), 48.
16 William E. Leuchtenburg, *The FDR Years: Roosevelt and His Legacy* (New York: Columbia University Press, 1997), 39.
17 Adelstein, "Islands of Conscious Power,"162.
18 Ellis Wayne Hawley, *The New Deal and the Problem of Monopoly: A Study of Economic Ambivalence* (Princeton: Princeton University Press, 1966), 17.
19 Sternhell, *The Birth of Fascist Ideology*, 31.
20 Quoted in Barry D. Karl, *The Uneasy State: The United States from 1915 to 1945* (Chicago: University of Chicago Press, 1985), 9.
21 Arthur M. Schlesinger, *The Coming of the New Deal, 1933–1935*, vol. 2 of *The Age of Roosevelt* (Boston: Houghton Mifflin, 1957), 550.
22 George Packer, "The New Liberalism," *New Yorker*, Oct. 17, 2008, 84–91.
23 Quoted in Richard Hofstadter, *The American Political Tradition and the Men Who Made It* (New York: Knopf, 1948), 428–30.
24 John Chamberlain, *Farewell to Reform: The Rise, Life and Decay of the Progressive Mind in America* (New York: Liveright, 1932; Chicago: Quadrangle Paperbacks, 1965), 220, 230–1.
25 Pells, *Radical Visions and American Dreams*, 82.
26 Jordan Schwarz, *The New Dealers: Power Politics in the Age of Roosevelt* (New York: Knopf, 1993), 134.
27 Edmund Wilson, "An Appeal to Progressives," *New Republic*, Jan. 14, 1931, 237.
28 John L. Shover's *Cornbelt Rebellion* quoted in Harvard Sitkoff, *Fifty Years Later: The New Deal Evaluated* (New York: Knopf, 1985), 13.
29 E. J. Hobsbawm, *The Age of Extremes: A History of the World, 1914–1991* (New York: Vintage, 1996), 133. Long's followers were

"The people from the red clay country and the piney woods, from the canebrakes and the bayous, the shrimp fishermen and the moss fishermen, the rednecks and the hillbillies and the Cajuns," according to Arthur M. Schlesinger, *The Politics of Upheaval, 1935–1936,* vol. 3 of *The Age of Roosevelt* (Boston: Houghton Mifflin, 1960), 52.

30 Schlesinger, *The Politics of Upheaval,* 43.

31 Steven Fraser, *Labor Will Rule: Sidney Hillman and the Rise of American Labor* (Ithaca: Cornell University Press, 1993), 357.

32 Leuchtenburg, *The FDR Years,* 103; Fraser, *Labor Will Rule,* 369: "Roosevelt and his closest advisers realized that the expulsion or excommunication of 'Big Business' was the key to holding together a coalition subject to disintegration from both the left and right."

33 Harold L. Ickes, *The Secret Diary of Harold L. Ickes,* vol. 1 (New York: DeCapo Press, 1974), 363.

34 David M. Kennedy, *Freedom from Fear: The American People in Depression and War, 1929–1945* (New York: Oxford University Press, 2001), 275.

35 Leuchtenburg, *The FDR Years,* 153.

36 Schlesinger, *The Politics of Upheaval,* 422.

37 Eric Foner, *The Story of American Freedom* (New York: Norton, 1999), 197–8.

38 Kennedy, *Freedom from Fear,* 242, 246.

39 Lizabeth Cohen, *Making a New Deal* (New York: Cambridge University Press, 2008), 264.

40 Hobsbawm, *The Age of Extremes,* 168.

41 Lionel Trilling, "Young in the Thirties," *Commentary* 41:5 (May 1966), 43–51.

42 David Brion Davis, *Inhuman Bondage: The Rise and Fall of Slavery in the New World* (New York: Oxford University Press, 2006), 248.

43 Kennedy, *Freedom from Fear,* 24.

44 William Isaac Thomas, *The Polish Peasant in Europe and America,* ed. Eli Zaretsky (Urbana: University of Illinois Press, 1984), 42.

45 Gary Gerstle, *American Crucible,* 16.

46 Glenda Gilmore, *Defying Dixie: The Radical Roots of Civil Rights 1919–1950* (New York: Norton, 2008), 193–4.

47 The UMW, ILGWU, and the building trades unions had mostly immigrant members.

48 Cohen, *Making a New Deal,* 333.

49 David Brody, *Workers in Industrial America: Essays on the Twentieth Century Struggle* (New York: Oxford University Press, 1993), 230.

50 The best book on American ethnicity, Werner Sollors's *Beyond Ethnicity: Consent and Descent in American Culture* (New York: Oxford University Press, 1987), ignores the role of the CIO. According to Sollors, ethnicity *naturalized* the immigrant's free choice; as a Detroit pastor explained, "Sweden is my mother, but America is my bride." The result was a kind of fictive kinship for American national identity. While this is illuminating in describing what happened *within* each ethnic group, it does not describe what occurred *between* them. The left harnessed ethnic and national identification to class-consciousness, showing what the immigrants had in common historically.

51 Cohen, *Making a New Deal*, 316–17.

52 Ron Rothbart, "'Homes Are What Any Strike Is About': Immigrant Labor and the Family Wage," *Journal of Social History* 23:2 (Winter 1989), 267–84.

53 James R. Barrett, "Rethinking the Popular Front," *Rethinking Marxism*, no. 4 (2009).

54 Ruth Milkman, *Gender at Work: The Dynamics of Job Segregation by Sex during World War II* (Urbana: University of Illinois Press, 1987), 34, 39, 41.

55 Leuchtenburg, *The FDR Years*, 240.

56 Brody, *Workers in Industrial America*, 82–3

57 William Leuchtenburg, *The Supreme Court Reborn: The Constitutional Revolution in the Age of Roosevelt* (New York: Oxford University Press, 1996), 157–8. With the denouement of the "Court Fight," "the curtain effectively rang down on the New Deal itself." David M. Kennedy, "How FDR Derailed the New Deal," *Atlantic Monthly* 276:1 (1995), 88.

58 Kevin K. Gaines, *Uplifting the Race: Black Leadership, Politics, and Culture in the Twentieth Century* (Chapel Hill: University of North Carolina Press, 1996), 20.

59 Gerstle, *American Crucible*, 169, 2.

60 Cohen, *Making a New Deal*, 252, 270–1.

61 John B. Kirby, *Black Americans in the Roosevelt Era: Liberalism and Race* (Knoxville: University of Tennessee Press, 1980), 204f.

62 Robert Korstad and Nelson Lichtenstein, "Opportunities Found and Lost: Labor, Radicals, and the Early Civil Rights Movement," *Journal of American History* 75:3 (Dec.1988), 786–811. By 1943 the Detroit NAACP was one of the most working-class chapters in the country.

63 Roy Rosenzweig and Barbara Melosh, "Government and the Arts: Voices from the New Deal Era," *Journal of American History* 77:2 (Sept. 1990), 607.

64 Wolfgang Schivelbusch, *Three New Deals: Reflections on Roosevelt's America, Mussolini's Italy, and Hitler's Germany, 1933–1939* (New York: Metropolitan, 2006), 102.

65 Alfred Kazin, *On Native Grounds: An Interpretation of Modern American Prose Literature* (New York: Reynal & Hitchcock, 1942), 378.

66 Pells, *Radical Visions and American Dreams*, 283f.

67 Morris Dickstein, *Dancing in the Dark: A Cultural History of the Great Depression* (New York: Norton, 2009), 18.

68 Quoted in ibid., 20, 28.

69 Ibid., 155.

70 Trilling, "Young in the Thirties," 47, emphasis added.

71 In 1919, James Weldon Johnson, the first black field secretary of the NAACP, called the strike "the mightiest weapon colored people have" and urged that it be directed against Jim Crow, and not just against labor exploitation.

72 Richard Wright, *Black Boy* (New York: Perennial, 2006), 135; Richard H. Crossman, ed., *The God That Failed* (New York: Columbia University Press, 2001), 131. George Fredrickson, *Black Liberation: A Comparative History of Black Ideologies in the United States and South Africa* (New York: Oxford University Press, 1995), 187.

73 Robin D. G. Kelley, *Freedom Dreams: The Black Radical Imagination* (Boston: Beacon, 2002), 54.

74 Gerstle, *American Crucible*, 163.

75 Herman Melville, *Redburn: His First Voyage* (New York: Harper Brothers, 1850).

76 Leuchtenburg, *The FDR Years*, 156.

77 Steve Fraser quoted in Michael Kazin, *The Populist Persuasion: An American History* (Ithaca: Cornell University Press, 1998), 158. New Dealers, wrote Robert Kelley, were "a young, shirt-sleeved crowd, self-consciously brainy and professorial, whose irreverent style offended WASP America." Robert Kelley, "Ideology and Political Culture from Jefferson to Nixon," *American Historical Review* 82:3 (June 1977), 522. Even the politics of homosexuality that became important later could be found in the Popular Front period, as in charges that "do-gooders, bleeding hearts and long-hairs" ran the government, or that TVA was pervaded by "the swishing of long wings" and by visions of "Green Pastures and De Lawd." Leuchtenburg, *The FDR Years*, 253; Michael Sherry, *In the Shadow of War: The United States since the 1930s* (New Haven: Yale University Press, 1995), 78.

78 Edmund Wilson, "The Literary Consequences of the Crash," in

Wilson, *The Shores of Light* (New York: Farrar, Strauss & Giroux, 1952), 498–9.

79 Pells, *Radical Visions and American Dreams*, 98.

80 William Stott, *Documentary Expression and Thirties America* (Chicago: University of Chicago Press, 1986), 291–3, 268–9.

81 The concept permeates much of Europe's writing of the late thirties, as in Orwell ("No one, now, could devote himself to literature as single-mindedly as Joyce or Henry James"), Auden ("Tomorrow the bicycle races/ Through the suburbs on summer evenings. But today the struggle"), and Brecht ("Ah, what an age it is/ When to speak of trees is almost a crime").

82 Malraux's interest, Kazin added, was not in Communism but in Communists. Alfred Kazin, *Starting Out in the Thirties* (Boston: Little, Brown, 1965), 20–2.

83 Norman Mailer, *The Armies of the Night* (New York: New American Library, 1968), 121–2.

84 Leuchtenburg, *The FDR Years*; 129; Karl, *The Uneasy State*, 174, 199.

85 Kirby, *Black Americans*, 193f.

86 Ibid., 172–3.

87 Thomas J. Sugrue, *Sweet Land of Liberty: The Forgotten Struggle for Civil Rights in the North* (New York: Random House, 2008), 3–31.

88 Sitkoff, *Fifty Years Later*, 94–5, 99.

89 Karl, *The Uneasy State*, 173.

90 Korstad and Lichtenstein, "Opportunities Found and Lost."

91 Daniel Horowitz, *Betty Friedan and the Making of* The Feminine Mystique*: The American Left, the Cold War, and Modern Feminism* (Amherst: University of Massachusetts Press, 1998), 111.

92 These included Nora Stanton Blatch Barney, a granddaughter of Elizabeth Cady Stanton, Susan B. Anthony II, Elizabeth Gurley Flynn, Gerda Lerner, Eleanor Flexner, Aileen Kraditor, Amy Swerdlow, and Claudia Jones, a Harlem Communist Party leader.

93 Kate Weigand, *Red Feminism: American Communism and the Making of Women's Liberation* (Baltimore: Johns Hopkins University Press, 2002), 98.

94 The pamphlet proved an important source for Eleanor Flexner in her seminal *Century of Struggle* (New York: Atheneum, 1972).

3 The New Left and Participatory Democracy

1 Paul Kennedy, *The Rise and Fall of the Great Powers* (New York: Random House, 1987), 358.

2 Quoted in Giovanni Arrighi, *The Long Twentieth Century: Money, Power and the Origins of Our Times*, new and updated edn (New York: Verso, 2009), 341.

3 Robert Keohane, *After Hegemony: Cooperation and Discord in the World Political Economy* (Princeton: Princeton University Press, 1984), 137.

4 Kristin Ross, *May '68 and Its Afterlives* (Chicago: University of Chicago Press, 2002), 2–3.

5 Philip Roth, *The Facts: A Novelist's Autobiography* (New York: Vintage, 1997), 123.

6 Michael Crozier, Samuel Huntington, and Joji Watanuki, *The Crisis of Democracy: Report on the Governability of Democracies to the Trilateral Commission* (New York: New York University Press, 1975).

7 For neo-Marxist social theory consider Immanuel Wallerstein, Eugene Genovese, Eric Wolf, Gabriel Kolko, William Appleman Williams, Fredric Jameson, as well as widely read British authors like Perry Anderson, Raymond Williams and E. P. Thompson.

8 Gabriel Kolko, *The Politics of War: The World and United States Foreign Policy, 1943–1945* (New York: Vintage, 1970), 3.

9 Quoted in William Graebner, *The Age of Doubt: American Thought and Culture in the 1940s* (Boston: Twayne, 1991), 20.

10 H. Stuart Hughes, "Why We Had No Dreyfus Case," *American Scholar* 30 (1961), 478.

11 Michael Kazin, *The Populist Persuasion: An American History* (Ithaca: Cornell University Press, 1998), 179.

12 David J. O'Brien, *American Catholics and Social Reform: The New Deal Years* (New York: Oxford University Press, 1968), 217.

13 Michael Rogin, *The Intellectuals and McCarthy: The Radical Specter* (Cambridge: MIT Press, 1967), 6; Richard Hofstadter, "The Pseudo-Conservative Revolt" (1954), in Hofstadter, *The Paranoid Style in American Politics and Other Essays* (Cambridge: Harvard University Press, 1996), 39.

14 Alan Wolfe, *America's Impasse: The Rise and Fall of the Politics of Growth* (New York: Pantheon, 1981); Charles Maier, "The Politics of Productivity: The Foundations of American International Economic Policy after World War II," *International Organization* 31 (Autumn 1977).

15 In this atmosphere, one figure gave Cold War liberalism its own moral depth, namely Freud. However, the liberals read Freud through a conservative lens. Reflecting the new ethos of mass consumption, which invested marriage and personal relations with an intensity comparable to that which the Popular Front put into the workplace, Cold War liberalism associated Freud with an anti-utopian "maturity ethic."

16 Daniel Yergin, *Shattered Peace: The Origins of the Cold War and the National Security State* (Boston: Houghton Mifflin, 1978), 241.

17 The duty of intellectuals, Chambers explained, was "to keep pointing out why the Enlightenment and its fruits were a wrong turn in human history." Michael Klimmage, *The Conservative Turn: Lionel Trilling, Whittaker Chambers and the Lessons of Anti-Communism* (Cambridge: Harvard University Press, 2009), 146.

18 Ibid., 94, 222–3, 146, 11. *Witness* created the core postwar persona, captured by the right, the witness. David Horowitz wrote of his New Left years, "I was like Whittaker Chambers . . . a young man inspired by the high-minded passions of the left who had broken through to the dark underside of the radical cause." Still later, Ann Coulter rallied Bush era conservatives: the liberals "have the media, the universities, the textbooks. We have ourselves. We are the witnesses." David Horowitz, *Radical Son: A Generational Odyssey* (New York: Simon & Schuster, 1998), 2; Ann Coulter, *Treason: Liberal Treachery from the Cold War to the War on Terrorism* (New York: Random House, 2003), 17.

19 "Our Country and Our Culture," editorial statement, *Partisan Review* 19 (May–June, 1952), 282–4.

20 One can grasp the difference between the New Right and the New Left by examining Ayn Rand's two famous novels, *The Fountainhead* (1943) and *Atlas Shrugged* (1957). Though replete with the adolescent rebellion against authority and the even more adolescent sexuality, shared by the New Left and the New Right, Rand's novels overflow with a Nietzschean contempt for "losers," "spongers," and "free-riders." The New Left, by contrast, was the child of the New Deal. Jennifer Burns, *Goddess of the Market: Ayn Rand and the American Right* (New York: Oxford University Press, 2009), 264.

21 Richard Gillam, "The Perils of Postindustrialism," *American Quarterly* 34:1 (Spring 1982), 465–6; Daniel Geary, *Radical Ambition: C. Wright Mills, the Left, and American Social Thought* (Berkeley: University of California Press, 2009).

22 Alain Touraine, *The Post-industrial Society* (London: Wildwood House, 1974), 8–9.

23 John Fowles in *American Scholar* 30 (1961), 612.

24 Robin D. G. Kelley, *Race Rebels: Culture, Politics, and the Black Working Class* (New York: Simon & Schuster, 1996), 173.

25 Morris Dickstein, *Gates of Eden: American Culture in the Sixties* (Cambridge: Harvard University Press, 1997), 53.

26 Ibid., 188.

27 Ronald Sukenick, *Down and In: Life in the Underground* (New York: Collier, 1988), 17.

28 David Halberstam, *The Best and the Brightest* (New York: Random House, 2001), 38.

29 Walter Laqueur, *Europe in Our Time: A History 1945–1992* (New York: Penguin, 1993), 315, 268.

30 William Taubman, *Khrushchev: The Man and His Era* (New York: Norton, 2003), 162, 424, 534.

31 C. Wright Mills, "Letter to the New Left," *New Left Review*, no. 5 (Sept.–Oct. 1960).

32 Robert F. Williams, Harold Cruse, and LeRoi Jones were the key figures.

33 Van Gosse, *Where the Boys Are: Cuba, Cold War America, and the Making of a New Left* (New York: Verso, 1996), 147–8.

34 Judith N. Shklar, *Redeeming American Political Thought* (Chicago: University of Chicago Press, 1998), 112.

35 Mary L. Dudziak, *Cold War Civil Rights: Race and the Image of American Democracy* (Princeton: Princeton University Press, 2002), 10.

36 Ibid., 185, 29.

37 Thomas Borstelman, *The Cold War and the Color Line: American Race Relations in the Global Arena* (Cambridge: Harvard University Press, 2003), 42.

38 Peter Kellogg, "Civil Rights Consciousness in the 1940s," *Historian* 42:1 (1979), 39.

39 Michael Schudson, *The Good Citizen: A History of American Civic Life* (New York: Simon & Schuster, 2011), 245–59.

40 Abdul R. Janmohamed, "Negating the Negation: The Construction of Richard Wright," in Henry Louis Gates and Anthony Appiah, eds, *Richard Wright: Critical Perspectives* (New York: Amistad, 1993).

41 Richard Wright, *Black Boy* (New York: Harper, 1945), 284.

42 William H. Chafe, *Civilities and Civil Rights: Greensboro, North Carolina, and the Black Struggle for Freedom* (New York: Oxford University Press, 1981), 7.

43 Ibid., 116–17, 138–9.

44 George M. Fredrickson, *Black Liberation: A Comparative History*

of Black Ideologies in the United States and South Africa (New York: Oxford University Press, 1996), 259.

45 David L. Chappell, *A Stone of Hope: Prophetic Religion and the Death of Jim Crow* (Chapel Hill: University of North Carolina Press, 2004), 46–7.

46 Thomas F. Jackson, *From Civil Rights to Human Rights: Martin Luther King, Jr., and the Struggle for Economic Justice* (Philadelphia: University of Pennsylvania Press, 2006), 47.

47 Fredrickson, *Black Liberation*, 261.

48 Jackson, *Civil Rights*, 88, 117.

49 Clayborne Carson, *In Struggle: SNCC and the Black Awakening of the 1960s* (Cambridge: Harvard University Press, 1995), 78.

50 Leigh Raiford, "Come, Let us Build a New World Together," *American Quarterly* 59:4 (Dec. 2007), 1129–57.

51 Allen J. Matusow, *The Unraveling of America: A History of Liberalism in the 1960s* (New York: Harper & Row, 1984), 77–8.

52 Constance Curry, Joan C. Browning, Dorothy Dawson Burlage, *Deep in Our Hearts: Nine White Women in the Freedom Movement* (Athens: University of Georgia Press, 2000), 342.

53 Matusow, *The Unraveling of America*, 310–11.

54 David Barber, *A Hard Rain Fell: SDS and Why It Failed* (Jackson: University Press of Mississippi, 2008), 96, 99–100.

55 Tom Hayden, *Reunion: A Memoir* (New York: Random House, 1988), 39.

56 Dominick Cavallo, *Fiction of the Past: The Sixties in American History* (New York: St. Martin's Press, 1999), 74–5.

57 Carson, *In Struggle*, 129.

58 Geary, *Radical Ambition*, 101.

59 Hayden, *Reunion*, 44.

60 John McMillian and Paul Buhle, *The New Left Revisited* (Philadelphia: Temple University Press, 2002), 164.

61 A good example is the Clamshell movement during which every imaginable form of inequality, such as gender, sexual orientation, age and physical disability, was taken into consideration in the attempt to shut down a nuclear power plant. Barbara Epstein, *Political Protest and Cultural Revolution: Nonviolent Direct Action in the 1970s and 1980s* (Berkeley: University of California Press, 1991).

62 Wini Breines, *Community and Organization in the New Left, 1962–1968: The Great Refusal* (New York: Praeger, 1982), xiv.

63 William H. Chafe, *Never Stop Running: Allard Lowenstein and the Struggle to Save American Liberalism* (New York: Basic Books, 1993), 205.

64 Matusow, *The Unraveling of America*, 78.

65 Thomas J. Sugrue, *Sweet Land of Liberty: The Forgotten Struggle for Civil Rights in the North* (New York: Random House, 2008), 288.

66 "The question nobody wants to say . . . is that the people around Dr. King, and Dr. King himself – we were all left wingers," added Reverend Wyatt T. Walker, King's chief of staff. Jackson, *Civil Rights*, 1–3, 50, 52, 105. King was also a typical representative of the Popular Front in that he sought to hide his politics. When Harper signed King to write *Stride toward Freedom*, published in 1958, it assigned an editor to him, Melvin Arnold, experienced in protecting liberal authors from red-baiting. When King wrote that capitalist materialism was "far more pernicious" than communist materialism, Arnold changed it to "as pernicious." When King wrote that socialism and capitalism each had a half-truth, Arnold changed it to "partial truth." When King used the word "collective," Arnold axed it because it had slave-labor connotations. When King wrote that the "economic power structure usually supports and controls the political power structure," Arnold had him take out the whole passage.

67 Peter B. Levy, *The New Left and Labor in the 1960s* (Urbana: University of Illinois Press, 1994), 32.

68 Doris Kearns, *Lyndon Johnson and the American Dream* (New York: American Library, 1977), 174.

69 Matusow, *The Unraveling of America*, 88, 140–1.

70 Sidney M. Milkis and Jerome M. Mileur, eds, *The Great Society and the High Tide of Liberalism* (Amherst: University of Massachusetts Press, 2005), 199; Matusow, *The Unraveling of* America, 110ff.

71 Milkis and Mileur, *The Great Society*, 438.

72 The New Left was the child of the New Deal. SDS, the most important New Left organization after SNCC, was a breakaway from SLID, the Popular Front-inspired Student League for Industrial Democracy. Among SDS's founding members, Al Haber was the son of a left-wing New Deal lawyer who had served in postwar Germany. Sharon Jeffrey's parents were both trade union organizers. Paul Potter's father had been on Truman's Council of Economic Advisors. Steve Max's father had been managing editor of the *Daily Worker*, the Communist newspaper. Tom Hayden came from a Catholic working-class background, at that point politically conservative but still the backbone of the New Deal. For several years the United Auto Workers would be the primary funding source of SDS, and the Port Huron statement was written at a UAW retreat.

73 Philip Roth, *American Pastoral* (New York: Vintage, 1988), 164.

74 Kearns, *Lyndon Johnson,* 304–7. In a 1965 article Bayard Rustin, who had been a communist in the thirties, and served prison time during World War Two as a draft resister, argued that the civil rights extremists were caught up in the same illusions as the liberals since their aim was to shock and therefore to expose the hypocrisy of the white liberals. The advocates of shock, Rustin wrote, "are often described as the radicals of the movement, but they are really its moralists. They seek to change white hearts – by traumatizing them." They praise Malcolm because "they think he can frighten white people into doing the right thing." They are apparently convinced that "at the core of the white man's heart lies a buried affection for Negroes." Nonviolence he added, "could absorb the violence that is inevitable in social change wherever deep-seated prejudices are challenged." Chappell, *A Stone of Hope,* 60–2.

75 Alexander Bloom, *Long Time Gone: Sixties America Then and Now* (New York: Oxford University Press, 2001), 106.

76 Both quotes from in Milkis and Mileur, *The Great Society,* 442.

77 Halberstam, *The Best and the Brightest,* 76.

78 "The perception of credibility trumped every other aspect of military strategy," writes Gordon Goldstein. Gordon Goldstein, *Lessons in Disaster: McGeorge Bundy and the Path to War in Vietnam* (New York: Times Books/Henry Holt, 2008), 166–7, 220–1.

79 Kearns, 154; Lloyd Gardner, *Pay any Price: Lyndon Johnson and the Wars for Vietnam* (Chicago: I. R. Dee, 1995), 96.

80 Barber, *A Hard Rain Fell,* 41.

81 Loren Baritz, *Backfire: A History of How American Culture Led Us Into Vietnam and Made Us Fight the Way We Did* (Baltimore: Johns Hopkins University Press, 1998), 34, 38.

82 Hughes, "Why We Had No Dreyfus Case."

83 Barber, *A Hard Rain Fell,* 37.

84 Marshall Sahlins, "The Future of the National Teach-in: A History" (1965), in Sahlins, *Culture in Practice: Selected Essays* (New York: Zone Books, 2000), 209ff.

85 Tom Wicker, *On Press* (New York: Viking, 1978), 16.

86 Michael Herr, *Dispatches* (New York: Knopf, 1977), 42.

87 Marilyn Young, *The Vietnam Wars, 1945–1990* (New York: HarperCollins, 1991), 196.

88 William James, "On a Certain Blindness in Human Beings," in James, *Talks to Teachers on Psychology and to Students on Some of Life's Ideals* (New York: Henry Holt, 1915).

89 Quoted in Louis Menand, *The Metaphysical Club* (New York: Farrar, Straus & Giroux, 2001), 372.

90 Gloria Emerson, *Winners and Losers: Battles, Retreats, Gains,*

Losses, and Ruins from a Long War (New York: Random House, 1976), 8.

91 Nat Hentoff, "Behold the New Journalism – It's Coming after You!" *Evergreen Review* 50 (July 1968), quoted in Michael Schudson, *Discovering the News: A Social History of American Newspapers* (New York: Basic Books, 1978), 187. "The pose of objectivity and the obsession with internal structure and imagery [gave] way to something wilder, more personal, more intense and apocalyptic." Dickstein, *Gates of Eden*, 66.

92 Michael E Staub, "Black Panthers, New Journalism, and the Rewriting of the Sixties," *Representations* 57:1 (Winter 1997), 55.

93 Emerson, *Winners and Losers*, 5, 10, 88,104.

94 Judith Thurman, "Walking through Walls: Marina Abramovic's Performance Art," *New Yorker*, Mar. 8, 2010, 28.

95 Myra MacPherson, *Long Time Passing: Vietnam and the Haunted Generation* (Bloomington: University of Indiana Press, 2001), 125.

96 Emerson, *Winners and Losers*, 50.

97 Tom Wells, *The War Within: America's Battle over Vietnam* (Berkeley: University of California Press, 1994), 163.

98 Hannah Arendt, *On Violence* (New York: Harcourt, Brace & World, 1974).

99 Emerson, *Winners and Losers*, 22.

100 Young, *The Vietnam Wars*, 202.

101 Jeremy Varon, *Bringing the War Home: The Weather Underground, the Red Army Faction, and Revolutionary Violence in the Sixties and Seventies* (Berkeley: University of California Press, 2004), 3; H. Bruce Franklin, *Vietnam and Other American Fantasies* (Amherst: University of Massachusetts Press, 2000), 60.

102 Emerson, *Winners and Losers*, 133.

103 Robert D. Heinl, "The Collapse of the Armed Forces," *Armed Forces Journal* 108:19 (June 7, 1971), 30–8.

104 Jonathan Glover, *Humanity: A Moral History of the Twentieth Century* (New Haven: Yale University Press, 2001), 50.

105 Baritz, *Backfire*, 6.

106 The policeman was the father of Jesse Helms, the well-known conservative Senator from North Carolina.

107 Mike Marqusee, *Redemption Song: Muhammad Ali and the Spirit of the Sixties* (New York: Verso, 1999), 127. Malcolm X called himself "one of the 22 million black people who are the victims of Americanism." "I don't see any American dream," Malcolm added, "I see an American nightmare." Dudziak, *Cold War Civil Rights*, 221; Barber, *A Hard Rain Fell*, 19.

108 Glover, *Humanity*, 58.

109 *New York Times*, Nov. 30, 1969.

110 *Nation*, Dec. 15, 1969.

111 Jefferson Cowie, *Stayin' Alive: The 1970s and the Last Days of the Working Class* (New York: New Press, 2010), 135.

112 Roth, *American Pastoral*, 206.

113 Kearns, *Lyndon Johnson*, 343.

114 Ibid., 328.

115 Gardner, *Pay any Price*, 180.

116 Wells, *The War Within*, 208.

117 Jules Witcover, *The Year the Dream Died: Revisiting 1968 in America* (New York: Warner Books, 1997), 138.

118 Rick Perlstein, *Nixonland: The Rise of a President and the Fracturing of America* (New York: Scribner, 2009), 230.

119 Kearns, *Lyndon Johnson*, 327, 281.

120 Edward Shils, "American Society and the War," in Anthony Lake, *The Vietnam Legacy: The War, American Society, and the Future of American Foreign Policy* (New York: New York University Press, 1976).

121 Lippmann, Sept. 1968, quoted in Gary Wills, *Nixon Agonistes: The Crisis of the Self-Made Man* (Boston: Houghton Mifflin, 1970), 66.

122 Daniel T. Rodgers, *Age of Fracture* (Cambridge: Belknap Press of Harvard University Press, 2011), 3.

123 Witcover, *The Year the Dream Died*, 488.

124 Ibid., 492–3.

125 Walter Benjamin, "Theses on the Philosophy of History," in Benjamin, *Illuminations* (New York: Harcourt, Brace & World, 1955).

126 Perlstein, *Nixonland*, 218.

127 Witcover, *The Year the Dream Died*, 475.

128 Cowie, *Stayin' Alive*, 123.

129 Young, *The Vietnam Wars*, 192.

130 Cowie, *Stayin' Alive*, 76.

131 Ibid., 8.

132 Godfrey Hodgson, *More Equal than Others: America from Nixon to the New Century* (Princeton: Princeton University Press, 2004), 141.

133 Barber, *A Hard Rain Fell*, 101.

134 Ibid., 115.

135 Such statements may seem to lend support to the now canonical view that women left the New Left because of the obstinacy and resistance of men, but this view is inaccurate. Women left the mixed-left insofar as they did because they wanted an all-women's

movement; they were not reacting to men's bad behavior, and would not have reacted differently had men behaved better.

136 Hodgson, *More Equal than Others*, 156.
137 Sara Evans, *Personal Politics: The Roots of Women's Liberation in the Civil Rights Movement and the New Left* (New York: Vintage, 1980), 204–7.
138 Karen V. Hansen and Ilene J. Philipson, eds, *Women, Class and the Feminist Imagination: A Socialist-Feminist Reader* (Philadelphia: Temple University Press, 1990), 7.
139 This is Catherine MacKinnon's formulation.
140 Jennifer Ring, "Saving Objectivity for Feminism: MacKinnon, Marx, and Other Possibilities," *Review of Politics* 49:4 (Autumn 1987), 471.
141 Catharine A. MacKinnon, "Feminism, Marxism, Method, and the State: An Agenda for Theory," *Signs* 7:3 (Spring 1982), 532.
142 Catharine A. MacKinnon, "Sexuality, Pornography, and Method: 'Pleasure under Patriarchy,'" *Ethics* 99:2 (Jan. 1989), 318.
143 Combahee River Collective, "A Black Feminist Statement" (1981), 212, quoted in Mary Louise Adams, "There's No Place like Home: On the Place of Identity in Feminist Politics," *Feminist Review* 31 (Spring 1989), 23.
144 Justin Suran, "Coming Out against the War." *American Quarterly* 53:3 (Sept. 2001), 465.
145 Arthur Marwick, *The Sixties: Cultural Revolution in Britain, France, Italy, and the United States, c. 1958–c. 1974* (New York: Oxford University Press, 1998), 725.
146 Shane Phelan, *Identity Politics: Lesbian Feminism and the Limits of Community* (Philadelphia: Temple University Press, 1989), 73–4.
147 Martin Duberman, *A Saving Remnant: The Radical Lives of Barbara Deming and David McReynolds* (New York: New Press, 2010).
148 Hansen and Philipson, *Women, Class and the Feminist Imagination*, 305.
149 Cynthia Griggs Fleming, *Soon We Will Not Cry: The Liberation of Ruby Doris Smith Robinson* (Lanham: Rowman & Littlefield, 1998), 117.
150 Emerson, *Winners and Losers*, 7.
151 Eli Zaretsky, *Capitalism, the Family and Personal Life* (New York: Harper & Row, 1976), 11.
152 David Harvey, *A Brief History of Neoliberalism* (New York: Oxford University Press, 2005), 12.
153 John Nichols, *The "S" Word: A Short History of an American Tradition – Socialism* (New York: Verso, 2011).

154 Martine Storti quoted in Ross, *May 1968 and Its Afterlives*, 189.
155 Luisa Passerini, *Autobiography of a Generation: Italy, 1968* (Hanover: University Press of New England, 1996), 1.
156 Douglas Rossinow, *The Politics of Authenticity: Liberalism, Christianity, and the New Left in America* (New York: Columbia University Press, 1998), vii.
157 Emerson, *Winners and Losers*, 112.
158 Thomas Wolfe, *Radical Chic and Mau-Mauing the Flak Catchers* (New York: Farrar, Straus & Giroux, 1970), 56.
159 Roger Sale, "Hurled into Vietnam," review of *Dispatches* by Michael Herr, *New York Review of Books*, Dec. 8, 1977.
160 Tim O'Brien, *Going after Cacciato* (New York: Broadway, 1999), 320.
161 Ibid., 14.
162 Tom Wicker, *One of Us: Richard Nixon and the American Dream* (New York: Random House, 1991), 423.
163 Thomas Frank, *What's the Matter with Kansas* (New York: Metropolitan, 2004), 8.

Conclusion

1 Thomas J. McCormick, *America's Half Century: United States Foreign Policy in the Cold War and After* (Baltimore: Johns Hopkins University Press, 1995), 164.
2 Thomas Frank, *What's the Matter with Kansas* (New York: Metropolitan, 2004), 10.
3 Eli Zaretsky, "Psychoanalysis and the Spirit of Capitalism," *Constellations* 15:3 (2008), 366–81.
4 According to *Time*, "no presidential aspirant since Huey Long has proposed so sweeping an economic change." *Time*, Feb. 14, 1972.
5 In 1971 "Freedom Buses" swept up Jews all over America to protest the treatment of Soviet Jews.
6 Samuel Moyn, *The Last Utopia: Human Rights in History* (Cambridge: Harvard University Press, 2010), 139, 159–60.
7 Bethany Moreton, *To Serve God and Wal-Mart: The Making of Christian Free Enterprise* (Cambridge: Harvard University Press, 2009), 5.
8 Hester Eisenstein, *Feminism Seduced: How Global Elites Use Women's Labor and Ideas to Exploit the World* (Boulder: Paradigm, 2009).
9 Wallerstein, "The Bourgeois(ie) as Concept and Reality," *New Left Review* I/167 (Jan.–Feb. 1988).

10 Daniel T. Rodgers, *Age of Fracture* (Cambridge: Belknap Press of Harvard University Press, 2011), 177, 193.
11 Christopher Lasch, *The True and Only Heaven* (New York: Norton, 1991), 21–2.
12 Thomas Frank, interview with Emily Udell, "Recapturing Kansas," *In These Times,* Jan. 12, 2005.
13 Obama's "evidence-based," "results-based," finance-department framing of "Affordable Health Care" is intended to reinforce a two-tier health care system. Phillip Pizzo, the Dean of the Stanford School of Medicine and one of the most prominent supporters of the bill, explained, "We can't afford to have a system like this. The cultural expectation is that we are in a community where the public – every individual – believes that she or he should get the most advanced health care kind of on demand. And the notion that it wouldn't be, that is sort of anathema and we've grown toward that over the years." More recently, Obama has endorsed the idea that Medicare should be means-tested.

Index